IDEA & EXPERIENCE

ERAZIM KOHÁK

IDEA & EXPERIENCE

Edmund Husserl's
Project of Phenomenology
in IDEAS I

The University of Chicago Press
Chicago and London

The University of Chicago Press, Chicago 60637
The University of Chicago Press, Ltd., London

Library of Congress Cataloging in Publication Data

Kohák, Erazim V
  Idea and experience.

Bibliography: p.
  Includes index
  1. Husserl, Edmund, 1859–1938. Ideen zu einer
reinen Phänomenologie. 2. Phenomenology.
I. Title.
B3279.H93I343   142'.7   78–661
ISBN 0–226–4501908

ERAZIM KOHÁK is professor of philosophy at Boston
University.

To the memory of Jan Patočka

who undertook the difficult task of carrying on Husserl's work in the land of Husserl's birth

Univ. Prof. PhDr. Jan Patočka, D.Sc., Ph.D. h.c. (Aachen), a student of Edmund Husserl, a scholar of distinction, and a noble human of unswerving moral vision, died in Prague on March 13, 1977, after eleven hours of police interrogation, having affixed his signature to a petition calling on the government of his country to observe those human rights guaranteed by the Universal Declaration of Human Rights and the laws of the Republic of Czechoslovakia.

Contents

4

Experience and Intersubjectivity
73

5

Reflection, Intentionality, Constitution
105

6

Method in Phenomenology
132

7

Phenomenology and Philosophy
152

8

The Horizon of Phenomenology
173

Preface

This study is predicated on the Heraclitean conviction that wisdom is "to know the *gnōmē*, the thought by which all things are guided through all." In the case of Husserl's project of phenomenology, that one thought, profound in its simplicity, is that, primordially and ultimately, *to know means to see,* or, as Husserl presents it in *Ideas I* § 19c,[1]

Das *unmittelbare "Sehen"* (νοεῖν), nicht bloss das sinnliche, erfahrende Sehen, sondern das *Sehen überhaupt als originär gebendes Bewusstsein welcher Art immer,* ist die letzte Rechtsquelle aller vernünftigen Behauptungen.	*Direct "seeing"* (νοεῖν), not merely experiential sense perception, but *seeing in general as the primordial presentive consciousness of whatever kind,* is the ultimate source of the validity of all rational assertions.

The primordial starting point, as well as the ultimate aim of all knowledge, is not speculation but that clear, evident insight which humans acknowledge with the startled exclamation, "Oh, *now* I *see!*" The purpose of this volume is to retrieve that clear, basic insight from the complexity of experience and the compilations of phenomenological scholarship and to bring it to that clear, evident grasp which is the basis of phenomenology.

We consider this basic insight equally crucial for understanding Husserl and for doing philosophy. In presenting that insight, Husserl fulfills, in Aron Gurwitsch's words, the "secret longing of modern philosophy."[2] He grasps the genius of positivism—the fundamental recognition of experience as the ultimate ground and meaning of all knowledge—but raises it to a new level. While the empiricists reduced experience to passive sense perception of discrete particulars, Husserl recognizes its full breadth as primordial awareness presenting all our being, its necessary structure as well as its contingent content, in the evident givenness which he comes to call *Evidenz.* In that recognition, Husserl fuses the cutting edge of positivism with the wisdom of Continental rationalism, that is, with its awareness that experience presents us not only with contingent contents but with necessary structures as well. Husserl, however, does not mistake those structures of experience for categories which a "mind" would impose on a docile "matter." Rather, he recognizes them as the intrinsic structures of transcendental experiencing, that is, of the one primordial reality given in lived experience and simply brought to thematic awareness and articulation in phenomenological reflection.

As the preceding paragraph testifies, that simple, basic insight, crucial to all of Husserl's work, becomes quickly obscured in elaboration. Husserl himself elaborates at length—in *Cartesian Meditations,* in *Formal and Transcendental Logic,* in *Experience and Judgment,* in *The Crisis of European Sciences*—and to good effect, resolving many specific problems and shedding light on numerous marginally obscure issues. At the same time, however, his elaborations, by their sheer complexity and volume, tend to obscure his basic insight, especially for those scholars who cannot devote a lifetime to the study of Husserliana. If we keep the basic insight clearly in mind, we can richly profit from Husserl's elaborations; but first we must retrieve that insight in all its primordial clarity.

The same holds true of Husserlian scholarship. Husserl's work profoundly affected the temper and direction of European philosophy. Among his successors, Husserl found numerous disciples—Eugen Fink, Aron Gurwitsch, Ludwig Landgrebe, Alfred Schutz, and a host of others. He inspired other thinkers, such as Merleau-Ponty, Paul Ricoeur, Jan Patočka, and many more, to continue his work in new directions. Finally, he challenged a whole range of thinkers, such as Martin Heidegger, Jean-Paul Sartre, and Hans-Georg Gadamer, who came to disagree with him but could not ignore him. All of the work of these men, together with that of the diligent scholars who—like Walter Biemel, Herbert Spiegelberg, Dorion Cairns, and others— labored to make Husserl's work available, provides a rich field of study when we approach it with Husserl's basic insight clearly in mind; but it can be quite bewildering if we lack that insight.[3]

That is why, in this volume, we shall not aspire to add to the wealth of Husserlian scholarship. Our aim is much more modest: to retrieve Husserl's basic insight and to bring it to the evident givenness of that clear perception which we can greet with the exclamation, "Oh, *now* I *see!*"

Since we are convinced, with Dorion Cairns,[4] that a genuine study of phenomenology must itself be phenomenological, we shall not (except in notes, which the reader can ignore at first reading) seek to speculate or to reconstruct phenomenology from the jigsaw puzzle of scholarship. We shall, rather, aim to *see* in the sense of the passage from *Ideas I* § 19 cited above: to win a clear, evident grasp of Husserl's basic insight. Following the advice in *Ideas I* § 18a, we shall create a methodological vacuum and focus within it on a sole text, Husserl's presentation of the project of phenomenology in the first of the three volumes which he subtitled "Introduction to Phenomenology," his *Ideas I*.[5]

Our reason for choosing that text rather than one of the two other "introductions"—*Cartesian Meditations* or *The Crisis of European Sciences*—is itself Husserlian. We are convinced, with Gurwitsch, that in this early work Husserl's insight can be most clearly *seen*.[6] We shall therefore look, as Husserl tells us to do in *Ideas I* §§ 66–69, seeking to bring the insight embodied in the text to full clarity. Since Husserl is speaking about lived experience rather than scholarship, we shall not (again, except in the notes) seek clarification in Husserl's other works or in those of his successors but in lived experience itself. When we encounter obscurities, we shall first ask, *what in experience,* lived experience at its most ordinary, is Husserl talking about? At the start of each chapter, we shall first survey a segment of our ordinary experience at its most ordinary, avoiding any but the most ordinary terms. Against that background, we shall then focus on the corresponding section of Husserl's text, letting the clear articulation stand out from it.[7] Throughout, we shall, like Husserl in *Crisis* § 7, seek not to teach but to see and to point out. The measure of our success will not be whether the reader will have learned some new "points" about Husserl but whether, at the end of our common work, he will be able to exclaim, "Oh, *now* I *see!*"

In *Formal and Transcendental Logic* § 59 Husserl points out that further seeing is the sole test of seeing. Since my aim was to see clearly, I owe a special debt to all my colleagues and students who have read my successive drafts, doodled question marks and scribbled in the margin, "I just don't see this." My philosophical indebtedness will emerge clearly in the text and the notes. But I wish to express my gratitude to three special colleagues and friends: to Paul Ricoeur, for inspiration, encouragement, and *citron pressé* when most I needed them; to Richard Zaner, for his painstaking analysis of my text, which combined the full rigor of scholarship with an unfailing good will; and to Peter A. Bertocci, for teaching me, in theory and practice, that subjects are Persons. Theirs let the praise be—let me answer for the flaws.

Erazim Kohák   *Boston University*
                                               Rogation Sunday, A.D. 1977

List of Abbreviations of Husserl's Works

C The Crisis of European Sciences and Transcendental Phenomenology (*Die Krisis der europäischen Wissenschaften und die transzendentale Phänomenologie*)

CM Cartesian Meditations (*Cartesianische Meditationen*)

E&J Experience and Judgment (*Erfahrung und Urteil*)

FTL Formal and Transcendental Logic (*Formale und transzendentale Logik*)

I Ideas towards a Pure Phenomenology and Phenomenological Philosophy (*Ideen zu einer reinen Phänomenologie und phänomenologischen Philosophie; Vol. I: Allgemeine Einführung in die reine Phänomenologie*)

IDEA & EXPERIENCE

Ordinary Experience and Common Sense

Why phenomenology?

Simply because, <u>as humans, we experi-</u>
<u>ence before we theorize, and what we</u>
<u>theorize about is primordially given</u> as lived
experience. I drink and am aware of
drinking; that lived experience is the
datum which enables me to go on to conceive of a world in which some objects
function as cups and I function as a
drinker. But that is already a second step
in reflecting. The primary experience is not
the cup or the "I" but the conscious act of
drinking. Without that, the world and my
acts therein would appear absurd, the "I"
as a subject, as an improbable hypothesis.
To provide a firm foundation for our
propositions about objects and subjects,
we need first to grasp clearly the lived
experience on which they are all ultimately
based.

That, at least, is the standard phenomenological argument. Let us accept it as a
working hypothesis and assume that the
core of phenomenology is indeed its insistence on the critical articulation of the necessary structures of lived experience. In the
context of our usual philosophizing, that
insistence can appear puzzling. On the one
hand, the emphasis on pure description of
lived experience sounds like a radical empiricism. Husserl, in a moment of fervor,
did actually proclaim himself the true positivist.[1] On the other hand, the conception
of experience as radically a subject's experience, eidetically structured, suggests a

strong kinship to idealism. Again, Husserl in his later years did identify himself as a true transcendental idealist.[2] Approaching phenomenology through traditional philosophy inevitably leads to puzzling conclusions, for the writings of other philosophers are not the subject matter of phenomenology—lived experience, at its most primordial and most overlooked ordinary, is that. We need to set aside our habits of historical scholarship and approach phenomenology from the viewpoint of lived experience.[3]

Habitually, we pass over that ordinary experience as philosophically trivial. We begin, instead, with a philosophical theory about experience —an empiricist, an idealist, or even a phenomenological one. A scrupulous examination of what and how we actually experience in our most ordinary daily living seems to us somewhat embarrassing, as a belaboring of the obvious, unworthy of true philosophers.

But the obvious is not always the evident. It is just as likely to be simply the familiar, heavily laden with traditional preconceptions and hasty conclusions. Premature theorizing can lead to a rude confrontation between the "obvious" conclusions of our elaborate ideologies and the recalcitrant ordinary experience which we had passed over as trivial. To protect against that danger, we have to risk setting aside our sophistication and to begin, quite naively, with the experience we actually live.

For that reason, we shall not begin even with Husserl's description of ordinary experience. Instead, we shall simply note some of the most ordinary characteristics of our actual experiencing. Only then shall we look at experience a second time, in the light of Husserl's text, noting what Husserl wishes to bring to our attention about it: the naive realism of our common sense (*I* § 1), its implicit denial of its own nominalism (*I* §§ 2–3), and the crucial role of the imagination in our understanding of even the most "real" reality (*I* § 4).

Common Sense in
Ordinary Experience

The trouble with any proposal to "return to experience" is that, as we live it, experience is highly elusive, and as we see it presented by the poets, the scientists, and the philosophers it somehow is not quite the same. As we live it, our experience is always *ours,* though it is by no means private. We live it as individual subjects, though in a public world which we share with others. That world seems "objective" to us, not simply a product of our imagination, but it is also structured by human values and intentions and laced with possibilities which confront us as real—though not as existing. We are its subjects, but we act out our lives on a stage set by something we call the "laws of nature" and, possibly, by something we identify vaguely as "fate."

As we observe that experience, re-presented by poets, scientists, and philosophers, some of these traits seem always absent. At the hands of the poets, experience loses much of its public, nonarbitrary character. It becomes subjective and private. At the hands of the scientists, it seems to lose all sense of being *mine,* personally meaningful and valuable. What the philosophers do to experience is usually too complex to be understood in ordinary terms at all; and if it is not complex, we assume it must be trivial.

The slogan "Back to experience" is intrinsically appealing, but experience is always someone's "mine." As a subject, each of us is an individual, with his own perspective. No two experiences duplicate each other precisely. Were we to return radically to actual lived experience, could we still speak of any common, transindividual experience? Or would we find ourselves locked each in his private world, waiting for poetry, science, or philosophy to construct a common reality for us?[4]

At first glance, that seems obviously a problem. Yet if we resist the impulse to start constructing theoretical "solutions" and instead look at our experience more closely, we shall note that even at its most ordinary it presents a great deal of evidence that, though lived individually, human acts do exhibit an analogous structure. Intersubjective understanding is an experiential given before it becomes a philosophical problem. The startling reality is not that misunderstandings and breakdowns of communication between individuals and cultures occur but that they are breakdowns within a basically common comprehension of our humanity. Motifs from civilizations long dead and far removed find ready parallels in our experience. The biblical triangle of David, Uriah, and Bathsheba could be replayed in its essential outlines here and now, even though its factual counterparts would be different. Love poems translated from ancient Egyptian hieroglyphics are not in the least dated. Even though a modern suitor is more likely to bring roses and chocolates than a lotus and a pomegranate, the sentiment is the same. Similarly, except for factual details, a photograph of a Bushman family, the mother cradling a child, the father's arm protectively draped around an older son, could be taken in Norway or Ohio. Facts may be culturally variable, but the basic structure of human experience does appear to be profoundly common.

The intricate step is from this intuitive homogeneity of experience to its articulation in reflection and verbal reports. It is an equally undeniable given of our ordinary experience that two persons in analogous situations will in all sincerity produce incompatible reports. They will yield to a fascination with facts, losing sight of the analogy of principles, and will assure themselves that life at other times and in other places was really entirely different because the "facts" were different—though the experiences were not.

This is largely the reason why the empirical sciences have shunned verbal reports as unreliable and have substituted objective observation of controlled experiments as their primary datum. But there is something missing in such reports as well. The subject does not simply exhibit economic behavior; he is trying to earn a living for his family. It would be misleading to dismiss that *intentio* as "merely subjective." It is a subject's experience, but it is in no sense arbitrary or private. We observe and can speak of a *behavior* rather than of an aggregate of discrete movements only because those movements exhibit the purposive unity of an *intentio*. Without it, economic activity would appear unintelligible and absurd, as it often does to the idle. Nor is that *intentio* private; it structures overt behavior in a public world.

It is to experience as lived by a subject—though not as "subjective" —that we need to return. We can do so because verbal reports do not *necessarily* distort; they can also be faithful expressions of the clearly given. But because they can distort, we must tread warily indeed.

Still, we can offer some observations about ordinary experience which are reasonably noncontroversial. Perhaps the most basic of these is that ordinary experience does *make sense* to its subjects, not necessarily in some grand "existentialist" manner but in the ordinary sense of being intelligible. The subject will report, "Yes, I know what I am doing," and observation will confirm his assertion. Humans in their ordinary doings do not grope about as in a daze. They move confidently and purposefully, as one moves in a rational, predictable, and familiar context. That context may appear familiar, predictable, and rational because of "human nature," because of social conditioning, or even because such rationality is an intrinsic characteristic of all possible experiencing. But, whatever the reason, it is a given. Ordinary experience, as we are initially aware of it, is intelligible.

A second reasonably noncontroversial assertion is that the usual articulations of ordinary experience, at least in all relatively complex societies, are predominantly object-oriented. Nouns are the basic counters in all Western languages. Verbs are variables, often derived from nouns. A common-sense account of an experience is typically a catalog of the *things* which allegedly "cause" the experience and which common sense regards as eminently "real." Even when speaking about himself, the average person will tend to use nouns and speak of things. Though he experiences, for instance, his home as a place of safety structured by human relations, he will habitually describe it as a house. This does not mean that humans are "materialistic" or anything else; it is simply a given of our experience. Our common sense is naively realist or, more precisely, naively *reist*.

But it is also the case that, in our daily doings, our common sense is not consistent in its naive object-realism. The average speaker may insist that objects are what is "real," but he will seldom act accordingly. Though "sentimental value" is normally pronounced almost with a sneer, it plays a crucial role in the way humans respond to their world. Even when dealing with objects of physical need (in excess of his basic requirements), a subject typically chooses in terms of a significance within a meaning-context—for instance, in terms of prestige within a peer group—rather than in terms of quantifiable, "objective" value. As demagogues and hucksters have always known, few things function in ordinary experience "as they are." Ordinarily, they function *as they mean*. Though common sense is emphatically realist in its pronouncements, it is far closer to being idealist in its responses. It regards meanings ("It shows she loves me . . .") as more basic than "facts" (". . . even though I really don't need a necktie").

What is more, there is also a reasonably nonproblematic consensus that such meanings are not ordinarily experienced as a whim or as something we make up. Whether we account for them as a result of social conditioning or as inherent in human nature or in the intrinsic structure of experience, we experience them as something we *encounter* rather than invent. Common sense makes a clear distinction between "genuine" experienced meanings and what it calls "put-ons," meanings which it takes to be arbitrary or artificial. When we state that X (Robert, Annabelle, Steier, Ara) is the *most beautiful* Y (man, woman, car, horse) in the world, we do not normally think we are deceiving ourselves and that X, in unadmitted fact, is a rather average Y. Nor do we ordinarily think of our statement as an objective report about the world, based on rigorous criteria and exhaustive comparison. We are, typically, aware of the existence of other, equally beautiful Y's. Rather, we are reporting that *in the context of lived experience, as we are aware of it,* X *functions as* "the most beautiful" Y. *Not* that we *think* so, not that it "objectively" *is* so, but that it *so functions*. The meaning, "most beautiful," is not discovered in the mind or in the world but in lived experience.[5]

Furthermore, in spite of the overt realism of common sense, in ordinary experience such meanings, though experienced *in* a given context, are also experienced as in principle independent of it. We encounter the concept "the most beautiful" in the context of a car or a woman, but it is separable from, and intelligible without, either. A frog or a gardenia can also be "the most beautiful." The meaning, as common sense grasps it, has a "logic" of its own and can serve to order other experiences as well. Ordinary speakers may disagree as to which objects are beautiful but will acknowledge as evident the reality of the experience of "the most beautiful." Common sense pays little attention to its ontological status or to its conflict with the realistic assumption that only things are real. It is content to claim that that simply is "the way it is."

All of this may seem far removed from the object-realism of common sense with which we are most familiar and which we habitually treat as the "experiential" basis of reflection. Yet it is clearly present in experience, there to be seen. Experience does present itself as an experience *of objects* to which common sense attributes primary reality. But, quite prior to any theorizing, those objects also function as endowed with meanings, and we are quite confident of our ability to grasp those meanings "in principle." That may seem inconsistent, but a philosophy of ordinary experience cannot simplify its task by imposing prior criteria which would disqualify the "inconsistent" parts of ordinary experience as inauthentic or merely subjective. It must start by taking experience in its complexity as a starting point.[6] Let us look at our ordinary experience once more, this time noting what it is that Husserl is pointing out within it.

Husserl's § 1:
What Common Sense
Takes for Granted

Start out, if you will, by reading the opening of Husserl's § 1. This is   § 1
a section that most readers and commentators usually omit, because
it seems both trivial and obscure: its topic is ordinary experience, but
Husserl's titles and text speak of "essences."

In part, this is a problem of translation. The term *Wesen,* usually
rendered as "essence," has very different connotations from the English
"essence" in ordinary use. We usually think of "essence" as a hidden
inner core, which has to be abstracted by an operation of the active
intellect, by a mystical intuition, or, in the case of the essence of
vanilla, by a corresponding chemical operation. By contrast, *Wesen,*
derived from the old Germanic verb for "to be," suggests something
overt, directly presented in experience. It is the "was-ing" or "be-ing"
of an entity, the way something is, or, more precisely, the typical way
in which a phenomenon presents itself in experience. Ordinary English
usage comes close to it in phrases like "Isn't that just like a man (or a
woman, an adolescent, etc.)," which identify not a hidden "essence"
but a *Wesen,* an overt, characteristic way of being, what an X is "in
principle."[7] Forgoing attempts at an exact translation, we can take
the chapter title, *"Tatsache und Wesen"* ("Fact and Essence"), as an
indication that Husserl is concerned with the relationship of particulars
and principles in ordinary experience. The significance of his terms is
best allowed to emerge from the text.

That text, again, will bear some attention. Husserl sets out to
sketch the assumptions which common sense—the *sensus naturalis,*   § 1
for which he uses the term "the natural standpoint" (*C* § 53c)—
makes about knowledge and experience. Yet the language seems re-
mote and the ideas far from ordinary. Perhaps the best way to start is to
cite the first three sentences in the original and supplement the English
translation available to the reader with a more colloquial paraphrase:[8]

Natürliche Erkenntnis hebt an mit der Erfahrung und verbleibt *in* der Erfahrung. In der theoretischen Einstellung, die wir die *"natürliche"* nennen, ist also	Common-sense knowledge begins with the awareness of objects and never goes beyond it. Within the theoretical perspective of which we say that it "comes	§ 1a

| der Gesamthorizont möglicher Forschungen mit *einem* Worte bezeichnet: es ist die *Welt*. | naturally" to us, all that any inquiry can deal with may be summed up in a single word: it is the "world" [in English, usually the "objective" or the "external" world]. |

| Die Wissenschaften dieser ursprünglichen Einstellung sind demnach insgesamt Wissenschaften von der Welt, und solange sie die ausschliesslich herrschende ist, decken sich die Begriffe "wahrhaftes Sein," "wirkliches Sein," d.i. reales Sein, und—da alles Real sich zur Einheit der Welt zusammenschliesst—"Sein in der Welt." | The sciences which operate within this primordial outlook are therefore all studies of the "world," and, as long as the perspective of "seeing things out there" dominates our conception of what it is to know, saying that something "truly is," that it "really is," or that it is "in the world" amounts to the same thing—in the last case because all that we encounter as "real" fits together in the unity of the "world." |

The point is clear even if the terms are unfamiliar. Husserl is acknowledging the naive realism of our common sense. We do in fact habitually assume that knowledge is a recording of "facts" or "objects" which we assume exist "in the world," complete with meanings, ready to be recorded indifferently by a knower or a camera. For common sense, to know a lot means to have recorded and to be able to recall a "lot of things."

§ 1b   To the extent that science is nothing but "common sense systematized," as C. S. Peirce is reputed to have said, it, too, becomes a matter of recording and ordering "facts about the world." This, too, is obvious enough, and Husserl simply acknowledges it: from the perspective of common sense, experience is "seeing facts," knowing is "recording facts," and science, even at its most theoretical, is "ordering facts."

But, while noting the obvious, Husserl calls attention to a crucial point: all this is obvious not as experience but only *from the perspective of common sense.* As he notes in the second sentence, the naive realism of common sense (which we shall later designate as its "thesis") is already a *theoretische Einstellung*—a "theoretical orientation." It is already an interpretation of experience, a low-level theory rather than a direct report (and, we might note, an interpretation that people without a Western schooling frequently do not share).

Nor does lived experience bear out that habitual interpretation. Take, for instance, the experience of lighting a cigarette in a non-smoker's house. After a few puffs, the subject looks anxiously for a place to deposit his ashes. There are no ashtrays. The subject casts about, settles on a seashell or a nut dish, and, with a mixture of anxiety and relief, knocks off the ash. He did not "find" an ashtray "in the objective world"; there was none there to be found. Rather, he constituted an ashtray in his act.[9]

Common sense, in ordinary reports, passes over this and, instead of reporting, *interprets* the experience as an encounter with an object out there in the world. Typically, it will report that "I *found* an ashtray." But there was no ashtray to be found; the smoker had to constitute it. Here "I found one" is *an interpretation,* so habitual as to seem "natural," but still not a direct report.

§ 1b

For the moment, Husserl does not examine the implications of this recognition but goes on to sketch the consequences of our common-sense realism. When we assume, with common sense, that knowledge means recording facts about the world and that science means making corresponding true statements about them, then it is the "things"—classes of objects studied—that will distinguish one science from another. Petrology deals with rocks, ichthyology with fish, and psychology presumably with things called psyches, while philosophy is not a science at all, because it has no set of objects of its own (unless it is the writings of philosophers). The business of each science will appear to be based on "firsthand observation," in which the observer "in-tuits"—takes in—the object as it is "out there," in the world.

In that way our common sense already suggests an uncritical epistemology. In our ordinary experience, as we actually live it, the primary source of knowledge (what Husserl here calls *"originär* gebende *Erfahrung"*)[10] is the awareness that accompanies our acts: I am aware of writing, and that involves an intent and a pen. In our uncritical reflections we take the source to be perception in, Husserl tells us, "the ordinary sense," that is, as a recording of objects: there is a pen; he is using it.

To our common sense, that seems quite obvious. Only the "outer" world, things that "really are," "out there," are observable. The rules of evidence in Anglo-American jurisprudence, Blackstone's monument to common sense, in fact exclude hearsay, opinion, feelings, or significance from admissible evidence. Only sense perceptions of objects and of their movements "in the world" are admissible. Even self-awareness must be interpreted as self-*observation,* modeled strictly on sense perception and, as such, necessarily defective, because it is not public. Common sense will not speak of awareness but of "looking within" and "seeing there . . . ," as if my mood or my memory were objects in an "inner" world. Not surprisingly, a great many acts which made sense in the living appear arbitrary in the telling.

§ 1c   Hence the conclusion of the last paragraph of section 1: For common sense and the sciences based on it, "the world" represents the sum total of all possible objects of experience and knowledge. Sciences based on the naive realism of common sense must treat their objects as *things in the world,* whether they deal with the physical world, in which case it may be appropriate enough, or with social and human reality.[11] Even psychology conforms to the model, speaking of psychic "facts" and treating dimensions of personality as psychic objects. Thus the dynamic dimensions of experience which we indicate by terms like *Ich, Es, Überich,* or by Jung's archetypes come to be interpreted not as dimensions or patterns of being but as psychic entities called *the* ego, *the* id, *the* superego, *the* anima, or *the* shadow, all objects in an "inner" world. By now, this conception of science, like the conception of experience on which it is based, is so familiar that it appears to us as "only natural." But it is based not on nature, only on habit, on the customary interpretation of common sense.

Husserl leaves another possibility open. Even though in actual practice the human sciences (*Geisteswissenschaften*) seek to conform to the naive realism of common sense, canonized by the natural sciences, they may in fact prove to belong to an entirely different type of science that we shall be able to recognize once we have formulated a viable experiential alternative to the "empirical" realism of common sense.

For the moment, however, we can sum up the assertion of Husserl's first section quite simply. Knowledge, as common sense understands it, is naively realistic, gathering true statements about things observed "in the world"; and this naive realism carries over to the sciences.

Husserl's §§ 2–3:
Particulars and Principles

In the second section, "Tatsache. Untrennbarkeit von Tatsachen und   § 2
Wesen" ("Fact. The Inseparability of Facts and Types"), Husserl
turns his attention to the "facts" that common sense posits as the sole
objects of knowledge and scientific inquiry. He continues to work
within the limits of ordinary experience, but is concerned to point out a
basic conflict. Common sense is naively realistic; it assumes that the
"real" thing is always a particular, a "this here rose." But it also
assumes as obvious that "this here rose" is *a* rose, a type of an object
which, "in principle," remains constant in spite of factual variations.
The givens of common sense turn out to be not only concrete particulars but also "meanings," functioning as instances of a *kind*.

In the first paragraph of the section Husserl acknowledges that   § 2a
ordinary perception does deal with its objects as with particulars. The
word he actually uses literally means "fact." Even the etymology is the
same: *Tat-sache* is a "deed-thing"; *factum* is the past participle of
facere, "to do." But Husserl is concerned with the concreteness and
particularity, the quality of "this here now" with which common sense
endows whatever it considers real. For that, the term "a particular"
might serve better.

Husserl is calling our attention to an aspect of the "this here now"
which we ordinarily overlook. We are accustomed to speaking of
facts as "hard," occasionally as "brute," and to assuming that, while
principles and values are somehow ethereal and relative, facts are
absolute and necessary. But, on a closer inspection, the opposite turns
out to be the case, even in terms of the most ordinary experiences.
"Facts" are necessary only in the very trivial sense that they are what
they "in fact" happen to be, and that is infinitely fortuitous. This chair,
as a concrete, particular "fact," is wooden and white, but it would be
no less a chair if it were constructed of aluminum tubing and drill
straps. Similarly, as a matter of fact, this triangle may be drawn in
chalk on slate, but it would be no less a triangle if it were made of
three jointed lengths of pine. What it is as a matter of *fact,* in its concrete particularity, is wholly fortuitous.

In our ordinary experiencing we recognize that contingency of   § 2b
facts; but, contrary to our common-sense bias, we also take a certain
necessity for granted. A chair can, as a matter of *fact,* be anything—

but, *in principle,* it must be capable of being sat upon. *That* things are may be utterly contingent, but *what* they are *in principle* seems unambiguously, universally valid even to people who never heard of Plato or Whitehead. Beer is beer, though none be brewed; a rose is a rose, whatever you call it; a triangle is a triangle, no matter how you draw it. As a particular, that is, as a matter of fact, this triangle happens to be drawn in chalk, but it might have been drawn in ink, scratched in sandstone, constructed of extruded aluminum, or even erased altogether. That is accidental; it just happens to be that way. But any triangle *must have* three sides: the relation between the ratio of its angles and the ratio of its sides has an eternal validity, just as a chair, whatever it is, must be sit-uponable. Each is the necessary condition of being a triangle or a chair.

The possibility of phenomenology hinges on this basic recognition. A particular is in *fact* what it is, but in principle it must meet certain conditions, *and our direct awareness includes not only particular, factual instances but also the necessary principles they embody.* In ordinary experience as I live it, I am aware of every object both as a particular and "in principle," as the instance of a type. I can speak of it in either mode: as a fact, making contingent "factual" assertions about it, or as the instance of a principle, meeting necessary conditions. Thus when I see an elephant, though it be the first elephant I have ever laid eyes on, I see not only "this animal" but also an instance of "this type of animal," even should it be the only instance there is. Should I be fortunate enough to see a second elephant, I would recognize it as the *same kind* of animal even without having studied biological classification. And, in speaking of it, I can say both "There is this elephant in the garden" and "An elephant must have a trunk," in the first case speaking of a particular and in the second case of a type.

Husserl, speaking of "essence," is not departing from ordinary experience but is questioning the easy nominalist assumptions of common sense—on strictly experiential grounds. Even ordinary experience operates with concepts which do not refer to concrete particulars. Even common-sense "knowledge" is knowledge only because it recognizes particulars as instances of a kind.

This second dimension of our ordinary experience, the awareness of an experience "in principle," as a type of experience, is what Husserl designates as *Wesensanschauung,* the awareness of a principle

or a pattern, of the *Wesen* which puzzled us earlier.[12] That, too, is
something we grasp in perception itself.[13]

Thus we literally *see* not only this *fact,* this brown, hard, square
chair, but also the principle of sit-uponability, with a "logic" of its
own, illustrated by but not dependent on this instance. Similarly, we
see not only a child slipping two extra jelly beans into his pile but also
the principle of greed.[14]

This, Husserl is pointing out, is a matter of seeing (more precisely,
of a direct grasp), not of judgment. On reflection, we might, in an
act of judgment, correct our initial perception: *this* is not a chair, only
a model; *this* is not greed, just carelessness. We might also correct our
initial grasp: a chair is not just a sit-uponable; greed is more complex
than we thought.

But such judgments do not operate in a vacuum, constructing
patterns out of chaotic bits. Their raw materials are already meaningful wholes, no matter how primitive or inadequate, with a "logic"
and an inner necessity of their own which we grasp in lived experience
as primordially as we see green. The fact of this chair and the principle
of sit-uponability are equally *givens*. This is *really* a chair; the principle of sit-uponability *necessarily* demands a flat surface.

Our example and Husserl's point are so elementary that it is easy to   § 3
grow impatient with them. But they have far-reaching implications.
When we spoke of behavior, first perceived as greed, exhibiting
characteristics of carelessness—which is well within the bounds of
most ordinary locutions—we implied that we know, in principle, what
carelessness is, without having an instance before us, so that we can
compare it with the instance perceived as greed. While we cannot
perceive a particular without perceiving it as the instance of a kind
(in other words, we cannot perceive a fact without perceiving a typical
way of being), we can consider such a typical way of being in isolation, apart from any instantiation. It is possible to know something
"in principle" without having any particular instance in mind.

The burden of Husserl's section 3a is to note that such "eidetic"   § 3a
knowledge is still a matter of seeing, not a matter of induction or generalization from a sample. In dealing with facts, general statements
can, of course, be a product of generalization. After noting that the
chairs in the offices of two-thirds of my colleagues are brown, I can
generalize that chairs issued by this university are brown. But, in

dealing with principles, the matter stands otherwise. If I grasp the "principle" of a parallelogram, I need only one instance (even an imaginary one) to *see*—not "infer"—that the opposite angles of *any* parallelogram *must* be equal, just as one (perhaps even imaginary) instance is enough to grasp the principle and inner necessity of sit-uponability.

Certainly, in our actual quest for knowledge, the *process* of grasping a principle is seldom a one-stroke achievement. Nor, as Husserl acknowledges (for instance, in *I* §§ 67–70), is any clear seeing a matter of a single casual glance. In actual knowing, "seeing" is a matter of looking and looking again, focusing, comparing perspectives; in short, it is a *process,* even when it is a phenomenological seeing. But the *necessity* of a principle is not a product of a compilation of evidence or of an induction from a sample. It is *there,* to be grasped, even in a single instance, no matter how laboriously we actually achieve such a grasp.

That is not a matter of phenomenological speculation but of the most ordinary experience. When I try, unsuccessfully, to squeeze a tennis ball into a wine bottle, I need not try several wine bottles and several tennis balls before, using Mill's canons of induction, I arrive inductively at the hypothesis that tennis balls do not fit into wine bottles. One instance is enough. I *see* not only that this tennis ball won't fit into this wine bottle but that, in principle, tennis balls do not fit into wine bottles, and, for that matter, I *see* that large objects do not fit into small openings. Without ever leaving the bounds of ordinary experience, Husserl, in sections 2 and 3, makes the point that, while our common sense is naively realistic, our ordinary experience is not nominalistic. It includes not only a perception of objects but a perception of principles (*eidē*) as well.

§ 3b,c   In the following paragraphs Husserl notes that while we do *see* not only particulars but also principles, such a grasp is not necessarily clear and immediate. What seems obvious need not be evident and necessary; it may be merely familiar. But that does not change the truth that I grasp the principle as well as the fact of a phenomenon in direct awareness even in unclear perception. When I see a cup indistinctly through colored glass, I am not seeing an imperfect cup or a non-cup. I am still seeing a cup, albeit imperfectly. Similarly, when I grasp a principle dimly or unclearly, I am still grasping a principle. As in sense perception, I may have to look and look again before I grasp the principle clearly, but I am seeing, not speculating.[15] Thus, in our example of the parallelogram, the fact and the principle can be present in one direct glance; colloquially, when you have seen one parallelogram, you have seen them all. Husserl uses the example of a tone to make the same point.

But that is not the case with, for instance, physical objects. Those inevitably present themselves to me from a particular perspective, incompletely, with an infinite possibility of new perspectival views.[16] Even in such cases, however, ordinary experience recognizes, and common sense speaks of, awareness on two levels, of the particular and of the particular as an instance, presenting an idea—say, the sense perception of a façade and an awareness of it as a façade *of* a house. In such a case I obviously might be mistaken "in fact"—what I took to be the façade of a house may prove to be a two-dimensional movie set. I need to look and look again to see "what it really is," to grasp adequately the "typical way of being" (the *Wesen*) of the phenomenon. But that *Wesen* is not a composite of such perspectival views; it is an idea presented through them and grasped directly, though perhaps inaccurately, even in a single exposure. Similarly, a *Wesen* which potentially could be grasped in one glance may be unclear and need to be looked at again and again—just what is the "inner logic" of jealousy? Yet what I do here is analogous not to speculation but to sense perception: it is a *seeing*, a direct grasp.[17]

On this basis, working entirely within the confines of ordinary experience, Husserl concludes that the *eidos*—the "principle" considered in its purity—represents a different kind of object altogether from the particulars which common sense recognizes as "real." It is not yet another "new" thing, but it is characterized by a different type of being than those we habitually recognize. Constrained by the naive realism—really "reism"—of our common sense, we have, for some three centuries, assumed that there are only real, "objective" things "in the world" and "merely mental," subjective ideas, private and relative to the thinker. But the "principles" of our ordinary experience, the inner necessity of a triangle or of sit-uponability, are neither private nor arbitrary. (I cannot make the angles of a triangle equal a quarter-circle or make a sharp point sit-uponable; each has a "logic" of its own.) Yet neither are they objects in the world, particular existing entities. Our grasp of them is a *gebende Anchauung*—a "giving" or synthetic awareness—yet it is not a recording of "facts in the world."

§ 3e

That again is not a matter of speculation but of a recognition of an experiential datum. In ordinary usage we do sometimes say of an experience, "I have figured out how to make sense of it"—usually when the experience offers us no "rhyme or reason" and we have to impose a pattern on it. Far more frequently, however, we will say, "I see how it makes sense"—that is, I have grasped the principle of it, what makes it tick, its *Wesen,* the *eidos* it embodies.[18]

Husserl underlined the entire paragraph 3e, and with reason. It is crucial for the possibility of phenomenology as a *systematic* study of reality in its *lived immediacy*. If only particulars were experiential givens, our knowledge could be either immediate and chaotic or systematic but speculative. A sociologist could present us either with an aggregate of "concrete" instances of marriage as lived or with his speculative generalizations about the nature of marriage. We can speak of the meaning of marriage, as such and as lived, only because the principle as well as the particular is an experiential given.

What § 3e asserts, though this is often overlooked, is again a matter of everyday, ordinary experience. We can, as a matter of that experience, not only reflect on but also *perceive* our experience from both a factual and an eidetic viewpoint, from the standpoint of preoccupation with particulars as well as "in principle," focusing our awareness on the principle an instance embodies. Looking up at the rafters of a snowed-in cottage, I can *see* these handsome old timbers, or I can *see* them as instances of types in typical relations (braced beams bearing certain stress), or I can grasp the latter entirely as a force diagram, calculating a theoretical breaking point.

§ 3f,g   Thus, even when we focus on the *Wesen/eidos* dimension of experience, we are still seeing; that is, our awareness is still a synthetic awareness. However, while in focusing on the fact dimension (the "things" as particulars) we reduced the richness of experience to the poverty of its material counterparts (say, love to bowls of goulash cooked and bouquets of flowers delivered per calendar month), in focusing on the meaning dimension we are seeing experience in all the complexity of actual experiencing. For, merely as fact, "reality" is a meaningless aggregation of fragments. It is intelligible only because, as experience, those facts actually present themselves, not as common sense interprets them, but as structured by an *eidos,* as making sense. In spite of the fact-realism of common sense, even in ordinary experience, reality is a matrix of meaning presented through contingent contents of sense perception.

When Husserl speaks of the inseparability of "fact" from "essence," he is stressing that sense perception and awareness of meaning are intrinsically but asymmetrically related. Though I can grasp the principle of a ship as such, I cannot see it except as an instance of a principle. Even the unity of something as concrete as a ship is the unity of an *eidos*. Without that, I should be confronted with an assemblage of boards and ropes having no more than a *unitas aggregationis,* and, on strict associationist principles of continuity, contiguity, and resemblance, could not even decide whether the gig, towing astern, is or is not a part of the object.

In all of this, Husserl has done no more than point out what we in fact experience, yet he has literally inverted our "obvious" assumptions about our experiencing. Our common-sense assumption may be that in knowing we simply record objects "in the world." In our actual ordinary practice, however, we experience objects as embodying a principle, a *Wesen,* which we can grasp separately. It is our awareness of a principle which enables us to see the raw data of our experience as intelligible objects rather than as a confusion of particulars. Or, colloquially, I see *this* object and see that it is *a ship;* with that recognition, the tangle of ropes and timbers begins to make sense, because any entity which is to perform the function of what we designate as a ship *must,* in principle, have a means of staying afloat, of being propelled and steered. It is ordinary experience; if it seems extraordinary, perhaps we did not look carefully enough until Husserl made us take notice.

Husserl's § 4:
The Role of the
Imagination

Husserl's §§ 1–3 make the point that lived experience is intelligible because it contains an awareness not only of arbitrary "facts" but also of principles which order them and which are not themselves arbitrary. *This* triangle could be wood, chalk line, or anything, but as *a* triangle it must contain angles equal to half a circle. Anything can provoke fear, but the experience of being afraid has, in principle, a "logic of its own." The project of phenomenology is an elaboration of that recognition.

The reason for adding § 4 to our consideration is that it is crucial to the systematic elaboration of phenomenology but is very subject to §4a   misinterpretation. It is here, in § 4a, that Husserl makes the claim that the *eidē* which phenomenology studies can be grasped in imaginary as well as in factual lived experience—and often more clearly in the former. Since we are accustomed to thinking of a science as constructing generalizations on the basis of observed "facts," that seems to consign phenomenology to the realm of the fanciful.

But if we bear in mind that phenomenology is a study of principles rather than facts and that it makes no factual claims, that assertion becomes almost a commonplace. We surely find nothing surprising in the recognition that the validity of the principle that the opposite angles of a parallelogram are necessarily equal does not depend on "factual" ("empirical") evidence. It is based on its own inner necessity, clearly grasped. An actual parallelogram, hastily sketched on a blackboard or copied freehand in a student's notes, may in fact not demonstrate that principle with nearly as much clarity as an ideal parallelogram, constructed solely in the imagination, of intersecting, perfectly parallel lines.

§ 4b   The point which Husserl was at pains to point out in §§ 1–3 is that not only parallelograms but also lived experiences have an eidetic structure, that is, demonstrate a principle. For instance, the self-reinforcing pattern of jealousy is not accidental; it has a structurally necessary "logic" of its own, which we grasp rather than deduce or construct. When, however, we seek to grasp it in an actual experience, it is often obscured by a myriad of contingent factors. An empirical report of the observed behavior of the commanding officer of the Venetian armed forces, his wife, and his chief of staff would yield a cumbersome mass of trivia about the life of military officers and their dependents. Shakespeare's fictional account of *Othello* cuts through all that, presenting an instantiation of the pure *eidos* of the complex phenomenon, jealousy. In principle, we can grasp the structure of the phenomenon far more clearly here than in our empirical reports.

Shakespeare's play does not "prove" that jealousy is, in principle, this or that, but our empirical data would not "prove" it either. As with the principle of the parallelogram, the principle of jealousy is not susceptible of any proof other than that based on its own intrinsic necessity. Instances, whether factual or imaginary, simply present it to be seen. They do not add to or subtract from its validity. That is either intrinsic and evident or it is not at all, very much as we either *see* a green surface or we do not.

It would be illegitimate to use such an eidetic grasp as the basis   § 4c
for factual assertions about contingent particulars. Phenomenology is not a mystical shortcut to empirical knowledge.[19] Grasping the self-reinforcing "logic" of jealousy does not entitle us to claim that Desdemona or her empirical equivalent on some forgotten army post was or was not unfaithful. But it does enable us to *understand* Othello's behavior, which, empirically described, would appear arbitrary. Only empirical observation can justify empirical assertions. A phenomenological grasp of the "logic" of phenomena makes particulars intelligible and so renders them susceptible to intelligent observation rather than mere mechanical recording. Imagination, finally, contributes no factual information, but it does provide a useful instance for grasping eidetic principles.

What is more, as Husserl suggests in the last sentences of § 4c, it also creates possibility. While he does not examine the implications of this in detail until the *Cartesian Meditations,* we can note it here because, again, it is not a matter of phenomenological speculation but of ordinary experience.[20] Given an identical situation, with the same assets and same limitations, individuals react in totally different ways. One child may find endless amusement in a box full of colored shapes, while another sits over it in frustrated boredom unless directions are enclosed. Similarly, one person may experience the world as a realm of endless possibility, while another person may experience the same or even a better-equipped world as a meaningless context into which he feels, in Heidegger's term, "contingently thrown."[21]

Ordinary usage distinguishes between the two reactions by speaking in terms of a person either having or lacking imagination. But that is not strictly accurate. Both individuals have imagination—what the second person lacks is *eidetic* imagination. The bored child normally can and does imagine additional facts, for example, another toy; the adult can likewise imagine another fact, perhaps dream of winning the first prize in a lottery. He cannot, however, imagine possibilities; or, more exactly, he can imagine a possible fact but not a possible *eidos,* capable of giving meaning, direction, and the dimension of possibility to the facts at hand. Should he win his million, he would be disappointed; the dream would turn into another "fact." As common sense knows, "unimaginative" people bore easily and, true to the thing-orientation of common sense, blame the world for being boring or frustrating.

This, incidentally, is why seeing many things does not expand the imagination but only stocks factual recall. Imagination grows far more with seeing the same thing in many perspectives and contexts. In a very real sense, as Husserl will tell us later, a fact is meaningful in virtue of "fulfilling" an "empty" eidetic possibility. Common sense recognizes this in the phrase "That's just what I needed," showing that the speaker knew "in principle" what he needed long before he actually saw a "fact" to fit that need. Without such knowledge, he would not even have recognized that "fact" as filling his need, unless it came with a label attached. Looking for something to "make do" presupposes a mature eidetic grasp.

In this context it is no longer startling when Husserl affirms that, while a fact is inseparable from an *eidos,* both the *eidos* and eidetic knowledge are in principle independent of all factual knowledge. Rather, it is a matter of seeing and noting what we in fact take for granted, in spite of the reistic bias of our *sensus naturalis.*

How to accomplish that is the basic topic of Husserl's presentation of the project of phenomenology in *Ideas.* His brief survey in the opening four sections makes the point that phenomenology is possible (because experiential givens include principles as well as particulars) and that it is needed (because our common-sense perspective focuses on particulars and overlooks the principles). Our task now is to see how we can break through the habits of common sense and regain an awareness of our actual lived experience.

In Search of Pure Experience

2

Husserl introduced the concept of phenomenological bracketing, or <u>epochē,</u> as a <u>means of focusing on experience in its lived immediacy, excluding all theoretical interpretation and distortion.</u> Perhaps no other concept in the project of phenomenology has proved as controversial. There is something inherently suspect about a conception of ordinary experience that can be reached only by extraordinary means, and the *epochē* has far too often been interpreted as esoteric indeed.

If the concept of phenomenological bracketing is to be justified—or even understood—it has to be grounded experientially rather than theoretically. Phenomenology, after all, claims to be *seeing,* not speculation. Both the need for a special focus and its possibility have to be there to be seen, in ordinary, not esoteric, experience.

But while the need for and justification of phenomenological bracketing must be *evident* in experience, they need not be *obvious.* As Husserl will point out later, seeing is not a matter of leaping to conclusions on the basis of a casual glance, and neither is phenomenology. Rather, <u>as with all seeing, it is a matter of looking, looking again, then again, each time with greater precision, until we reach a clear, evident grasp.[1]</u>

In dealing with the conception of bracketing, we shall return to the familiar territory of ordinary experience. The old landmarks will all be there: the initial awareness that accompanies our acts, the distinction between particulars and principles, the possibility of grasping principles directly in experience, and even the possibility of examining the structure of experience in its purity, isolated from all factual counterparts, in imagination. This time, however, we shall look more precisely, asking ourselves what in ordinary experience makes a special focus necessary and what makes it possible.

Specifically, we shall look for answers in ordinary experience itself; if they are not there, it would be vain to look for them in Husserl's writings. Only then shall we look at experience through the eyes of Husserl's text, noting his analysis of the habitual bias we need to set aside (§§ 27–30), the actual operation of "bracketing" by which he seeks to achieve this (§§ 31–32), and, finally, the extent and effect of such bracketing (§§ 56–62).[2]

The Metaphysical Bias of Common Sense

As we have noted, there is something about scientific descriptions of lived experience that evokes protest:

> No, I did not offer my son positive reinforcement. I was just glad to have him back. Yes, I did kill the fatted calf and bought him a new suit—but that's not the point. I *welcomed* him, quite spontaneously. It seemed so obvious at the time. When you talk about it, it just doesn't sound the same . . .

Even though the language of the description may be familiar, the facts and even the feelings all duly recorded, the experience somehow just isn't there.

It is not simply that the description does not reproduce the vividness of the experience. That we could accept. A description is not supposed to reproduce; it is supposed to describe. But it should do so faithfully, and too often the ordinary descriptions we unreflectingly accept as true simply fail to do that.

Take, for instance, the way we speak of marriage. As lived, marriage is first of all a *way of being*: being toward each other in freedom and commitment. "Married" is what we *are*. Certainly, there are feelings— but how they fluctuate in the course of a lifetime! There are the living arrangements, the rights and obligations, the economic and social ramifications; but none of that is *our marriage* as we live it.

Yet when a sociologist or a lawyer speaks of our marriage, and, often, even when we speak of it to our single friends, the lived reality of being-married seems to evaporate. Its accidental "objective" counterparts are what comes to the fore. We speak of the housekeeping arrangements, of the financial advantages, of mutual claims and obligations. Those are "the facts." We might speak of our "subjective" feelings as well, but even those appear as "facts." What we live as an essential act we describe in terms of contingent facts: we have a house, I earn, she cooks, and we love each other.

Or consider the case of fear. As an experience, that, too, is a subject's way of being: in this case, being-afraid. It is a way of understanding myself and my world and of orienting toward it. Certainly, it is expressed by behaving in a particular way and is registered in terms of certain feelings, but the primary experience which makes behavior and feeling alike intelligible is that of being-afraid. Yet when we speak of that experience, its expressions become primary. "The subject exhibited avoidance behavior and reported feelings of anxiety." That statement is accurate, but what it describes is no one's experience, only a reconstruction of one. The primordial experience that subjects actually live, being-afraid, seems to disappear.

Strictly on the surface, the difference might appear as one of perspective. As lived, experience is always our act. The world is not the initial reality; the act is. The world is its stage, and our behavior, feelings, and objects are the stage props through which we act out ourselves. The primordial reality, however, is the role, not in the sense of a prewritten sequence of actions, as in a play, but as in a commedia dell'arte in which the actor is given a character and an intent to act out as he will. As I enter my workshop, I have a purpose: I will make a cradle. My presence gives the shop a unity as the context of my act; my purpose gives meaning to its contents: ash stock for the rockers, knives to carve the end panels, geraniums in a window box to cheer my day. As we live our experiences, we are always aware of them from the center of the action.

When we describe our experiences, our viewpoint shifts as we habitually assume the role of an observer. There was a shop, he went in . . . : we are no longer conscious of the intent being acted out. Instead, we focus on the world of objects, of behavior, or, if we are introspective psychologists, of the feelings through which we act out ourselves. Reality is no longer the experienced, the lived, but rather the "objective," as if in a game of chess we saw the pieces and the moves but considered the player's intent—say, the Sicilian defense—as "merely subjective."

In ordinary discourse that inversion can be frustrating, but for most purposes ordinary speakers are resigned to it and compensate for it automatically. When a speaker states, "My Jimmy, he's a real fine boy; he helps me around the house and goes fishing with me," his hearers know that he is not saying that he values his son as an unpaid yardman or oarsman but that he is speaking of the joy of being-a-father and having-a-son as a way of being. The distortion in expression is automatically corrected as we take facts as a shorthand for lived experiences.

If, however, we were to record the conversation and others like it on tape and submit the material to a computer analysis, those facts might well obscure the intent. We might, for instance, conclude that "the lower classes" are unfeeling and materialistic in their relation to their children, since they speak of their usefulness. Outsiders, not familiar with the shorthand which Americans inherited from their huddled masses, will frequently conclude that Americans are grossly materialistic because they habitually express their compassion through effective material aid. Similarly, college students whose parents provide them with everything from tuition to pocket money can still feel unloved if they fail to see all they receive as an expression of loving care. Losing sight of the lived reality through fascination with the "facts" embodying it can be a source of tragic personal misunderstandings.

That myopia of common sense becomes dogmatic when it claims the authority of "science," whether that science is theology, sociology, or nuclear physics. The reality with which the sciences begin is a lived experience, whether of the holy, of human coexistence, or of the need to manipulate a resisting environment. The constructions they build upon it, whether systematizing our religious experience or our conception of the world as physical, can be most useful. We have learned by experience that we can work our purposes most effectively when we assess our situation objectively. A drowning person can save himself if he can master the urge to get out of the water and instead can float with only his nostrils breaking the surface. The objectifications of our sciences are a powerful tool. But if we lose sight of their experiential grounding, we might well end up dismissing our lived reality, in the name of science, as "merely subjective" or evaluating it in terms of our objective constructions.[3]

So, for example, the basic thrust of being-human (as distinct from merely surviving), which we experience as the desire for freedom and dignity, is quite naturally expressed "objectively" in the quest for the objects and the conditions which we consider conducive to them. But if we were to lose sight of the lived experience and to treat those objects and conditions as reality itself, we might come to conclude that, given a choice, we must sacrifice the "merely subjective" freedom and dignity to preserve the "objective" reality. Or, more simply, noting that free men are happy at their labor, we might conclude that we shall make men happy by forcing them to labor. George Orwell and Alexander Solzhenitsyn know something about that, both in fiction and in fact.

It is not phenomenological theory but the experienced distortion of lived experience in ordinary description that leads us to look for "brackets"—for a procedure which, for the moment, would set aside all our theoretical assumptions about the nature of reality, including the uncritical objectivism of our common sense, and allow us to see and describe experience in its lived purity. The need for bracketing arises from experience.

Similarly, the possibility of such a focus cannot be derived from phenomenological theory unless it is already present in experience. Phenomenology cannot invent; it must *see,* grasp directly, the primordial given of awareness. It may point out the experienced *epochē* to us, clarify it, purify it of uncritical assumptions and contingent factors, but it must first look for it in ordinary experience.

Here we might well look to those moments of crisis about which common usage will say that "the world ceased to exist for me; I could only think of X." Consider, for example, the perspective of a parent whose child is threatened by an abductor and who gladly pays the fortune demanded for his safe return. Objectively, a child is far easier to replace than a fortune. Even subjectively, for the purposes of emotional satisfaction, warm cuddly babies are virtually interchangeable. But a parent does not think in those terms. "Nothing mattered," he/she will tell us; "I could only think of my baby."

The world, strictly speaking, did not cease to exist, but it did lose its explanatory force. It could no longer provide the criteria of greater and lesser worth. In that moment, its value and relevance appeared clearly derivative from the lived reality, the being-toward-another of parent and child. That was what made the fortune valuable or the cuddling emotionally satisfying. When it was threatened, the illusory autonomy of the world disappeared, and the world appeared as we live it, in the perspective of experience.

In a crisis situation we recapture the primordial experiential perspective quite spontaneously and unsystematically. But we also do it consciously and systematically, still wholly in ordinary terms, in the theater. As the circus presents a vision of a world redeemed, so the stage presents us with an almost literal vision of phenomenological bracketing.

Basically, in the theater, the object-world is again suspended. It exists, but it explains nothing. The fact that the lead actor was suffering from acute indigestion cannot serve to explain why Othello strangled Desdemona. The explanation must come from the role, that is, from pure experience. Here the world becomes literally a stage, deriving its reality from human acts: spilled catsup becomes blood, and painted canvas an impenetrable wall, according to its relation to the role. The world as "real" is bracketed; it remains as lived. It is no longer the *explanans,* explaining human acts. It becomes the *explanandum,* deriving its meaning from them.

The theater in effect presents experience in reflection, conceptually available, but in the way in which subjects actually live it rather than from the viewpoint of an observer. It also presents a model of the way we can and do break the hold that the common-sense conception of the world as "objective" has on our understanding: by treating it as a stage. The world does not disappear, but it loses its authority. Analogously, we can break through the screen of our special sciences, from theology to physics, to the lived experience at their core, placing them in a human perspective rather than reducing ourselves to the perspective of the sciences as authoritative. We can even break through the dogmas of our fundamental *scientia,* philosophy, rediscovering, for instance, the experience of will and obstacle at the root of our usual assertions about "the mind-body problem."

There is only one sticking point. We can—and at times do—treat both the world and everything in it as a stage, but we cannot suspend the I that perceives and brackets it. What we can suspend is the I as a natural subject, one being among others. The "myself" we see in a mirror, we can suspend, much as the actor loses himself in the role he plays. But the role as lived is never anonymous. It is always someone's "mine." That "someone" is not a body, not a *res cogitans* or a psychological or theological entity like a psyche or a soul. It is simply the sheer I-hood of all experience. Look to your own experience: though you convince yourself, with Tirse de Molina, that life is a dream, there is always *an I* dreaming it. No matter how objectively we look, even at ourselves, there is always *an I* doing the looking. That *I* may at times lack all self-confidence, may feel pathetic, impotent, and insignificant; without it, however, there would no longer be experience but only a set of meaningless events. A camera lives no experience; it simply records events. As lived, experience is irreducibly a *subject's* experience. It need not be subjective in the sense of private, arbitrary, or illusory. The marriage I live is as objective as our daily experience, the Sicilian defense is as objective as my *Chess Handbook;* but as lived, it is always a subject's experience, it is meaningful and intelligible as such.[4]

We need a special focus on experience to see it as it is lived and meaningful, in a subject's perspective. We know that such a special focus is possible because we encounter it in crisis situations and in the theater. What we need to do is to formulate it as a rigorous, self-conscious procedure.[5]

Husserl's §§ 27–30:	§§ 27–30
The Thesis of the	
Natural Standpoint	

What Husserl undertakes in the opening chapter of the second part of his *Ideas*[6] becomes most intelligible when we read it not as an esoteric speculation but as a rigorous, systematic description of the needs and possibilities of the experiential perspective which we have already noted superficially in our survey of ordinary experience.

Notice that Husserl starts out by switching to the first person. It is not the intimate first person of private personal experience but rather something we could call the "first person indefinite" of common human experience, for which in English we ordinarily use the first-person plural. For his "I am aware of a world" we could substitute *"An I* is aware . . ." (or "We are aware . . .") because all experience,

§ 27a

even experience we share, is in the first place something *an I* lives, only secondarily something an observer can describe in the third person. Locutions such as "the subject exhibits an awareness" already interpret experience. As lived, its form is always that of "(an) I am aware . . ."

§ 27b   But, as Husserl notes, experience even in the first person is not private or arbitrary but has definite generic characteristics. Perhaps the most pervasive of these is that experience invariably confronts me as an encounter with a world "out there," which is real independently of me. On this level we experience no Cartesian doubt.[7] Though we may mistake particulars, in principle persons, animals, and objects confront us as something we encounter as *there* to be seen, touched, and heard, *not* as something we invent.

Not only that: we also encounter the objects of our experience as interrelated and as ordered, near and far, lower and higher, constitut-
§ 27c   ing a spatial matrix which includes them and shades off indefinitely toward an all-embracing horizon. Similarly, we experience them as ordered in time. Though our actual experience, including present memories and anticipations, is always present, its objects, clearly, are not. They are extended in time as they are extended in space, in an order
§ 27d   of long ago, just now, in a while, yet to come. Finally, they are ordered in value terms as well. Though we may have to alter such initial valuations, we do not have to invent them. *Ab initio,* the objects of our world present themselves as friendly or hostile, helpful or adverse, exhibiting a whole range of values. Together, they appear to us as the illuminated segment of a continuum, of whose presence we are aware but which exceeds our direct awareness, stretching endlessly in time and space to form the horizon of our world.

§ 28a   Within this world we are aware of ourselves as well, as among the objects present to our awareness, each of us one person among many in the world. I, too, am "there" to be seen and touched. But I am aware of myself in a second sense as well, as everything that Descartes lumps under the term *cogito.* I am doing the seeing: it is I who sees, feels, touches, and gives meaning to this world. The world is there *before* me and *for* me, as my sphere of activity. The sterilized instruments on the tray would, by themselves, be just dumb, meaningless things, one after another. It is my presence as a surgeon that gives them unity and meaning.

§ 28b   My role as a subject stands out most clearly when I consider the other "worlds," other contexts which I can constitute, like the world of mathematics (which Husserl mentions) or the world of my daydreams (which he does not). These, too, are worlds, coherent systems around me. Yet there is a difference. The natural world is always there, whether I will it or not, resisting me and including me. My ideal worlds, though not arbitrary, are totally dependent on me. In relation to them, I am purely a subject.[8]

Common sense, we might note in the margin, is never quite sure what to do about my presence as a subject. My presence as a body is simple enough: I can always stand outside myself and figuratively look down upon myself, "there" in the world. But what about the subject who does the looking? He is real, yet never an object I can see as "out there." Common sense resolves the difficulty by positing a "soul," which it imagines as "just like" an object though not quite an object, in the world yet not of it. The conception of a sheer I-hood is too difficult for it. In common-sense imagination, the "soul" provides the sheer I-function with a substantive pseudo-body which makes it thinkable.[9]

This is especially handy when we come to deal with other humans.   § 29
They are there, like chairs, cups, and teddy bears, but, unlike these objects, they have a spontaneity of their own. They, too, are subjects, constituting worlds around them. The world of their daydreams or the world of their mathematics may be different—especially if one of them happens to be Riemann or Boole. Yet common sense is quite confident that their "objective" world is the same as mine and that they fit this common world as bodies or, in the case of their subjectivity, as "souls."

All of this is familiar from our earlier survey. Husserl reports it far more systematically; but though his terminology is at times unusual, what he reports is not. This, indeed, is the world as we ordinarily describe it, and, as such, it is reasonably nonproblematic.

But then comes § 30, in which Husserl calls our attention to the   § 30
fact that our common sense, which he speaks of as the *natürliche Einstellung,* goes significantly beyond such simple description.

To grasp § 30 clearly, we have to note first, and note emphatically, that the *natürliche Einstellung,* usually rendered "natural standpoint," is in fact the conventional, habitual standpoint that ordinary English usage describes as "common sense"; it is not some biological necessity of our perception. Similarly, when Husserl speaks of "the natural world," he is not speaking about a biological "world of nature" but about the image and conception of the world which are so familiar that they "come naturally" to us.[10]

"Natürlich," like "natural," can mean "of or pertaining to nature," but it can also mean "the familiar," "the customary," "the matter-of-fact." When a German speaker answers your request to use his telephone with "Aber natürlich," "Naturally," he is not saying that it is a matter of a natural ability or a biological necessity. He is saying that it is a matter of course; "naturally" you may use the phone. Similarly, in English, when we speak of someone acting "naturally," we do not mean that he is driven by natural instinct but that he is acting without conscious effort, in a familiar, habitual way, though his behavior may represent an acquired convention of our particular subgroup.

This is crucial. If the "natural standpoint" really designated some biological necessity of our perception, bracketing it would distort, not reveal, lived experience. But that is not what Husserl's "natural standpoint" means. Rather, it designates the centuries-old habit of Western thought that is so ingrained in us that we slip into it effortlessly, "naturally." It is what older philosophy used to call the *sensus naturalis*— and which usual English designates as our "common sense."

Thus, when Husserl speaks of the natural standpoint, he is not claiming that some biological necessity forces a metaphysics upon us but simply that the ingrained habits of our common sense, without our even being aware of it, lead us into a metaphysics. Precisely because our common sense is habitual and quite free of self-conscious reflection, because it is preoccupied with the world it encounters as "out there," it assumes that *reality* itself is "out there," only passively recorded by the subject "in here." The shift is subtle but significant. As lived, reality is the *experiencing of* an object. As common sense interprets it, the reality is *the object;* the experience is incidental to it. That is no longer a datum; it is the unacknowledged theoretical postulate of common-sense knowledge. Husserl calls it the "thesis of the natural standpoint": the world is "out there," only its reflection is "in here," so that, if I am to understand what is "in here," I must look for an explanation "out there"; or, in sum, lived experience is what is to be explained, and the world is what explains it. To understand my experience, common sense assumes, I need not know what I am experiencing but must discover *what in the world* is causing it.

It is this elementary theoretical postulate, adopted uncritically by the sciences, that makes a behavioristic or a physicalistic model of scientific explanation appealing. Yet in terms of actual experience that postulate is problematic. Think back, for a moment, to the example of lighting a cigarette in a nonsmoker's house. There was no ashtray there. The ashtray that the smoker confidently reports having found "out there in the world," though clearly not existing "merely in the mind," actually exists *in his experience* rather than in any "objective world," independent of any subject.

That is also a crucial point: the world is indeed "there" *in lived experience,* but that experience is not an ephemeral, transparent nonrealm between a "subjective" mind and an "objective" world. Nor is it a passive "subjective" report of an autonomously existing "objective" reality. It is *reality,* the only reality that is actually given in experience rather than constructed in speculation. As such, it is very much *a subject's reality.* To be sure, it is not "subjective" in the sense of being entirely private or arbitrary, invented by the subject *ex nihilo.* Few things, except perhaps mental states, are actually that. But experience is *a subject's* activity: its characteristics, though neither private nor arbitrary, still relate to a—any—subject.

So, for example, the spatial ordering of my experience as near and far, large and small, certainly is not subjective in the sense of being "only in the mind," subject to arbitrary manipulation. The bookshelf is not farther than the desk "because I think so"; no amount of thought will reverse that order. The bookshelf is "really" farther. Yet, at the same time, the bookshelf is farther only in relation to the experiencing subject. Even the entirely "objective" characteristic of spatial location describes the "objective" world with reference to a subject. Experience may be "objectively ordered," but it is so *as a subject's experience.*

The same is true of temporal location. Again, sooner or later is not simply a "subjective" matter. Next Wednesday will come before next Friday and no amount of thought will change the sequence. But the sequence of sooner or later is contingent on a now. Wednesday will come before Friday because today is Monday. Temporal structure, too, while not "subjective," describes *the context of a subject's experience.*

Similar observations apply to the value-structuring of experience. Things are not good or bad simply because thinking makes them so; no amount of thought will make salt water good to drink. Yet neither are they simply "objectively" so. The quality "good to drink," though "objective" in the sense of nonarbitrary, is so only in relation to a possible drinking subject. Things really are good or bad, though in the context of *a subject's*—any subject's—experience.

Such observations are, in a sense, quite trivial, noting no more than we all take for granted. Still, they must be made because the experience they express is wholly incompatible with something else we take for granted, the uncritical metaphysical bias of our common sense. According to the "thesis of the natural standpoint" as Husserl described it earlier, a whole range of lived experiences, for instance the experience of value, would have to be dismissed as illusory. That thesis holds that reality is "out there in the world"; its reflection, variously classified as illusion or "merely mental reality," is said to be "in here," "in the mind." There is nothing else. Common sense in its theorizing recognizes no experienced beauty. At times it claims that beauty is real, "objectively" out there in the world, in a flower or a painting. A subject's impression (and subsequently idea) of beauty simply records it, more or less accurately. Alternately, common sense dismisses beauty as "merely subjective," a matter of preference with no intersubjective significance. Values and all generic characteristics of lived experience fare the same way; spatial and temporal location are rescued only by a putative "objective" space and time. The thesis of the natural standpoint—that reality is out there in the world, that the world explains experience—permits no other possibility. Common sense is a true heir of Descartes: whatever is real must be a *res extensa* or a *res cogitans—tertium* simply *non datur*.

As has been noted earlier, common sense, in its daily practice, pays little attention to its own theorizing. Though it may declare, for instance, values to be illusory, it recognizes and respects their reality in practice and expects a like respect from others. Though it may dismiss, say, justice, as "only an idea," it retains the ability to subordinate material gain and personal prejudice to a conception of "what is only fair." Though ordinary speakers may theorize that a dowry is real and all else "merely subjective," they do marry and, more painfully, do divorce "for love."

Common sense can afford its facile objectivism because it does not have to raise the question of ultimate reality. Adequate functioning is enough. As philosophers or as special scientists, we cannot avoid that question. We may be able to describe human acts equally well on the assumption that they constitute a closed stimulus-response system or on the assumption that they are the expression of human freedom. But we need not only to describe but also to choose. Our assumptions commit us to priorities that have widely different consequences. We cannot simply let them happen. We need a critical foundation rather than the haphazard one provided by the habitual thesis of the natural standpoint. To secure such a foundation, we need to see reality as given, as actually lived—or, as Husserl puts it, to look at it "in brackets."

Husserl's §§ 31–32: The Idea of Phenomenological Bracketing

§ 31

Husserl speaks of bracketing (reduction, *epoché*) rather freely, without always specifying exactly what he has in mind. While describing ordinary experience in §§ 1–3, he used the generic term *epoché* in the specific sense which at times he distinguishes as *eidetic*. There it refers to the suspension of particulars. It is the operation of looking through instantiating particulars to grasp a phenomenon in principle.

This is not a uniquely phenomenological operation. When a child adds six apples and six apples and gets eleven apples ("If I had so many, I'd lose one—my basket is too small . . .") and the teacher urges him to forget about apples and think of the sum, $6 + 6 = 12$, she is asking him to impose an eidetic *epoché*. She is not doing phenomenology; the eidetic reduction is common to all knowledge. Were we able to grasp only the fact that *this* triangle has angles adding up to 180° and not the principle that this is so *necessarily,* we should live in an Alice-in-Wonderland world in which anything could happen. That we do not live in such a world we owe to our ability to grasp principles, or, in Husserl's terms, to impose an *eidetic epoché*.

The *phenomenological epoché* which Husserl introduces in § 31 is a very different matter. It refers again to a suspension, but this time of the common-sense thesis that a transcendent reality "explains" experience. It is the operation of treating phenomena as we in fact encounter them, as subject experiences.

The *eidetic* reduction (seeing in terms of principles) is obviously crucial for the phenomenological-transcendental reduction. If we were to apply the shift to a radically experiential viewpoint (the *phenomenological epoché*) simply to factual, particular experiences, the result would be a solipsistic subjectivism, a purely private perspective on purely private experiences. The shift to the subject viewpoint is not subjectivistic because experience, grasped in principle (in *eidetic* brackets), is not purely subjective. The sum $2 + 2 = 4$ is a subject's sum, but it is not subjective; in principle it is independent of the size of my basket. The "solipsism" of phenomenological shift to the subject, as Husserl points out in the fourth *CM* (note esp. §§ 34, 40), is harmless because subject experience, if seen in principle, has universal validity. (Or, in the technical language of phenomenology, the phenomenological *epoché* is transcendental insofar as it subsumes a previous eidetic *epoché*.)

But, for all that, the eidetic "seeing in principle" is not of itself phenomenology. Phenomenology in the strict sense begins only with the radically experiential turn of the *phenomenological* (transcendental) *epoché*—the rigorous, self-conscious suspension of the "thesis of the natural standpoint." It is a refusal to accept the assumption of common sense that "reality" is the objective, posited as existing "out there" and "explaining" the given, lived reality—while that lived reality is "merely subjective." In brackets, any transcendent reality—that is, reality posited as "objectively existing" rather than as experientially given—is denied any explanatory value.

Quite simply, I see a glass. That is a given. I can, on that basis, form a hypothesis that a glass is there. But I cannot, on the strength of that hypothesis, conclude that the glass is "reality" and my experience of a glass mere subjective impression. Similarly, I may legitimately speak of tables in terms of molecules or of fear as avoidance behavior, but I cannot claim that such constructs constitute the reality of my experience of tables or of fear. That experience must be understood as lived before I can legitimately go on to theorize about it.

The terms that Husserl uses indicate his intent. He speaks of bracketing, of abstention, of *epoché,* of phenomenological reduction, as well as a host of other terms, creating the illusion of a complex of multiple operations. In fact, differences in precise definition are implicit in the text. But the basic move is the same; it is perhaps best characterized by the term *Ausschaltung*. Literally, the word means "switching off," as when we switch off an electric lamp. The lamp is still there, but now as one of the objects in the room, not as that which illuminates everything else. This is what the phenomenologist does when he "switches off the world" or, more precisely, the common-sense assumption that the world explains experience. The world, like the lamp, is still there, but no longer as that which makes experience "visible" (here, intelligible). The presence of the subject does that. The world remains as a datum, but now as a datum to be explained, not as that which "explains" experience. For, metaphysically, as we know from ordinary experience, the fact that I see a sharp steel object pointed at me is hardly the reality of deadly fear.

Husserl insists that he is not pretending that the world does not exist or even doubting whether it does.[11] Even less is he claiming that the "mental pole" of the common-sense polarity of the mental and the physical is somehow really real, or more real than the physical. That would not be phenomenology or even critical idealism; it would be no more than materialism stood on its head. The purpose of phenomenological bracketing is to break free of the entire categorical schema introduced by common sense and to recognize the reality of the world as neither "subjective" nor "objective" but *as experience* or, in Husserl's terminology, *as phenomenon*.[12]

Such a radical shift of viewpoint is possible, as a pretheoretical propaedeutic rather than a theoretical proposal, because the thesis of common sense is not the result of a judgment but rather a habitual stance we assume toward the world. We do not examine experiential evidence and come to the conclusion that the reality, say, the ashtray, is "out there" and thus accounts for the presence of the idea "in here." If we examined the evidence, as we did in our earlier example, we would not come to that conclusion. The ashtray is first in experience. Rather, we make the assumption, quite unthinkingly, that since we encounter the world as there before us, it must explain experience; and we build our theories on it, overlooking the real constitution of our ashtray in experience.

§ 31b

But we do not *have to* make that assumption. Once we become conscious of it, we can modify it in various ways. We can doubt it, as Descartes does; we can modify it in imagination, as Santayana thinks we in fact do; or we can bracket it, as Husserl proposes to do. But Husserl is not Descartes. Even when lecturing in Paris and using Descartes as a bridge between himself and his French audience, Husserl sees the sole value of what he styles Descartes's *attempt* at universal doubt (*der allgemeine Zweifel*versuch) in its making the point

§ 31c,d

that the habitual objectivism of common sense is not inherent in some "human nature," much less in reality itself, but is really no more than a habitual assumption.

§ 31e,f   Husserl's intent, however, is radically different from Descartes's, as we have already noted (p. 37, n. 11). The phenomenology that Husserl proposes is in no sense Cartesian. Descartes doubts the existence of the world in order to assure himself of it. His concern is with the existence (or nonexistence) of the world. Husserl, by contrast, does not doubt the existence of the world one bit: he treats that as an experiential given. But he is supremely uninterested in it. What interests him is how to *understand* it. That is why he does not propose to doubt it but rather to *bracket* it, that is, to abstain from using it as a principle of explanation so that we can understand how it is constituted as experience.

This is a crucial difference but, for all the apparent obscurity of its philosophical formulation, not really an obscure one. Say, for instance, that we are studying the cargo cults.[13] We observe Polynesians marching in makeshift uniforms, carrying mock rifles. From our natural standpoint, it is tempting to "explain" this as a reflection of a reality existing out there: European armies had been there, and the natives are imitating their behavior. But such an explanation yields little understanding. Why are they imitating this and not something else? Why did the European presence become a motive? How do the natives' acts *make sense* as subject experience? The question is not What do they "feel"? but What are they doing, as subjects? To answer the question, we need to put "the world" into brackets—seeing it not as a fact, as *explanans,* but as a phenomenon—and then pose the question How do the subjects experience this behavior? What does it mean in the context of their experience? What is it *as a human way of being in the world?* On that basis we can understand the concept of "cargo," and of ritual as a means of procuring it, and we can then go back and see why the natives are imitating just this behavior. Having uncovered the intentional structure of the experience, we can even take the world, so ordered, out of brackets and construct a "causal" explanation of the *particular form* the experience takes.[14]

Or we can take an example in philosophy. If we are studying, say, the traditional "mind-body" problem, it is also tempting to claim that the problem arises "because" humans "have" bodies and minds or perhaps "because" past thinkers have written what they have about the subject. But such an explanation again yields little understanding. Why does the question persist? We have to bracket the world (here, the history of philosophy), refrain from attributing any causal efficiency to it, and ask what in lived experience leads us to raise the question. We might, for instance, note the experience of thwarted effort, of disappointed expectation—whatever. The point is that we have first to understand the mind-body problem in primordial experience. Only then can we return to the history of philosophy and construct a "causal" explanation, showing why we in fact articulate the problem as we do.

Such examples, however, take us much too far afield. Husserl was hardly thinking in sociological terms. His concern, as he himself stresses,[15] was with the principle of explanation: bracketing the existence of a transcendent, "objective" world as a principle of explanation so that we can see human experience, and indeed *all* consciousness, in its intrinsic intelligibility, as a phenomenon.

Phenomenology, as Husserl presents it, is not a study of "mere appearances." It is a study of experiences. The world as phenomenon, as we shall see in detail later (*I* § 33, below), is not the world as appearance but the world as experience. Its implicit metaphysical claim is simply the radically experiential recognition that experience is the only given reality; all else is abstraction. What is significant for sociological explanation is not hunger as a low caloric intake, as the materialists would claim, nor the "Hunger as Idea" of Hegelian dialectics, but hunger *as a human experience.* Husserl, in turning to the world as phenomenon, is seeking to return to lived experience.

That, finally, is what the phenomenological *epochē*—our "bracketing"—is all about. In the *epochē* we do not doubt the world's existence but bracket it, suspending the thesis that the world "out there" is what makes experience "in here" intelligible. We know the world exists, we know there are sciences that describe it as existing, but we choose not to use any of this as a principle of explanation. It is the intelligibility of experience that makes the world intelligible, not vice versa.

§ 32

Imposing the phenomenological *epochē,* finally, means no more than treating the contents of our experience *as experience* and rigorously refraining from attributing to them the significance of images of or indices to some hidden transexperiential "reality." Bracketing the ashtray of our earlier example means not *doubting* but *recognizing its reality as experience* instead of treating it as a "mere appearance" of some putative real ("objective" or "mental") ashtray. Or, in the case of the human and social sciences, it means setting aside "reality" as the dogma of a science and rediscovering it as a human way of being-in-the world. The contents of consciousness, whether physical, social, or human phenomena, are primordially human acts, not natural events. Phenomenological brackets "switch off" the dogma of the "natural world" to rediscover the world as experience.[16]

Husserl's §§ 56–62:
The Brackets
in Practice

§ 56a   If Husserl's presentation of phenomenological bracketing in §§ 31 and 32 is clearly seen, it should require no further explanation. But seeing is rarely accomplished at a glance, especially when noting something we habitually overlook. To look at the world as experience, we need to overcome more than three centuries of habitual reliance on objective explanation and on the sciences based on such explanation. Which of that familiar fund of ideas can we retain?

§ 56b   We have suspended our habitual reliance on the "world of nature"; its objects, we noted, become intelligible in and as experience and so cannot explain experience. But that is true, as Husserl points out, of our cultural objects as well. With the advent of cultural relativism, we become less likely to attribute human acts to an "instinct," such as a territorial imperative, and more likely to attribute them to cultural conditioning, say, to "class consciousness."

Such entities, too, have to be suspended in phenomenological bracketing. It may, for instance, be the case that the moral code generally accepted in our society requires compensation for unprovoked injury. But, except in the most trivial sense, we cannot use that fact to "explain" the sense of obligation to replace a borrowed pen we have broken. Our moral code itself requires explanation. To say that humans do X because "society" or its "mores" demand it involves us in a vicious regress. We need to ground our explanation in the primordial experience on which the entire personal and social superstructure of morals is based. To do this, we need to grasp the primordial moral dimension of lived experience—the *eidos* that unprovoked injury creates an obligation to make amends—in all its lived clarity and immediacy. Thus here, too, we need to bracket our moral code as a putative given reality so that we can understand it as an expression of a primordial lived experience.[17]

Very roughly, we are familiar with this need from ordinary experience. The lived experience of having something we cherish wantonly destroyed enables us to understand laws against vandalism. The existence of such statutes does not explain why we condemn acts of destruction. And, while the example is approximate, it exemplifies Husserl's principle: lived experience makes cultural constructs intelligible, not vice versa.

With the suspension of the "natural (and cultural) order" as an explanatory principle, a different kind of objectivism suggests itself. Our bracketing brings to the fore precisely those aspects of experience which have usually served as the basis for theism—its value, its structure, its purposiveness. With the world and the naturalistic explanation bracketed, a theistic explanation becomes tempting.[18]

§58

Yet such an explanation, too, must be bracketed. That is not a matter of denying or affirming God's existence any more than that of the world. But while the experience of the holy is as much an experiential given as our experience of the world, the God of theology is no more a given than the world of physics. To "explain" our experience by saying that "God" causes it yields no more understanding than to say that it is caused by the physical or cultural world. Theology, like sociology or physics, is a special science. It builds on experience, and its conclusions are significant only from the standpoint of the lived experience on which it builds.

Phenomenology can quite legitimately deal with religious experience, but it cannot look for help from theology, except as one of the data of our cultural experience. The putative "cause" of religious experience may be the encounter with the true living God; it may also be an overdose of mescaline sulphate or a projection of a father image. Personally, I happen to hold the first theory, but that is irrelevant. The cause is suspended; the experience is what matters. Our task, finally, is not to "explain" religious experience but first to understand it.

Not only the sciences of transcendent reality but even the formal sciences, Husserl tells us, fall within the brackets—at least in their role as *mathesis universalis,* the ultimate explanatory principle, though not as a pure description of the evident structure of thought. We shall continue to rely on logic to make unambiguous communication possible, but we shall refrain from using it as an explanatory principle.

§59

§ 59a   The difference is crucial, though not new. We have not explained the experience of a disappointed expectation by symbolizing it with a "~" or the experience of inescapable choice by symbolizing it with a " $\widehat{v}$," though these are handy notations. To the contrary, it is the respective experiences which make it intelligible why humans construct conceptions of negation or disjunction.

But logic is more than a formalization of experience in an empirical sense. It is also an expression of a clear grasp of the eidetic structure of that experience whose necessity is structural rather than empirical. The insight that $\sim (p \cdot \sim p)$ is not an empirical hypothesis whose validity would be contingent on empirical evidence. It is a pure eidetic insight with its own intrinsic necessity. As such, it is intrinsic to experience as its necessary condition and can no more be set aside than experience itself. Our brackets set aside all that is contingent, not what is necessary. Or, to illustrate quite naively, $2 + 2 = 4$ not "because" adding two pomegranates to the two already in the basket yields four pieces but because we can see that, in principle, it *must* be so, which is why the "new math" is possible. It is this basic insight that enables us to make sense of the multitudinous world around us—in which, incidentally, two and two objects do not necessarily add up to four objects: witness hungry cats and fat mice.[19]

§ 59b   This is what leads Husserl to distinguish two types of principles (or "patterns" or "structures"; in German we would speak of *Wesen*). One type he designates as immanent, the other transcendent; these equate roughly with the necessary structures inherent in experience as such and the generalized traits of empirical evidence. Since the purpose of bracketing is to exhibit experience in its lived immediacy, the *epochē,* or brackets, does not touch immanent essences but exhibits them in their clarity—precisely by suspending, as explanatory principles, the transcendent essences which we construct rather than grasp directly or, in our metaphor, "see."

The category of transcendent essences includes a wide range of principles, from commonly accepted prejudices to the "laws" of empirical science. They can be harmful, as in our habit of describing as "only natural" human behavior which we cannot justify on moral grounds. They can be neutral, like our categories of reflection, "subjective" and "objective." Or they can be most useful, like the constructs of the special sciences which enable us to deal effectively with our world. But in all cases they are transcendent, describing a putative object world rather than experience itself. The concept of the Oedipus complex, for instance, may be a useful way of describing certain patterns of experience for therapeutic purposes, but it is not an experiential datum. Its validity is derivative, and so it must be set aside in the search for primordial lived experience.

By contrast, immanent essences are principles inherent in lived experience itself. These are crucial. As Husserl has stressed throughout, our experience as lived is already intelligible, to its subjects rather than to theorists only, because not all principles are transcendent. Some are intrinsic to experience, constituting its initial intelligibility. They include, for instance, the intrinsic value-structuring of experience which Brentano uses as an example: the goodness of love and the badness of hate. Husserl's favorite example is the necessary relationship of the opposite angles of a parallelogram. Our own example is the necessary subject-orientation of lived experience. Since such principles are intrinsic to experience, bracketing all transexperiential constructs does not affect them.

This distinction, Husserl tells us, applies to the bracketing of logic, §§ 59b–60 mathematics, and all the "material eidetic disciplines"—the theoretical sciences of the empirical world such as theoretical physics. What we bracket in them are all constructs, no matter how useful, that are based on observation and generalization. What we retain are the evident principles, immanent in experience, which we can grasp clearly in terms of their own necessity.

With that distinction in mind we can return to § 57, which we §57 passed over earlier, and to the topic of bracketing the subject of experience. The distinction between the "natural" and the pure ego is basically the distinction between the transcendent and the immanent. Husserl's basic point is that conceptions like "man," "rational animal," "soul," "homo faber," are all ways we describe rather than live our being and so have to be bracketed. To say, for instance, that humans become attached to a homeland "because" they are territorial beings yields no understanding. It obscures the lived by the conjectured. The given is the lived experience (and principle) of self-actualization through identification with an objective counterpart. To exhibit it in its purity, we have to set aside all our theoretical conceptions of "human nature."

But, as we noted earlier, do what we will, even if we conceive of all of our experience as a dream, we cannot escape a basic subject perspective or, in Husserl's terms, the *pure ego*.

The sheer I-ness of our experience simply cannot be bracketed. The primordial experiential given, that all of my experiences are an I's experiences and intelligible only as such, is an immanent principle, a condition rather than a content of my experience. Without that I-hood, experience becomes fundamentally unintelligible.[20]

Husserl's recognition of immanent *sheer I-hood* as a necessary condition of all experience lends itself to misinterpretation, especially in translation. The term Husserl uses is *reines Ich,* literally, the "pure I." In English or French this becomes "pure ego," *l'ego pur.* The translation is formally unexceptionable, but the connotations of the Latinism "ego" are altogether different from those of the vernacular *Ich, I* or *je. Ich*—I—is something I *am*. "The ego," by contrast, suggests something I *have*. Ordinary usage speaks of someone's "having an inflated ego," as if there were two entities, the person and the ego *he has*. The term "pure ego" does not usually suggest to us the sheer I-ness of our acts but rather some soul-like entity which the subject has and to which he attributes his acts.

Against the background of such connotations, it is not difficult to misinterpret Husserl's "pure ego" as a piece of metaphysical furniture and to conclude that the conception of such an unbracketable "pure ego," over and beyond the contents of our experience, is a superfluous hypothesis.

§ 57b

Yet Husserl is quite aware that the "pure ego" is not an entity and is never an object of experience. It can, he tells us in *I* § 57b, *"in keinem Sinn als reelles Stück oder Moment* der Erlebnisse selbst *gelten"* (it can "in no sense figure as a part or a moment of lived experience itself"). As we know from experience, whenever we try to look at the I which is doing the observing, that "I" retreats a step back, as the perennial subject. Husserl does not claim, as his critics assume, that the subject *has* an aspect or an entity called "the pure ego." Rather, he points out, on rigorously experiential grounds, that *the subject* is not only a "natural subject"—a body, a mind, or a soul—but also, more fundamentally, a sheer I-hood of all experience.[21]

Here the experience of which his text speaks may prove a better guide than the text itself. What Husserl is pointing out is the commonplace of experience, that all of my acts in fact are, and are intelligible, *as mine.* I function as their subject. Lived experience never takes the hypothetical form of an anonymous "streetcar-to-be-caught." In Ricoeur's words, it always includes a self-imputation. No matter how hard I am running, my awareness is always one of a "streetcar-to-be-caught-*by-me*"; otherwise I would stop running.[22] Or, as Husserl quotes Kant as saying, "The 'I think' must be able to accompany all my presentations."

§ 57c

This sheer I-ness of all experience, as Husserl acknowledges, is never a component *within* it. To the extent to which it does have a factual counterpart, like my physical presence running after a streetcar or like my personal history, which gives an idiosyncratic twist to my interpretation, it is a part of the "natural" world and so is subject to bracketing. The sheer I-ness of my experience has no content, is not a part of anything, yet is always with me. Speaking in popular terms, I can never find the I *in* my experiences; the I is always doing the experiencing. Yet I do not arrive at a hypothesis of sheer I-hood by speculation; it is not only the necessary condition but also the most persistent given of my experience.[23] While transcendent in the sense of being the condition rather than the content of my experience, the sheer I-hood (*reines Ich*) is also radically immanent, given in experience itself, and so defies bracketing. I can and indeed must bracket myself as what Husserl will later call a "natural subject," but I can understand experience only as long as I recognize the fundamental I-orientation of its intelligibility. Whatever I *have* can be bracketed. The pure ego is what *I am,* as a sheer I, when all that I *have,* body, soul, and spirit, has been bracketed.

The significance of the irreducibility of the sheer I and the bracketing of all transcendence, natural, divine, or subjective, is, finally, not a shift of focus from the "objective" man, God, and world to a "subjective" consciousness, least of all to a soul-like "pure ego." Rather it is a shift from explaining experience as the recording of a set of entities, physical or psychological, said to be located autonomously "out there," to understanding it as a constituting process which renders its contents intelligible.

§ 61b

What Husserl claims to have done is to make our observation of experience consistent with the way we actually live it. Of course that is not enough. The special sciences, designed to deal with special needs, will have to develop special perspectives. Phenomenology is no substitute for theology, sociology, or physics. But if the special sciences are to serve rather than mislead, our general *scientia,* philosophy, has to provide them with a clear initial vision of experience in its lived reality and intelligibility.

The World As Experience

3

The phenomenological proposal to set theories aside and base our knowledge on lived
experience can intuitively be quite appealing. After all, being driven by libidinal
compulsions or by a revolutionary instinct
is not how we experience falling in love or
flying into a rage. In the same way, looking
back at a particularly difficult decision, we
might say that, all things considered, we
were "bound" to choose as we did, but we
resent having someone else tell us he had
known it all along. We know better: as we
lived it, the choice was not inevitable. We
had no comforting certitude to relieve the
agony of choosing. We had to choose, and
any explanation which denies the reality of
the choice distorts our experience. We want
to be recognized in our role as subjects.
Any proposal that promises to speak of
experience as we live it rather than as others
observe it can be sure of a spontaneous
welcome.

But our doubts are no less spontaneous.
We know that what we live is real to us,
but we suspect it may be so only to us. Our
lived experience seems to lack the reassur-
ing solidity of the "objective world." We
will often repeat even highly questionable
assertions confidently if they seem "objective"—say, claims about our alleged
"territorial instinct" that are based on
observations of animal behavior. By contrast, our own clear awareness of basic
ways of being-human—for instance, our
firsthand experience of the self-assurance

we derive from making a house a home—seem too insubstantial to qualify as "scientific evidence." Isn't it "merely subjective," real only "for us"? We welcome the idea of a humanistic explanation, but we doubt its ability to speak about the "real world."

That doubt is as primordial and pretheoretical as lived experience itself. Nor is it altogether groundless. Attempts at a humanistic study of human and social phenomena have in fact often been well meaning rather than effective. The ability to focus on lived experience may be the precondition of a humanistic understanding, but the acid test is its ability to deal with the world of our experience and to make interpersonally valid statements about it.[1] Without that ability, there is little to keep it from becoming a series of private confessional statements of little interest to anyone but the speaker.

Is there, finally, anything but purely internal, private feelings to study when we have focused on pure experience and bracketed out the world and everything that is in it? Or, in Husserl's terms, what is the phenomenological residue after the *epochē?* All that is left is what Husserl calls "the region of pure consciousness" and what we have called lived experience. What exactly is it?

This, again, is a question we cannot answer in terms of phenomenological theory. Phenomenology can only point out what is there to be seen; it cannot speculate and invent. We shall, therefore, turn first to ordinary experience and describe, quite naively, how the objective world appears in it as experience. Only then shall we turn to Husserl's text, examining his characterization of lived experience as a "transcendental consciousness" (§§ 33, 34–38). Next we shall follow what he points out about the place of the "objective" (more accurately, transcendent) reality within such transcendental consciousness (in our words, about the world as experience) (§§ 38–41). Finally, we shall examine the experiential grounds of his claim concerning the dependence of objectivity on the experiencing subject (§§ 42–45, 46).[2]

The Experience of the World

A "healthy distrust" of subjectivity is one of the most pronounced traits of our ordinary experience. When St. Augustine tells us to turn within or Husserl counsels us to bracket the transcendent reality, the ordinary person within each of us responds cautiously: "Yes . . . but you mustn't overdo it." Perhaps every one of us has had the experience of being swung out of control by his emotions, yielding to the vertigo of doubts, fears, and hopes. At such times, the external world in its clear objectivity appears as a refuge of sanity. The need to go on, even in an emotional trauma, chopping wood, drawing water, digging potatoes, has almost a redemptive value. The shiny blade cutting through the clean white wood, the weight of the yoke, and the feel of cool water splashing on our feet can save us from vertigo and bring us back to a manageable reality.

Far less dramatically, we have all had our experiences with the irrelevance and unreliability of our deeply held convictions and with the unyielding reality of the world. In everyday, popular terms, the world is simply there, clean and objective, while our subjectivity, by contrast, appears involuted and unreliable. If we were to elaborate the thesis of common sense, it would probably be that the world is real out there, while lived experience, apart from that world, is intense but vacuous.

The second part of that thesis has a direct experiential grounding. It reflects the awareness that even our lives as subjects become actual only as we act them out in a world. I may not simply be my body, but I would not be much without it. The apostle Paul acknowledges as much when he tells us that, in glory, we shall receive "spiritual bodies." My most personal acts, such as loving my daughter, become actual as I cook for her, braid her hair, and sew on her buttons. Even my identity is inseparable from my relationship to others—to persons, objects, and places. Take away all that and there would be little left to say.

That recognition, however, suggests something that our ordinary unthinking reflection tends to overlook, which is that our experience, even "pure" experience, strictly as lived, has the world very much built into it. Whatever it is, it is not empty. Its object may be illusory, like the meeting point of the railway tracks on the horizon, or it may be imaginary, like the burglar I fear when the wind rattles the shutters and the hounds, chained without, howl at the moon, or it may be as mundane as the cup cited in our examples, but it is there, *in* my experience, as lived.

This is something that is hard to fit into the Cartesian categories with which our common-sense theorizing operates. In a game of Twenty Questions of common-sense reflection, the first question would inevitably be, Is it a real thing or just an idea? Things and thoughts, as common-sense versions of *res extensa* and *res cogitans,* constitute the basic conceptual apparatus of our common sense.

But while the "natural" standpoint of our common sense may be Cartesian, our ordinary lived experience is not. Think of your own ordinary day—kindling the fire, hitching the horses, hauling wood, saying prayers, blowing out the lamp, or, for that matter, reading a book or studying philosophy. These are not thoughts, but neither are they things. They are acts, irreducible to either *res cogitans* or *res extensa.* It may seem "natural" to dismiss lived experience as purely subjective; it is not a thing and so must fit the category of mere thought. But, as we are aware of living it, it is neither; it is an act that includes both awareness and the object within itself. I do not begin with a subjective inner experience, "hitching," and wonder how I can reach my team in the world. I begin with the overt subject act, hitching my horses, which includes, *ab initio,* both my awareness and my team.

To our common sense, that recognition seems suspect. The team *in my experience* has, so to speak, crossed the barrier between thing and thought, from reality to idea. We distinguish accordingly: there is the real team in the world, and the appearance of that team in my perception; the first is real, the second apparent. The team, after all, does not change as I move from place to place or as the light changes or as I put on my spectacles, but what appears to me does. Step by step, common-sense reflection works itself unwittingly into a two-tier conception of reality: there is the world we see, only skin deep, while behind it there must be the "real" world, the thing in itself, unseen yet causing us to see.

It is this reasoning that leads common sense to its mystical moments, to musings about the real rose, not just the petals we see, and to questions about the real nature of the world. It is also this reasoning that leads it to interpret science as an esoteric gnosis which penetrates past the mere appearance to the unseen "true reality." Then we can easily conceive of molecular and psychic structures not as convenient ways of speaking about tables and acts but as the "real nature of things."

With that reasoning our common sense also becomes exceedingly uncommon. For, in our ordinary experience, appearance does not function as a mental double, hiding and hinting at an unseen reality. Here appearance is reality appearing, the real object presenting itself in experience. Speculation aside, in ordinary experience to be real means to appear as real in someone's experience. To say that a rock is *really* hard means that we will experience its hardness when we lean against it. Water is not H_2O which appears as a beverage. Its reality in our daily life is the way it appears, a liquid we drink and wash in. Its molecular structure is a convenient way of describing that reality, though from a special viewpoint and for a special purpose. Ordinary usage even speaks of what it overlooks as "unreal," precisely in the sense of not entering experience.

This is true of ordinary experience quite generally. Here objects are as they appear, as they, so to speak, function in the context of lived experience. What we respond to in our acts are not "mere appearances" but reality appearing in experience. We do not kneel at the Communion rail for a snack of wine and wafers. We receive communion, the bread of life, the cup of salvation; that is the lived reality.[3] Quite apart from all theorizing, strictly in the most ordinary terms, when we focus on experience we are not focusing on some vacuous interiority but on a lived act which includes its object. That object is not a mere appearance but reality entering experience—our world as experience. Our experience is not isolated within our mind, nor does it stand in first place in the world. Initially, as we act, the world is *in* experience.[4]

But then what of the real world, the logs which we are sure go on burning behind our backs, the trees which we are sure make a noise as they fall unseen in Siberia? In our primary awareness, that assurance, too, is a primordial datum. While the objects of our experience are there *in experience,* they present themselves within it as entering from without, as transcendent, or, in ordinary usage, as real, in experience but not simply of it. While it is our experience, it seems also independent of us.

Here we will do well to start out by noticing precisely how such transcendent objects present themselves in our experience. Immanent objects, such as the experience of pain or the principle that $\sim (p \cdot \sim p)$, are never "out there"; we experience them as "in here," grasped at once, within. A transcendent object like a table, a house, or a ship is different. We speak of "seeing a ship," but that is not what we actually experience. We have to row around it, and what is actually presented is never a ship as such, but always one side of it—timbers, cordage, canvas—from a particular perspective; and any one of those perspectives could actually be a two-dimensional movie set. Yet we are also aware of that perspectival view as the side *of a ship,* as if there were a ship, never actually seen itself, which was showing us its sides, one at a time.

With that recognition, the metaphysical temptation once again becomes almost irresistible as we start wondering whether the reality we experience might not be, after all, merely the effect on us of an object which is truly transcendent, not only in the sense of being experienced as independent of our experience but as essentially beyond experience so that we can come to know it only by a theoretical reconstruction from appearances. In fact, in our ordinary dealing with the world, we seldom bother to see and grasp clearly what we are experiencing; instead, we take the question of "what is causing it" as basic. "What is it you are saying?" is already a philosophical question; ordinary speakers are far more likely to ask, "What makes you say that?"

That kind of a perspective renders suspect any humanistic approach to understanding. For if we focus on experience and bracket out its alleged hidden causes—as when we focus, for instance, on the lived experience of justice while bracketing the alleged dialectic of class struggle—we would seem to be studying epiphenomena.

But here again our ordinary experiencing is at odds with our common-sense metaphysics. Our common-sense reflection assumes that reality is a peach, hiding a hard core beneath the skin and the pulp. Ordinary experience, however, suggests that reality may in fact be an onion, made up entirely of skins. Just what is that "concrete," objective reality, not as we speak about it but as we in fact encounter it in our daily doings? Think again of rowing around the ship. What we encounter is a series of exposures as on a filmstrip, each with its characteristics; wooden, real, brown. They are not random. Even if we were to cut up our filmstrip and shuffle the pieces, we could still rearrange them in order, fitting them together in a composite image of a ship.

But that bundle of contiguous impressions still is not "the ship," any more than the boards, oakum, cordage, and canvas constitute a ship. The unitary reality, a ship, enters our experience only with our purposive act: I will sail. In that moment, the aggregate of hemp, canvas, and lumber bobbing at anchor in the harbor becomes *a ship.* Had I boarded her with a different purpose, I might well have en-

countered a different object: a year's supply of firewood, a unit of a
fleet. The boards, ropes, and canvas are there, with all their characteristics, their reality, navigability, whatever else. But the unitary "thing-
in-itself" is there only *in lived experience,* not as a bundle of perceptions but *as a synthetic unity constituted by my purposive presence.*[5]
Without it, only a pointless aggregate would remain, meaningless as
the abandoned violin lying in the mud beside the dead fiddler.

The point of noting such dimensions of our ordinary experience is
not to doubt the reality of the ship. Here our experience is quite
emphatic: few things are as real as tarred oak beneath bare feet as
the yards creak, the sails fill, and the ship comes alive, heeling and
answering her helm. The transcendent object is not imaginary: reality
is one of the traits with which it presents us.

The point, however, is that the full undenied reality of the ship is a
reality *in experience.* It is no less real for it. The ship is real; but the
real ship is also experienced, not hidden.

In that way, ordinary experience offers answers to the doubts it
raises. In its lived purity, experience is not vacuous; it includes its
objects within itself. The world as experienced is not apparent or
epiphenomenal; it is a real world, as we really live it. In everyday
terms, when we switch to lived experience and speak of being afraid
rather than of "manifesting avoidance behavior," we are not discard-
ing reality. Quite the contrary; we are bringing it into focus as it is
really present in experience, setting aside all speculations about what
that reality would be like if it were not experienced. Though useful and
valid, such speculations can provide us only with special ways of
speaking about lived reality; they do not "reveal its true nature." To
look for the primordial reality, we must first look to experience.

Here, however, we are going beyond our basic survey of the world
as experience, and, as long as we are doing phenomenology, the way
to "go beyond" is to look again, with greater precision. We will be well
advised to look again, this time through the eyes of Husserl's text.

Husserl's §§ 33–37: Experience As Consciousness

Look, for a moment, at Husserl's § 33.[6] The point Husserl raises is
familiar from our common-sense survey: what is left to be studied

once the entire natural and cultural fact-world has been bracketed?

§ 33a   The answer seems simple: with the world bracketed as fact, what remains is the world as Idea. But that is *not* Husserl's answer. Though, as we have noted, certain ideal mathematical structures do survive the bracketing, Husserl wants to focus our attention on a different residuum, on the world-as-experience, which, he tells us, constitutes a "new region of being."

That phrase has frequently been something of a stumbling block to understanding. In our ordinary experience we are, of course, aware of the difference between the world-as-experience and the world conceived as existing independently of it—as "transcendent," both as fact and as Idea. When we deal, for instance, with the behavior of survivors in a lifeboat, we automatically set aside the "objective" properties or "ideal" value of a flask of water as irrelevant to explanation. The relevant reality is reality in experience, what the flask of water meant to the survivors. It really was worth a life. Even ordinary usage distinguishes between objects described "objectively," from some special viewpoint, such as that of physics or economics, and objects as they really function in lived experience. The claim that, to understand the behavior of the survivors, we need to consider the flask of water in its lived significance is nonproblematic even for common sense.

But when Husserl speaks of the flask in experience as a new region of hitherto undiscovered being, he evokes visions of a transexperiential world peopled by metaphysical entities, better fit for the occult sciences than for a workaday sociology or psychology. This is unfortunate, because Husserl's intent, in spite of his terminology, is radically experiential.[7] First of all, a region, as he uses the term, is an experiential, not a quasi-spatial, concept. A region is constituted—as it is in ordinary experience—by a subject's intentional orientation rather than by spatial location. My saw is still a part of the region constituted by my work (the workshop), even though it is currently miles away, being repaired. Less crudely, physics is a regional science because it defines its subject matter by the *intentio* of constructing a physical description of the natural world as such; its region includes all information relevant to the task, and only that. Similarly, the "new region" of which Husserl speaks is that constituted by a radical awareness of lived experience, prior to any special standpoint, and so consists of objects-in-experience, as such and only as such. (In that sense, incidentally, philosophy as phenomenology is a general, not a special, science.)

The "new being" of which Husserl speaks—and, since he insists that it is a region of individual being, we could even speak of the "new beings"—is similarly an experiential concept. It does not refer to any hitherto undiscovered physical entities, but rather to what we have called "objects-in-experience." There is reason for treating what we encounter in experience as a distinct type of being rather than as a "subjective" impression of an "objective" entity. The two survivors in our earlier example did not kill the third for a worthless object which they merely "thought" valuable. They killed him for what really was a supremely valuable object-in-experience. That water-worth-a-life is not simply a survivor's "subjective impression" of an "objectively" worthless entity. Rather, it is a different kind of entity whose being is not physical or mental but experiential.

Recognizing this explicitly as a "different being" is easier in German than in English. In German, *sein* is a verb; in English, "being" is a gerund. As we ordinarily use it, "being" indicates *a* being, an entity, *something* that is, such as "a human being," a particular existing entity having the differentiating characteristic of "humanity." Here common usage predisposes us to reism.

Still, even in English, a verbal rather than a substantival usage survives in expressions like being-human. Here the suggestions of a noun are absent. Being-human is not a thing but rather a mode or way of being, a typical way of functioning. While the phrase "I am a being" suggests something I am, the construction "I *am being* the cook tonight" suggests something I do.

In Husserl's usage, the verbal connotations are basic to the substantival ones. I *am* a cook because I *do* the cooking, or, less naively, I am a human because I am being-human. The act is basic to the fact, because it is the act which is the direct experience, giving meaning to the "facts" reconstructed in reflection.[8]

Husserl uses the term "being" in this sense. Since his entire perspective is radically experiential, his basic counters are not physical entities but acts of being. The object-in-experience is, in experience, a *being* distinct from the putative natural object because it *be's* (functions, presents itself) differently.

Notice that here Husserl's usage in fact conforms to the way we experience, though not to the way we unthinkingly speak of our experience. The reality we experience in communion (to the believer, the Blood of Our Lord) is entirely distinct from the reality of sherry before dinner, though both could be poured from the same bottle. The reality we experience in each case is entirely different.

In ordinary usage we obscure that distinction by speaking of "the same wine," but that is neither the experience of the cocktail hour nor that of the communion. That is the experience of the vintner, the wine merchant, or the chemist. What we do in speaking of "the same wine" is to elevate one particular experience to a privileged position, though without any experiential warrant whatever. In experience, the primary reality is that of "cocktails" or "the Blood of Our Lord," and the distinction between them is a distinction between two distinct *entities*.

Yet, for all that, it is not a distinction between two distinct *things*. We have admitted to pouring from the same bottle; more drastically, alcoholics have been known to take communion for the sake of a drink. We are here dealing with a distinction largely overlooked in much of traditional philosophy, a distinction that is a real one though it is not a distinction between things; rather, it is a distinction between modes of being, between distinct ways in which objects *are*.[9] It is their distinctive *ways of being* that are the primary realities of our experience. In that sense, though his stylistic justification may be slender, Husserl has full experiential justification for speaking of objects-in-experience as a region of hitherto overlooked *beings*.

The example is, admittedly, trivial, but the point is not. For the purpose of understanding social and human phenomena, the relevant datum is the being-in-experience, not the "thing" which appears in
§ 33c   neutral description. While the usage may be awkward, Husserl has a reason for speaking of the residuum after the bracketing, the region of pure experience, as a "new region of being." It is the region of the *objects-in-experience* of which we lost all awareness in our Cartesian polarization of reality between *res extensa,* the neutral objects of physical description, and *res cogitans,* the mental objects which we regard as "merely subjective" but to which we in fact orient our acts. Bracketing opens before us the region of reality as experience, and of experience as reality.[10] Husserl's answer to the question of what remains when we have enclosed natural reality in phenomenological brackets is *everything,* though not as thing but as pure experience, as consciousness.

To clarify this, Husserl opens the following paragraph with another §33d turn of the phenomenological spiral, returning once more to a radical description of experience at its most ordinary, without any reference to phenomenological bracketing. In ordinary experience, he points out, I am conscious of myself as a natural being, part of a natural world, and §33e so consider even my act-experiences, my *Erlebnisse,* as part of that world. This conception, though so familiar as to seem "natural," is problematic even on its own level. The agony of remorse I suffer over some long-ago triviality is strictly internal. Even though it might affect my behavior, it is clearly not itself an event in the world. But common sense applies the Chinese-box principle—that internal *Erlebnis* is "in my mind," the mind is "in me," and I am "in the world."

Thus, as Husserl points out, we come to think even of ourselves in §33f the third person, not as a subject but as a "subject-type" object, with our subjectivity enclosed in our body, perhaps in the form of a soul. Then when we come to consider what Husserl has called the "new region of being" (the objects-in-experience), we automatically think of it as a new set of *objects*—perhaps "our subjective impressions," which, like all of our consciousness, are presumed to be in the world by virtue of the Chinese-box principle.

When, however, we place the world in brackets, we become aware §33h of the consciousness of our lived experience as something quite different. Now it can no longer be a distorted reflection of natural objects; those have been bracketed. In terms of our earlier example, we can no longer think in terms of a physical entity, like "alcoholic beverage," existing in the world beyond experience and "causing" our subjective impressions. Rather, we need to recognize as primary the actual objects-in-experience: the cocktails or the sacrament—or wine *in a vintner's experience.*

The actual passage in which Husserl makes the point, § 33h, bristles with the terminology of *Cartesian Meditations* and might well appear puzzling. Here he describes reality-as-experience as the region of absolute transcendental subjectivity. The description is, incidentally, quite matter-of-fact and accurate. The terms, however, are sufficiently loaded with unfortunate connotations that it takes a special effort to avoid the impression that Husserl, as the rumor about *CM* would have it, is turning from phenomenological description to the kind of abstrusely speculative idealist metaphysics which he criticized in *I* §§ 21–23. He is not.[11] He is still giving a phenomenological description, from a purely experiential perspective, calling our attention to the generic characteristics of our lived experience as such, as we in fact live it. While his description has metaphysical implications, it also has a clear workaday significance.

§ 33i First of all, as Husserl emphasizes, the terms "consciousness" and "pure experience" (*Erlebnis*) are functionally equivalent. Consciousness, as he uses the term, has none of the usual connotations of privacy, of "in my mind" as against "out there in the world." It is an experiential term. If anything, its connotations are just the opposite: consciousness extends to cover all actual and possible experiencing. The clock I see is neither "in here" in my mind nor "out there" in the world. If anything, it is literally *out there in my consciousness.* So is the class I anticipate teaching tomorrow or the tree I planted yesterday. In rigorously experiential terms, whatever is, is *out there in consciousness.* In that sense, experience as lived is a consciousness-region.[12]

Speaking of my experience as consciousness neither adds to nor subtracts from its contents. What it does do is call attention to the fact which both common-sense reflection and the sciences based on it tend to overlook—that reality as experience is always structured with reference to a subject who lives it and is aware of living it. Lived experiences, the phenomena lived by subjects, and studied, usually from without, by sociology or psychology, are never "objective" in the sense of existing neutrally as discrete givens. They always fit together in the unity of a subject's experience. It is surely no metaphysical tour de force to recognize that even transcendent objects are ordered—as near and far, as soon and long ago, or as the motives or implications of an act—only with reference to a subject, and are intelligible only as such.

Our slums, for instance, can be described as "the breeding ground of crime," not as such but only from the perspective of an actual or possible criminal act, or at least from the perspective of a sociologist studying their significance for a human subject. The point is that any other description, in terms of inhabitants per square meter of floor space, incidence of rodents, or availability of sanitation facilities, while most useful, is not sufficient. It describes, but it does not help us to *understand,* to grasp the internal coherence, the intelligibility of the facts which makes them add up to "a breeding ground of crime." Facts fit together as a meaningful whole that can become a reason for action only in the context of a subject. In *this* sense, and not in the sense of private sentimental emoting, reality as experience is a realm of subjectivity, meaningful in terms of *a* subject.

The use of the indefinite article in speaking of *a* subject requires emphasis. The furniture of our experience, intentional objects (which we have been calling objects-in-experience, though beings-in-experience would have been more accurate), have their being and so are intelligible only as a subject's context. A book, not as the physical object, paper with markings on it, but as a *book,* has being only in the context of subject experience. Yet that being is not arbitrary; several readers will, independently, read the same words. Similarly, the being-in-experience in our earlier example, the wine and the sacrament, has being only in a human context, that is, in reality-as-experience. Yet again that being is not arbitrary. While it is not a product of some objective "nature," neither is it a matter of individual preference. The function, wine as a sacrament, emerges quite understandably in any community worship. It is a product of human subjectivity but not of individual idiosyncrasies; its roots lie in the structure of human being-subject as such. The subjectivity of reality as experience, which Husserl calls pure consciousness, is neither particular nor private. It is, in Husserl's terms, a *transcendental subjectivity.*[13]

So understood, Husserl's characterization of the phenomenological residuum, reality as experience, as consciousness, that is, the realm of transcendental subjectivity, can appear as a rather matter-of-fact description of our experience (for example, the subject matter of social and human sciences) in spite of the unfamiliar terminology.

One other term in Husserl's description requires explication. When Husserl speaks of experience as lived (and so seen in brackets), he describes it as *absolute* transcendental subjectivity. Once again, he is not speculating or bestowing metaphysical attributes but is simply describing. He is calling attention to the difference between the statement of fact, "Whatever it is I see, I think *it is* a bear"—which, no matter how long and carefully I look, remains at best a highly probable hypothetical statement—and the absolute affirmation, "Whatever that may be, *I see* a bear." Objects-in-experience, like the "bear-I-see," are given in themselves, *ab solo,* not as hypothetical constructs on the basis of partial observations but as immediate data of consciousness. It is a matter of probability that the object I sense in the darkness is a fearsome bear; it is an absolute datum that (I see a bear and that) *I*

§ 33j

am afraid. The experience, fear, is wholly contained in the awareness of fear. Lived experiences are, in that sense, really given absolutely, indubitably.

Thus when Husserl describes the phenomenological residuum, reality-as-experience, as the region of absolute transcendental subjectivity, he is not doing metaphysical speculation, though what he says may have metaphysical implications. For our purposes, he is simply giving a remarkably lucid description of the generic characteristics of the experiential data on which alone we can and in fact do base our social and human sciences. It is experience lived by and intelligible as *a subject's* experience (hence *subjectivity*). But it is not a function of arbitrary personal preference. Its basic structure is given by our being-a-subject, in principle (hence not a particular, natural subjectivity but a *transcendental subjectivity*). Finally, that experience is not a product of speculation or deduction but is given in our primordial awareness, underived, wholly in itself, and as such, *ab solo*

§ 33k   (hence *absolute transcendental subjectivity*). The transcendental reduction does not alter our data; it simply presents them for study as they are lived, as the objects-in-experience of a subject-in-principle, directly given and fitting together not as an "objective world" but as an *Umwelt,* a meaningfully ordered context of consciousness.[14]

If Husserl is right (and we have yet to examine, in §§ 34–46, the detailed evidence he presents), then the natural-science model would have limited applicability as a general matrix for the study of social and human phenomena, even though it might remain indispensable as a special perspective within a subject-centered matrix. The fundamental ordering of our experience would be that of a "realm of subjectivity," of *Erlebnis:* a teleological ordering of meaning rather than a mechanical ("objective"), causal ordering of objects. Adequate understanding of social phenomena would demand a grasp of their *ratio* rather than a description of their alleged causes. In order to understand, for instance, a phenomenon like suicide, we could not begin by analyzing alleged "causal" influences; an event such as a business failure becomes a *reason for* suicide only as an event-in-experience. We would need to start with the subject experience, asking, for instance, what kind of self-understanding would, in principle, make suicide appear as a reasonable alternative for dealing with personal problems. Then we can ask how, in the context of such a consciousness, objects-in-experience would be constituted, and what kinds of objects-in-experience would function as reasons for suicide.

In introducing that example, though still within the implications of Husserl's analysis, we are going far beyond what Husserl suggests in § 33 and even farther beyond what he actually says. As usual, Husserl presents his basic insight in the pivotal § 33, then returns to it in detail in subsequent sections.

First of all he leads us to look at the being of consciousness, in his § 34 sense of being. In experience, consciousness is always a primordial datum and so an *explanans,* not an *explanandum.* The idea of "explaining" consciousness as if we were capable of standing outside it can arise only when we shift our viewpoint from experience to theory. Phenomenological bracketing protects us from that confusion: here consciousness is a datum, not a problem.

But while we cannot "explain" consciousness in terms of the world, this does not mean we can say nothing about it.[15] Even apart from bracketing, consciousness "as a psychological datum," as a fact, exhibits a definite structure.[16] Whatever its mode, whether perceiving, remembering, or doubting, consciousness is always a consciousness *of* something. Husserl, following Scholastic usage, will speak of this characteristic as the *intentionality* of consciousness. The term can be misleading in English, in which "intentional" has a native meaning of its own, but it is too crucial to avoid. The best we can do is to introduce a caveat: intentional, said of consciousness, does not mean "done on purpose"; it means, solely and precisely, being necessarily related to an object. Consciousness, Husserl is pointing out, is intentional in that sense: it is always a consciousness of . . . That is its *Wesen,* its typical way of being.[17]

When we examined the problem in ordinary terms, we used examples in which there is a clear distinction between the object-in-experience (now we can use the more precise term, the intentional object) and the object described as transcendent: the sacrament and sherry. Husserl, however, proposes to take his example from the experience of being conscious—the act of cogito in the widest Cartesian sense of all mental operations—to make the point: every lived experience has what ordinary usage calls its "meaning," or the "point of it," which gives it its unity. It is an experience of . . .—not a static datum but a typical way of constituting an object.

The example that Husserl selects in § 35a is the basic experience § 35a of seeing a sheet of paper. Note first of all that the experience is not the paper but the act, seeing-a-paper, and it is this experience, rather than the object, that has the typical structure (essence, *Wesen*) of being a *seeing of* . . . For us the important point, however, is that the object of the paper-seeing experience is not the sheet of paper as a physical entity but rather the paper-in-experience, the seen-paper, rather like the valued-flask in our lifeboat example. The seen-paper is not a physical object, presented by a natural world—even if we had not bracketed the world. It is an object constituted in the context of the experience.

§ 35b,c   The evidence comes from experience. First of all, even in our awareness of putative natural objects, it is the act of seeing that singles out an object; the world does not do that for us. Second, we are capable of introducing what Husserl calls an "inactuality modification"; that is, in memory, imagination, or anticipation we can still encounter a sheet of paper, though now as "inactual." An *Erlebnis,* lived experience, clearly is not a passive reception; it is an act, giving rise to ("constituting," in Husserl's sense) an object defined by the *way it functions* (the way it *"be's"*) in a subject's experience—in other words, an intentional object.

§ 35d   That, incidentally, is true not only of acts of perceiving but also of acts of volition (constituting, for instance, *the desired,* which can be quite specific and nonactual) or of affectivity (constituting, for instance, *the cherished*). In all our conscious acts, we are focusing on a segment of the phenomenal field ("intending it") and constituting it as an object, rather as we focus on six tiles on the floor and see a triangle. The other tiles are still there, as a marginal fringe, but are not in focus and so are not presenting any patterns.

§ 35e   In that sense, the "wakeful self"—the "conscious self" of ordinary discourse—is the focus of our experience. It is as such a self that I am aware of experiencing as the constitutive ("intentional") subject of my experiences, making experiences mine by recognizing them as my acts, something I do or suffer. There may, of course, be "absent-minded" acts, like lighting a cigarette out of habit in a nonsmoking area, which are mine in the sense of being susceptible to being brought to awareness as mine. But there are no "unconscious acts"; an event which I can in no way bring to consciousness as something I have done, though it may involve me, like performance under narcosis, remains a happening, something that happened to me, not one of my acts.[18]

The point, however, is the intentional structure of consciousness: consciousness is always a subject's way of *intending* (going toward and constituting) an object. For the purposes of the human and social sciences, it is crucial to note that this is not a variation of the old theme of "subjective awareness" of "objective entities." Intentionality is an internal structure of lived experience. The "object" is always an object-in-experience, the object of consciousness. The peasants rebel against the czar-experience, not against the czar; the czar, as a transcendent object, neutrally apprehended, is vastly irrelevant to understanding the revolution. That revolution is intelligible as an intentional act, giving meaning to the entire stream of lived experience, even though, as Husserl notes in § 36b, much of that stream may be tangential to the *intentio* itself. § 36a § 36b

Here we need to note a bit more closely what we have been calling the neutral apprehension. In every act of cogito, I as subject direct myself toward an intentional object; I see paper, in a mode that is appropriate to the act—seen-paper in seeing, imagined-paper in imagining, etc. But my awareness also includes intentionally neutral contents, what I, in Husserl's phrase, also "have in view" (*Im geistigen Auge haben*), as the survivors in our earlier example are presumably generally aware that the precious water happens to be contained in a plastic jug. If this in no way affects their plans, they are aware of the jug in a neutral mode, as an *apprehended* object, as distinct from objects-in-experience (intentional objects). § 37a

Now the point is that the intentional object and the apprehended object, even though they may be interpreted as *distinct beings of the same entity,* remain formally distinct in the technical Scotist sense: their being is distinct. I value the valued as such: the water as promise-of-survival. It would take a special act to note it neutrally, apart from the lived experience, as H_2O. Humans are notoriously capable of intentional relations to an intentional object (say, the beloved in love) without the least awareness of the object simply as apprehended, in what we called a neutral mode (can she cook?). The intentional object is always primary, which is why social and human scientific explanations cannot be based on the natural-scientific model: their primary data are intentional objects, not natural objects in neutral description.

To be sure, the simple apprehension is also, strictly speaking, two intentional objects: the object-valued and the object-apprehended. § 37b

What is crucial for our purposes is the primacy of the object-valued, or, more generally, of the object-lived. The object-apprehended is the object of a special, second-level operation in which we constitute our conception of the "natural world." And, while that second-level operation can be useful, it is distinctly secondary. I have to notice something, within experience, before I can subject it to a neutral description. Seeking to explain the act-in-experience in terms of the object-in-apprehension puts the cart before the horse.

Husserl's §§ 38–41:
Reality in Perception

Everything that Husserl has pointed out so far is confirmed by our ordinary experience. Our conscious acts are in fact structured as ways of dealing with an experienced reality, and that reality does present itself to us as a reality-in-experience. What we call "objective" reality clearly is an abstraction from the reality of our concerns.

But there is another side as well, namely, the spontaneity of the reality we experience. I see a tree: it is *I* who sees it; it is a tree in *my* experience; I, by focusing on it, single it out and constitute it as a tree. Yet, even in my experience, it bears fruit in its season, quite independently of me. Surely that is not just my perception; that tree is real.[19]

Of course it is. Perception is not imagination. But the question is whether I can best understand the tree-in-experience *in terms of my tree-experiencing* or as the product of some tree-*an-sich*. In a more familiar example, the question is not whether humans commit acts of aggression (only too clearly, they do) but whether we can best understand such acts as human ways of being-toward-others (which we experience) or as reflections of a biological instinct (which we posit).

The point at issue really is not the metaphysical one, whether there is a reality which is not the product of my imagination. There is. The other in my experience, as Husserly insists in *CM* V, is really other, given and experienced as such. Rather, the issue is epistemological: is the transcendent other what explains experience, or vice versa? Does our knowledge of the territorial behavior of a biological organism give us an adequate understanding of human aggression, or our knowledge of physical sexual needs an understanding of human love? Or is it the lived experience, whether of love or aggression, which makes observed biological behavior meaningful? The nature of experience, not the nature of the world, is the relevant topic for our inquiry.

Here our first step must be to distinguish between what Husserl calls the immanent and the transcendent *Erlebnis,* or the difference between seeing red in the metaphoric sense of feeling enraged and seeing a red ball. What precisely is the nature of the "seeing" in the two cases? § 38a,b

Husserl's terms "immanent" and "transcendent" suggest a spatial metaphor—"inner" and "outer" experience—which is quite misleading. "Inner" experience can be transcendent, as in the case of remembering past memories (see § 38f). Conversely, transcendent experience is not "outer" in the sense of reaching beyond experience to some transexperiential real object. If we must have a metaphor, "analytic" and "synthetic" experience might be more helpful, though that, too, is flawed. Our best resource is to eschew metaphors and to examine the experience itself.

Immanent acts of consciousness are basically acts in which I bring an immediate given to awareness. I become, literally, *self-conscious.* I *become aware of being* in pain, or, less dramatically, I *become aware of seeing* white (whether anything is white or not). These are entirely immanent acts. Such acts are, to be sure, *experiences* rather than judgments, but they can be considered analogous to Kantian analytical judgments insofar as the essence of the intentional object (being in pain) is wholly contained in the essence of the experience (being aware of pain).[20] As such, they are absolute and indubitable. When a subject reports that she feels exploited or guilty, a sociologist or psychologist might question her natural-standpoint assumption that something or someone is exploiting or condemning her, but it would be folly to try to convince her that she does not "really" feel what she (truthfully) reports feeling. Immanent acts of awareness are absolute, indubitable givens precisely because they represent a direct *Erlebnis.* § 38c

In this respect, acts of immanent awareness differ radically from *transcendent* acts, which bring to awareness not the experience itself (as in the immanent act of becoming aware of being in pain) but rather the experience of others. While in immanent acts the perceived and the perceiver can be separated only in abstraction, in transcendent acts they are presented as distinct. In Husserl's terms, the essence of the perceived is not contained in the essence of the perceiving. Or, simply, I cannot derive seen-paper just from the act of seeing. The § 38d

§ 38e

§ 38f

seen-paper, to be sure, is always present within the stream of my lived experiences, my *Erlebnisse,* but is not derived from it. The world, so to speak, is always present to me, there for me, but it is not of me.[21]

§ 39a   The problem, especially acute in the social sciences, is what to make of this double nature of social phenomena. To posit them as objective entities, after the manner of natural science, is problematic. Even hunger functions as an explanatory factor only *as experienced,* that is, experienced as an injustice rather than as the hand of God or a normal condition. Yet hunger is not simply a thought; thinking ourselves sated does not increase caloric intake any more than thinking ourselves educated can keep SAT scores from plummeting. How, then, do we make sense of transcendent perception?

§ 39b   Common sense deals with this largely by ignoring the problem. It takes perception as the normative model of all experience and assumes that there is a bodily presence, a thing, "out there" which by some unspecified means is conveyed, through impressions, to my consciousness "in here."

§ 40a   Popular science, basing itself on common sense, distinguishes "primary" and "secondary" qualities—say, basically "subjective" color sensations said to be caused by "objective" primary qualities, like the reflection of light. The "real" object is then conceived as something one step removed, the "objective" reality behind the appearances

§ 40b   registered by the senses. But since the distinction between primary and secondary qualities will not survive Berkeley's objection, true reality retreats a step further to the status of complex mathematical equations or dialectical triads, while what we experience with our senses is said to be but a sign pointing to this alleged "true reality." Somewhat ironically, the "realism" of science would reduce experienced reality to the status of an appearance while attributing reality to an essentially

§ 41a   unperceivable formula. Perception, then, would not deal with the "real thing" but only with appearances—which, however, would be merely subjective. If we followed our unreflecting assumptions to their consequences, perception would appear impossible.

§ 41b   Yet we do perceive. How do we actually do it? Husserl devotes another pivotal section, § 41, to this question. He proposes to bracket all the problematic assumptions of comon sense together with their scientific elaborations and deal only with our actual awareness of transcendent objects, which, though linked with the subject as his perceptions, are not identical with him.

Take as an example the perception of a table. Unlike pain, a table is not something I grasp directly. Rather, I walk around it, recording one perspectival exposure after another. I am aware of perceiving the "same" table, though my actual perspectival views of it change. The unitary conception, table, "of" which each of my particular views is said to be a perspectival perception, is an intentional synthesis of a potentially infinite series of particular perspectives. Only in the intentional consciousness is the table one; in the actual perceiving, the given is necessarily a series of perspectival views.

This is a crucial point and deserves belaboring, since we are contending here with the powerful habit of thinking that, after all, there still really "is" a table "of" which these are perceptions. Yet if I, as a perceiver, refrain from performing the synthesizing act, there literally *is* no table. If I am a carpenter looking for lumber, or a cold man looking for firewood, my synthesis will be quite different. When we come to deal with phenomena like behavior or social institutions, this becomes even more evident. Experiential *consciousness* of a given reality, whether a table, the Park Service, or the Church, is in fact unitary, but the object is presented through a potentially infinite series of variations which consciousness unites in an act of synthesis.

The real nature of perception is not that of a mysterious recording or second-guessing of an objective entity, the thing, but rather one of synthesizing perspectival views. The vaunted "objective reality," the thing, is in fact an intentional synthesis of perspectives of which we are conscious as being identical. That act, to be sure, is not an arbitrary one. Husserl speaks of the unity of apprehension as being grounded in the essential being—the typical way of presenting itself—of what is unified as well as in the synthesis of identification. In ordinary language, given a series of perspectival chair-views, there is a limited number of ways in which I can synthesize them in the conception of a "thing." But even if there were only one, that would not change the basic fact that "the thing" is not a perceptual given but a product of a synthesizing *Erlebnis,* an intentional experience.

For the practical purpose of seeing chairs, tables, and typewriters that changes nothing, but for the purposes of scientific explanation it changes a great deal. For if "the thing" is in reality an *Erlebnis,* a product of a synthesizing act rather than an existing entity mysteriously conveyed to our awareness, we cannot use that entity to explain our

§ 41c–d

§ 41e

experiences. Quite the contrary. It is experiences which make entities understandable and are the *ab solo* starting point of inquiry. Again, that experience is not arbitrary, but neither is it simply a passive reception. It is a constitutive act. *Lived experiences, finally, are the "hard" reality; transcendent objects are a product of constitution.*

Husserl's §§ 42–46: Reality As Experience

The consequences of Husserl's presentation of the real nature of perception are clear and direct. If our sciences wish to be empirical, they cannot be conceived as a study of putative "objective" realities or of our "subjective" impressions of them. They have to be, first and foremost, sciences of human experiences whose subjective and objective correlates are intelligible only from the perspective of those experiences. "Things" as such cannot be "given in perception"; they can only be constituted in an intentional synthesis: these boards become a bench when I sit on them. Only experiences can constitute a discrete event and so serve as the primordial basis of a science.

§ 42   The difference between an experiential perspective and a reistic one lies in what each of them takes to be the fundamental given. For the former it is "Being as consciousness," that is, the way reality presents itself in lived experience. For the latter it is "Being as reality" in Husserl's sense of that term as a putative set of transcendent entities. Husserl chooses the experiential perspective for a very good reason, namely, that it is only lived experience, an *Erlebnis,* that actually presents itself directly as a given rather than as a product of our synthesizing activity. A pain-experience ("I am hurting") or a chair-experience ("situponable") are each genuinely a given. By contrast, the conception of a pain or of a chair as events in an "objective" world is something we arrive at by a process of intentional synthesis of a series of perspectives. Literally, they represent something *taken from* experience rather than *given within* it.

§ 43   This is not simply a matter of the way we, as contrasted with some higher consciousness, happen to perceive it. It is an essential trait of all spatial entities. A synthesis of aspects is what a thing *is.* Thus it is not a matter of a limitation of our consciousness that we do not grasp the "soul" or the "true being" of a chair, for there is none. The "thing-in-itself" is only what it is in experience, a synthesis of ways of being-present. Literally, a thing is as it does; its "appearance"—in the strong sense of its presence-in-experience—is its reality.

Metaphorically, before we can speak of the "objective nature of the revolution" or the "nature of God" we have to grasp clearly what a revolution or a god really is, that is, the typical way of being of a revolutionary or of a religious experience—not "how they feel" but how they function, how they are lived. We might note, for instance, the disintegration of faith in the efficacy of effort as one component in revolution-as-way-of-being. Another component is the shift in conception of authority from one of a finite tool to one of an omnipotent will. A third may be a shift in the relative valuation of freedom and perfection. In sum, we can grasp the "logic" of a revolution as a way of being: a substitution of an armed will for purposeful labor as a social strategy. Analogously, an awareness of the experience of the sacred dimension of being, of the teleology of the cosmos as challenging the human and answering his aspiration, can enable us to grasp the meaning of God in experience. Only then can we speak intelligently of what revolutionary movements or churches do and believe.

More mundanely, this is also how we first grasp and understand other objects of our experience, including other humans. In trying to understand a paranoidal patient, we need first to grasp the "logic" of his acts. How, as we perceive his acts, can we make sense of them as a *way of being* (the profound meaning of the concept "behavior")?

This does not mean or imply in the slightest that the other person is nothing but a sum of the uses we make of him. Quite the contrary; it recognizes that the movements of the Other do not confront us as a random aggregate but exhibit an intentional unity, confronting us as an intelligible whole, *behavior,* whose "logic" we can grasp.[22] The other gives unity to his *Erlebnisse* as the acts of a self and so is an ego-subject. Husserl clearly recognizes even animals as ego-subjects.[23] His point is that the unity of a being is not some occult soul-substance hiding behind its acts but an intentional unity of experience. In encountering another person, I do not encounter an appearance hiding a true self; rather, I encounter a self incarnate, a self in bodily presence.[24] The difference between that self and my self is that I am aware only of my self immanently, as *Erlebnis,* while I am aware of the other self—person, animal, plant, or any transcendent object which is not simply my thought—only as embodied, in space, and thus perspectivally, so that my awareness of it remains hypothetical and dubitable.

The point, Husserl points out, is not, as some mystics would have it, that our knowledge is defective, so that a "higher" or an "expanded" consciousness could grasp the other self in a single insight. Rather, it is the very nature of a self, mine or another's, that it is actual only as it is acted out and so is "perspectival" even in itself. Metaphorically speaking, even God knows me as the series of acts in which I act out myself (though in His case, presumably, these become simultaneous *sub specie aeternitatis*) because that is the way *I am*.

In claiming that we know the other only perspectivally, Husserl is not denying the integrity of the other or the adequacy of our knowledge. Rather, he is recognizing that the other, whether it is a person or a thing, is not an occult entity hiding behind the acts we witness but is present in and through those acts. Perspectival knowledge is wholly appropriate to the sequential being of any transcendent entity.

More than all the specific texts we have cited, this assertion, together with its repetition in § 45, clearly confirms Husserl's rejection of any mystifying interpretation of phenomenology. The essence of mysticism is the promise of revealing the "true" being of the "thing (person) in itself," beyond its actual ways of being present. Husserl's strong claim is that precisely the true being, and the only true being, *is revealed in ways of being-present*—with the caution that whatever we know through ways of being-present, as transcendent (thus everything except our own immanent self-awareness), we know hypothetically. What I know through my dealing with you *is* your true self, though I may not know it truly. The promise of knowing you not in your actuality, in your acts, but "in yourself" is an illusion, as § 43 indicates. Your "in yourself" is *in experience,* though *your* awareness of it is immanent, *mine* transcendent.

This affirmation has far-reaching consequences. The dehumanizing tendencies in modern thought are ultimately founded on the conception of a subject's consciousness as a false consciousness, capable of grasping only the overt appearance, not the latent "reality," so that reality must be revealed by theory rather than experience. Husserl's claim that the reality of the actual is overt rather than esoteric—or, less abstrusely, that reality is in itself a human reality—in principle denies the conception of false consciousness. While the amount of information actually available to any particular subject at any particular time may vary, *in principle* truth is accessible to individual consciousness, and that consciousness *in principle* is not a false con-

sciousness but the only true consciousness and the one reality we
have. Not a superior insight but a clear awareness is the basic foundation of understanding.[25]

We shall postpone these implications, of which Husserl may well
have been quite unaware while writing *Ideas,* to the concluding chapter, since they clearly constitute an amplification, rather than any kind
of explication, of his text.[26] In §§ 44–46 the text turns to another
spiraling review of the pivotal § 41. Here Husserl stresses the contrast.
A transcendent being—a thing—he points out, is necessarily given as   § 44
incomplete, with a potential series of future perspectives. An *Erlebnis,*
by contrast, is given ab-solo-utely. The process of becoming more
clearly aware of it—say, of pain—is not one of adding new perspec-   § 45
tives but of clarifying awareness. Not by accident. It is the intrinsic
nature (Husserl speaks of *Seinsart,* "mode of being") of a transcendent
object to be present as a series of perspectives, so that an unperceivable
object is a contradiction in terms. By contrast, it is the intrinsic nature
of an *Erlebnis* to be available for awareness, not in perspectival views
but as such. It is immanent in consciousness even if, as presumably in
the case of animal consciousness, it is never reflectively articulated.
Perceiving a thing means always bringing new content before us;
becoming aware of a lived experience brings to focus what is already
present.

These considerations lead Husserl to the inevitable conclusion: § 46
experience is an absolute datum; transcendence is contingent on it. All
claims about transcendence—say, that not only do I *see* a chair but
that *there is* a chair, not only that murder *is* wrong but that a *given act
is* a murder—represent a second, hypothetical level of awareness and
so are not a datum but a conjecture. It may be a very well-warranted
conjecture indeed, but its givenness is always a matter of contingent
fact, not of essential necessity. Only the immanent, the awareness of
the I and of its stream of lived experiences, is given absolutely. Even
if all the objects of my experiences were fictions, *they would still be
the reality to which I respond.* Imaginary guilt can drive humans to
suicide; "objective" guilt, never experienced as *Erlebnis,* cannot.

Husserl's conclusions in turn lead us to ours. Phenomenological
bracketing—the consistent refusal to accept objectifications of lived
experiences as "explanation"—does not deprive our sciences of their
subject matter. Quite the contrary; it enables them to focus on their
real subject matter, subject experience and its objects-in-experience.

As an instance, the key to understanding a revolution, including its alleged "objective" conditions, is an understanding in principle of the subject as subject-in-revolt and of such a subject's world-in-experience as reason (not "cause") of revolution.

Husserl concludes § 46 with a phrase that sounds a bit ironic. He pronounces the problem solved, with only some easy finishing touches still to be provided. Given the penetrating clarity of his vision, this may have been true, even though those "finishing touches" produced several major volumes. For us, however, the chapter poses an immediate, equally major problem. We have shown that what we rather carelessly call a "humanistic approach" to knowledge—more precisely, a transcendental experientialism—is not in principle empty of content. While bracketing all conception of an "objective" reality, together with the consequent attempt to explain the subject as itself an object, it retains the entire scope of reality as experience, intelligible from the perspective of the experiencing subject. Instead of simply describing the sequences of human behavior on the model of the natural sciences, it can *understand them in their intrinsic rationality as human acts*. Silence—being rather than thinking—is not humanism, and humanism need not be silent.

But the recognition of reality as reality-in-experience, while making reality intelligible, also threatens to make it viciously subjective. Experience is always a subject's experience. Is it ever more than *this* subject's experience? Is the world-in-experience ever more than my world, only accidentally overlapping the worlds of other selves? Humanistic approaches to the study of social phenomena have at times produced platitudes rather than knowledge; perhaps even more frequently they have produced idiosyncratic confessions. Having concluded that the proper subject matter of the human and social sciences is the human as subject and reality as experience, we must next inquire why and how a science based on a transcendental experientialism can claim intersubjective validity.

Experience and Intersubjectivity

4

The humanistic turn signaled by the *epochē* raises two questions. So far, we have focused on the first, whether a science conceived as a critical elaboration rather than as an inversion of first-person experience would have anything to study besides purely inner moods.[1] With Husserl, we answered yes, it would have *everything,* though everything *as experience.* The foundation of an experientially conceived science is consciousness as the region of absolute transcendental subjectivity.

Those words need no longer intimidate us. We have rigorously excluded their mystified connotations and have given them back their workaday meaning. We know now that they refer to lived experience, as directly experienced, considered in principle as any subject's experience.

But that explanation does not dispel our second question: How can a science so conceived claim intersubjective validity? Each of us experiences individually; therefore, would not a radically experiential orientation yield as many realities—and sciences—as there are subjects? The objectivist bias of modern sciences is not fortuitous.[2] Like the dogmatism with which post-Tridentine theology (including Lutheran scholasticism) sought to overcome the relativity of individual religious experience, the "natural science model" in modern science reflects the need to escape the relativity of individual experience. The objectivism against which the existentialists protest was, in its day, itself a protest.[3] Husserl may have shown that individual experience includes a lived world within itself. But can a science of a lived world avoid a subjectivistic relativity which naturalism, whatever its flaws, seeks to overcome?

The question breaks down into two parts. The first is critical: Can naturalism fulfill its promise of interpersonal validity?[4] The second is positive: What is the experiential foundation of intersubjective validity?

We shall examine the problem first as it appears in ordinary experience at its most disdained ordinary. Phenomenology, as we have noted repeatedly, claims to *see,* not to invent, the structures it describes. If they are not there to be seen in experience, its claim is vain. Subsequently, we shall look at that experience again through Husserl's text, noting first the role which the "natural" world in fact plays in experience (§§ 47–50), and then the real nature of intersubjective validity (§§ 51–54). Finally, we shall examine Husserl's double conclusion: "All reality exists through the dispensing of meaning" and "No subjective idealism" (§ 55).

The Testimony of
Ordinary Experience

Ordinary experience, as we noted in our last chapter, sustains the Husserlian claim that an experiential reorientation not only does not deprive our sciences of their subject matter but actually puts them in touch with reality. After all, the reality of human lives, as we actually live them, consists of lived experiences, not of natural entities. Ordinary experience is a "region of absolute transcendental subjectivity" precisely from a radically experiential standpoint.

From a theoretical standpoint, however, that recognition appears problematic. If it is accurate, then would not reality in each instance be entirely private and individual, a "reality-for-me"?[5] Could we still make intersubjectively valid statements?

In ordinary discourse, making such statements poses no particular problem. We do it all the time, effectively and successfully. Nor are such statements all on the order of "This table is brown." Ordinary experience is not primitivistic; it includes the full richness of human life. Even an ordinary speaker, sipping his beer, might not confine his statements to "I see a glass." He might, for instance, comment on the absence of a habitual hunting companion: "Sure, when your kid gets killed, you don't feel like doing much of anything."

Such an observation, common enough in ordinary discourse, is not, in form or intent, an expression of a personal opinion, valid for the speaker alone. It is clearly presented as intersubjectively valid: for any subject, it is the case that the loss of a loved one produces a temporary paralysis of habitual interests. Yet neither is it presented or understood as an inductive generalization. The speaker does not claim, "I have observed that all of my friends who suffered a grievous personal loss exhibited a decline of interest in their hobbies and I expect to encounter a similar correlation in future incidences," as if he were simply observing behavior without any grasp of its inner logic. He knows intimately how it fits together. The principle appears to him as evident. If you suffer a loss, you lose other interests as well. His entirely commonplace observation is in fact a pure eidetic description of a necessary structure of human experience. It is not just the way Charlie acts or just what "I think." It is the way it is. In principle, necessarily, the structure of human experience is such that a grievous personal loss makes other activity appear pointless.

In debates over beer, the intersubjective validity of such universal statements is seldom challenged. When it is, the response is again likely to take the form of an appeal to the necessary structure of consciousness: "Can't you *see* it? It *stands to reason*—after all, he's *human,* he's *bound to* feel that way." If anything, it is the particular statements of fact which appear questionable, contingent on the information actually available to the speaker and so subject to discussion. "Was it really Charlie's kid that got killed?" "I hear they were drinking . . ." The discussion will become rambling, full of conjecture and hearsay evidence, until it butts up against another statement of essential necessity: "When you start thinking you can get by with anything, you're bound to get in trouble."

Ordinary usage in effect distinguishes two types of intersubjectively valid statements. One type, typically introduced by the phrase "It's a fact," is a matter of consensus and includes all statements referring to "objective" reality, from the height of the Empire State Building to the second baseman of the 1927 World Series Yankees. Here, all types of evidence, from *The Book of Records* through yesterday's newspaper to the opinion of a knowledgeable bartender, are admissible. The basis of interpersonal validity is assumed to be "reality," the "way it really is." That reality, however, is established by a compilation of evidence which is always subject to doubt and potentially open ended, so that such "truth" remains always subject to revision in the light of new information.

The second type of intersubjectively valid statements recognized in ordinary usage pertains to what is rather misleadingly described as "human nature." Such statements are typically introduced by the prefix, "It stands to reason." The basis of their intersubjective validity is, once again, said to be "reality," the "way it really is." However, here that reality is not established by a compilation of evidence but rather by evident insight. Standards of fair play and equity, bases of interpersonal relations, the principle of veracity and its limits, such as the tendency of fishermen to exaggerate their catch, or propositions concerning, for instance, the importance of self-esteem—all such matters are ascribed to "human nature" and held to be interpersonally valid as directly accessible to the insight of every reasonable person.

Thus ordinary usage establishes something of a hierarchy of validity. It treats certain statements, usually those of taste and preference, as in principle "subjective" and only individually valid—*de gustibus non est disputandum*. Others, pertaining to contingent particulars, it treats as capable of being established as intersubjectively valid by a compilation of evidence. Still others, conceived as principles of "human nature," it treats as intersubjectively evident and as providing the possibility of establishing the intersubjective validity of statements describing "objective" truth: "It stands to reason my buddy would not lie to me—if he does, he's no friend of mine." For all the objectivism of common sense, even here the evident insight into "human nature"—more accurately into the necessary structures of subject consciousness—is basic to establishing the intersubjective validity of "objective" reality.

This does not, to be sure, mean or imply that what ordinary discourse designates as "objective reality" is somehow less than real. Not in the least. As we in fact experience it, that reality confronts us as most emphatically real. It is not private, it is not subjective, it is not contingent on our wishes or preferences. Though imagination may be experience, experience is not imagination. The world is what it is, not what I would like it to be or what I imagine it to be. Nor is its reality simply a matter of arbitrary consensus. It is, rather, a matter of the coherence of evidence. We may agree on it, but even if we were to disagree our common sense still retains its stubborn animal faith that our disagreement does not change reality: white is still white, right is right. We constitute a world by experiencing, but we do not invent it.

That is a basic experiential datum. Our experience is such that we cannot avoid positing a nonarbitrary reality. Surrounded by the artifacts of our cities or the flexible consciences of our central committees, we may indulge in intellectual games, speaking of "ashtray-for-me/ nut dish-for-you" or of "freedom as the dialectical recognition of necessity." But away from our docile contexts, confronted by the granite grandeur of our mountains and the gray vastness of the autumn ocean—or, alternatively, by the workers of Csepel or Kolben-Daněk—those games become infinitely trivial.[6] White is still white, right is still right. No intellectual gymnastics can transform aggression into fraternal aid or necessity into freedom. Reality is what it is, not what we wish it to be. The greatness of authentic science is precisely its commitment to the autonomy of that reality, above and beyond all wishful thinking.

But what exactly is that "autonomy of reality"? When we experience something as "real," we experience it as autonomous from our *individual* experience (or a contingent consensus of such experiences), but emphatically not as independent of experience as such. Quite the contrary. In calling something "real," rather than imagined, wished for, remembered, or merely thought, we are identifying it as in principle experienceable by a (any) possible experiencer. Ordinary usage speaks of the real as "there for all to see," and that phrase is quite accurate. The distant mountain and, more humbly, the hidden cup are real even if no one sees them *because anyone could.* Perhaps they are real only in principle, as the snows of yesteryear, or perhaps only indirectly, as subatomic particles; but still they are real. If anything were *in principle* inexperienceable, such as a cup or a mountain said to be there only as long as no one is looking, ordinary usage would call it unreal. Not as a matter of philosophical theory but as a matter of our ordinary experience at its most ordinary, the real is the experienceable.

That relation between reality and experience, however, is essentially asymmetrical. Again, that is not a matter of philosophical speculation but of ordinary experience. Reality must be experienceable, but experience does not similarly require a factual counterpart. Even without it, it still retains all its basic structures. Fear, joy, guilt, lived through in a dream or vicariously in fiction, experienced in memory or in anticipation, are recognizably the same experiences as when they are lived by the waking cogito. Much of the appeal of literature lies precisely in its ability to let us live through a range of human experiences which have no factual counterparts in our lives. It is not only the coward who dies a thousand deaths; every imaginative person does. Only the person without imagination dies but once.

The basic asymmetry is that reality is essentially related to experience (anything real is real as experienceable) while experience is essentially related to nothing: the fear I feel now is given absolutely as such. It is fear, whether on closer inspection it turns out to have been justified by external circumstances or not. The *cup I see* on the table, *as experience,* remains the same whether closer inspection proves it to be a real cup or an illusion.

For that matter, it is quite clear that we can imagine things we have not experienced—or, more precisely, we can experience, in imagination, things which have no factual counterparts. It is far less clear that we can experience things we have not imagined. Much of the time we go through our lives like a wayfarer in a far country—or, less poetically, like a soccer player at a baseball game—seeing but not grasping. We must, in principle, understand what we are seeing in order to see it. Otherwise, as in seeing an inscription in a foreign language, we shall not see the inscription but only strange marks. If the script is unfamiliar enough, we may not even be aware that we are seeing writing rather than fancy scrollwork. Because we see an inscription, we conclude there is an inscription there. But we might not see it, though it is there, and we might see an inscription, though none is there. Our experience is primary. It is our experience which leads us to posit reality as objective, not vice versa.

Once again, this does not mean that the world of our experience is imaginary or private. The growing experiential coherence of our experience attests overwhelmingly that perception is not imagination and that the world we perceive we do share with others. But the shared reality of our world is a reality shared in experience. Thus we cannot explain the intersubjective validity of our perceptions in terms of the undenied reality of the perceived world. Our common recognition of certain contents of our experience as real presupposes a shared experience and so cannot explain it. Crudely, the world is what it is because we experience as we do, not the other way around. The basis of intersubjective validity must be present in experience, or else we should never "find it" in the transcendent world. The reality of the world, though undeniable, does not explain our experience.

So stated, that observation may appear speculative, but it reflects an evident datum of ordinary experience assumed by ordinary usage. In such usage, for instance, we will speak of a man being "driven to suicide" by a business failure or a wife's desertion. But these are not causes. A business failure might equally well be a reason for having a profitable fire and retiring prematurely to a farm; a wife's desertion might be an opportunity for remarriage or for joining a religious order. It is the experiences—the way we live them—that constitute "the facts" as reasons and so as explanations of a suicide. We can understand the suicide if we understand *the experience,* but without such understanding "the facts" would explain nothing. Our objective reality presupposes a common, intersubjective understanding but does not explain it.

This, finally, holds true whether we conceive of that objective reality as material or as mental. The latter alternative is by no means a mere fancy of idealistic philosophy. Everyday reflection resorts to it readily when dealing with realities like moral norms, which are clearly nonarbitrary but are not physical objects. An ordinary speaker might be quite aware that his emphatic conviction that "It isn't right to torture animals" is in no sense a reflection of any "objective reality." Yet he will stoutly resist all attempts to reduce it to a matter of preference. He can sense that there is something fundamentally wrong with torturing animals. Though frequently not a conventionally religious person, the ordinary speaker will, with Bishop Berkeley, claim for his moral norm the objectivity of an idea in God's mind: "It's against God to hurt animals."

But, whether true or false, such common-sense Berkeleyanism does not resolve the immediate problem of intersubjective validity.[7] Even if transcendent reality were ultimately "mental" rather than material, there would still be the problem of how we, as individual subjects, could secure a commonly valid grasp of it. The endless debates as to what God in fact wills and forbids provide sufficient testimony that the interpersonal validity of our conception of "God's will" is no more obvious than that of the materialist dialectics. The foundations of intersubjective validity must, in the last instance, be found in experience, not beyond it.

That, in fact, is where ordinary experience finds the basis for the intersubjective validity of its statements—not in a common world but in a common humanity. I, too, am human, I understand; or, more precisely, because I am human, I am in principle capable of understanding the acts of other humans. The application of that understanding to any particular instance remains subject to empirical confirmation, since empirical statements cannot be derived from eidetic statements alone. Even the eidetic certainty of $2 + 2 = 4$ does not guarantee that, if we add two hungry cats to two fat mice, we will end up with four animals. But it is my initial grasp of being-human in principle that makes my understanding possible.

This is a crucial point. The assumption, borne out repeatedly in practice, that we can understand others and can make ourselves understood by them, is not and cannot be based on the claim that we experience "the same world," because, strictly speaking, we do not. Facts, in their facticity, are always particular. It is our basic ways of experiencing them, as human subjects, that are analogous. The food we eat, as fact, does vary widely, but the experience of hunger and satisfaction is a structural constant. What sustains human self-respect similarly varies, yet the need for self-respect is a constant. So is the need for truth, for security, for freedom. The common locution "You know what I mean" attests to the recognition of ordinary experience that, though the contents of experience may vary, its basic structure is in principle common in virtue of our shared being as self-conscious subjects in a world.

To be sure, ordinary usage finds it almost impossible to distinguish the habitual from the necessary. Very frequently, the expression "It stands to reason" refers not to reason but to custom, to the structures of a culture rather than to the structure of our common humanity. Equally frequently, common usage takes psychological generalizations for essential necessity. A social science based on an uncritical generalization of the evident could very easily degenerate into a codification of the contingent. But the significant point is not that this is possible, as indeed it is, but rather that it is not necessary. We can focus not only on the way we have in fact structured our world but on the way that a subject, any subject, necessarily structures a world.

Here examples are not hard to come by, even on the most ordinary level. Take the universally human significance of freedom, understood as the possibility of voluntary action. We cannot justify the recognition of freedom as a basic human need in terms of cultural conditioning. Most societies, at most times, considered slavery natural and legitimate, and all societies at all times concern themselves, legitimately and necessarily, with the regulation rather than the fostering of freedom. On uncritically empirical grounds, we could at most conclude that freedom is a luxury indulged in by some members of some societies at some times, or that it is a fleeting moment in the periodic exchange of roles between master and slave, not a human need.

Yet our lived experience as subjects directly contradicts such a conclusion. We need but imagine the difference between performing a task, even one we regard as intrinsically pleasurable, voluntarily and under coercion. The metaphor of love and rape is trite but apt. We experience voluntary action as self-constitution, and the same act under coercion as self-destruction. In lived experience, freedom presents itself as crucial to the constitution of human identity.

To explain this by positing a pseudobiological "freedom-instinct" explains nothing. It is, at best, a groping articulation of our awareness that the desire for freedom we experience is not a matter of personal taste but something far more basic, universally applicable. We experience it as an instance of subject experience as such. To be a subject means precisely to be a self-constituting being, giving meaning and unity to one's experience. Deprivation of freedom is equivalent to destruction of subjectivity. It is this necessary connection that we recognize in our experience and use to understand the experience and behavior of others.

The significance of identifying with a place provides another example. To posit a quasi-biological "territorial instinct" is again a groping description rather than an explanation of human experience, and a description which would become problematic if it were used to justify aggression as a quest for *Lebensraum*. Genuine explanation needs once more to begin with lived experience, in this case the crucial personal significance of the ties that a person establishes with a context recognized as uniquely "his."

That experience is again significant, not simply as this particular experience but as an instance of an experience in principle. To be a subject means to be particular. The quest for a place is a necessary component of self-actualization. Once we have grasped that principle, we can understand why, for instance, humans endure rather than emigrate or why a human can identify with a group of persons, a language, or a religious faith in place of a territory. We can also apply the principle to understanding the behavior of animal subjects and thus give some intelligible content to the phrase "territorial imperative." In both cases, understanding is based on a necessary principle of being-a-subject, the choosing and having of a home, which we act out in our personal experience and can use to understand the experience of others.

In our ordinary experience, we sum up all of this by speaking of our "human nature," which enables us to speak of subjectivity (that is, human experience) and yet claim "objective" (that is, nonarbitrary, common) validity for our assertions. The basis of interpersonal understanding, we would say, is our common humanity. Not, to be sure, humanity as fact, the customs and conventions we happen to share with our actual neighbors in space and time. Rather it is the humanity we share necessarily, as self-conscious subjects in a world, that makes it possible for us to understand events from which millennia separate us, to speak of universal human rights, and even to communicate the particular content of our experience to others. The necessary structure of subject experience as such makes intersubjective assertions about subjects possible and our individual experience meaningful.

Finally, if we sum up the testimony of ordinary experience, two points emerge clearly. The first is that human reality is indissolubly tied to human experience. Bracketing all metaphysical connotations, we can even say that whatever functions as real in experience does so inasmuch and insofar as it makes sense, presents itself as meaningful. That is why intersubjectively valid statements about human and social phenomena are possible. The second point is that the meaning—in the generic sense of subject intelligibility rather than in the specific sense of personal significance—is not arbitrary; it is a function not of my individual personality but rather of my individually lived yet radically shared *humanity*. Intersubjectively valid statements about human and social phenomena conceived as human acts are possible in the first instance as statements about (any) human experience *as such*. It is these statements that serve as the intersubjective referent for statements about particular instances of human experience.

Ordinary discourse takes our common humanity for granted. That is why it finds intersubjective communication unproblematic. But ordinary reflection does not provide an adequate articulation of its own assumptions. True to its objectivistic bias, it transforms common human experience into a "human nature" which either must be interpreted as an animal "nature," reviving the vain attempt to explain experience in terms of objects, or becomes altogether vacuous. The principles of a science conceived as transcendental experientialism are present in ordinary experience, but they require a self-conscious, critical articulation. For that reason, having looked at them in their naive givenness, we need to look at them again, this time in terms of Husserl's critical analysis.

Husserl's §§ 47–51:
The Relativity of the
Object World

Husserl's analysis of reality as experience—or, in his words, as "The Region of Pure Consciousness" (§§ 47–55)—has been used as evidence both for an idealistic and for a realistic interpretation of phenomenology. Not without reason. In § 49d, Husserl declares explicitly that to doubt the reality of the world would be absurd,[8] while hard upon it, in § 50, he declares no less explicitly that the act of experiencing is primordial, the reality of its contents derivative. His conclusion, which we shall examine in detail later, is prefaced by a peremptory *Schluss* ("That's that") but sounds simply self-contradictory. Its first part asserts what, especially in the English translation, sounds like a classic idealist thesis: "All reality exists through the dispensing of meaning." The second part asserts, equally emphatically, "No subjective idealism."[9] The contradiction between the metaphysical implications of the two assertions seems blatant.

Yet reading Husserl's text as metaphysical speculation is always misleading. Though most readers are loath to believe him, Husserl is really doing what he claims to be doing, not metaphysics but descriptive phenomenology. He is not arguing a case for realism; in § 52 he explicitly argues against it. Nor is he arguing for idealism; the second clause of the title of § 55 really means what it says. The entire chapter, we shall submit, is best read as a phenomenological description of actual experiencing.

That much should already be evident from the way in which Husserl presents his acknowledgment of the reality of the world in the opening paragraph of the chapter. He does not offer a deductive argument in the manner of Descartes. Nor does he claim that the reality of the world is intuitively evident. Rather, he observes that the nature

§ 47a

of our experience is such that, *as a matter of fact,* it compels us to attribute "physical truth" (both the term and the quotes are his) to the objects of our experience. His claim is strictly experiential: our experience overwhelmingly presents its contents to us as real rather than as imaginary.[10]

But while that is a fact which it would be folly to deny, it is only a fact, not an essential necessity. We can have experiences without attributing reality to their objects. A subject, after all, really sees railways tracks converging in the distance even though he does not credit their convergence with reality. Or, in Husserl's example, a subject can become fixated at a childlike stage of development and never advance beyond treating reality as an extension of his preferences. The experience of such a subject will have the full coherence and range of ordinary experience without positing reality as objective. Similarly, in the case of neurosis or fanatic dogmatism, the subject can attribute physical reality to an experience which in no way corresponds to actuality. A paranoid schizophrenic's experience of the world as a hostile conspiracy against him can have all the complexity and coherence of ordinary experience without having any objective counterparts. In both cases, the meaning of experience is independent of the reality of its object.

Husserl's presentation here is complicated by the interweaving of two distinct themes. The dominant theme is the intrinsic intelligibility of experience. Throughout the chapter, Husserl will insist that experience is equally intelligible whether its object is posited as real or not. The experience of fear, for instance, retains the same basic structure (albeit not the same intensity) whether the subject is really threatened or not. This is why intersubjectively valid statements about *any* subject's experience of fear are possible. The structure is common; only the factual content is particular and so different in each instance. Or, concretely, the person who is afraid of scorpions can understand the person who is afraid of dentists by virtue of the shared *experience* of fear, even though the transcendent object is different in each case.

But there is a contrapuntal theme as well—that even though the meaning of experience is independent of its transcendent counterparts, we can still distinguish between veridical and nonveridical statements, between, say, a real and an imaginary threat. Succinctly—and inaccurately—stated, all reality is experience, but not all experience is reality. The reality of the threat to a paranoid schizophrenic is an *experienced* reality; the subject experiences himself as threatened. But the experience is not reality; there is in fact no threat.[11]

The criterion for such a distinction is inevitably empirical. Whether we should attribute transcendent reality to the object of experience is a matter not of essential necessity but of probability; it is the growing empirical coherence of our experience which justifies the attribution of reality. Thus Stalin's experience of being threatened by a universal conspiracy was, presumably, real enough as his experience. Tens of thousands paid with their lives for not taking it seriously. Yet it was a paranoidal rather than a veridical experience, as Khrushchev was to admit years later; it was not coherent with the entire body of other experiential evidence.

What an experience is—for instance, the structure or "logic" of paranoidal fear—is an experiential rather than an empirical question. We grasp it in experience seen from a subject's standpoint. We cannot deduce it, induce it, or construct it out of third-person observation of "objective" movements. Even behaviorism begins with a conception of *behavior,* of movements as constituting an intelligible unity. Similarly, even analytic philosophy and ordinary language philosophy begin with a conception of language as meaningful, as expressing an intentionally structured subject experience. But *whether* a particular set of events can or cannot be best understood as an instance of that type of experience—for instance, of paranoidal fear—is an empirical question. That is something we cannot "intuit," grasp directly, as we grasp the logic of fear. Here scrupulous compilation of empirical evidence is needed.

Throughout the chapter, Husserl presents both the point and the counterpoint: the essential autonomy of meaningful experience from any specific factual content and the factual possibility of distinguishing veridical from nonveridical assertions about that content. It is, concretely, possible to speak of the generic structure of fear independently of the question whether such fear is justified in a particular individual experience. This is what makes possible, in principle, intersubjectively valid statements and, for that matter, an eidetic science of even social and human phenomena. But it is also possible to distinguish between justified and unjustified fear in particular cases, which is what makes an *empirical science* of such phenomena necessary.[12]

The point of Husserl's exposition is not to doubt the reality of the world. The evidence is too overwhelming for that. It is simply to § 47b recognize that whatever things are, including "real," they are as things of experience. We cannot think away experience and retain the reality of the world, but we can think away the reality of the world without changing the structure of experience. It makes no sense, for instance, to speak of a cold, hard cube which no subject could possibly perceive, remember, imagine, or experience in some mode. But it is entirely possible to hold that the cold, hard cube, 30 x 30 x 30 cm, which I see on my desk is only imaginary. The experience remains constant: the cube, though imaginary, is still cold, hard and measures 30 cm to a side. When the iceman actually delivers a block of ice, that block contingently "acts out" one of my possible cube-experiences. Were I, for any reason, incapable of imagining a cube, I could not recognize the block of ice as one; I would, instead, subsume it under an available possibility, say, as a very imperfect ball. My actual experience is meaningful only as acting out a possibility of experience—an "empty intention."

Thus, not metaphysical speculation but our ordinary experience makes Husserl's basic point, *the primacy of the possible*. To speak of "learning from experience" is, strictly speaking, inaccurate, except in the sense that experience triggers in the subject an awareness of an essential possibility. Simply as fact, the contents of experience are meaningless and so can teach nothing.[13]

This applies not only to the perception of cubes but also to lived experiences like fear. Here again, the characteristics of fear as experience are independent of any particular threat, while experiencing a threat is contingent on a recognition of its possibility. The fearlessness of those who do not recognize the possibility—what we have earlier called the Androcles syndrome—is notorious. Androcles may be killed by the lion, but he cannot fear him. By contrast, a subject capable of imagining a lion as a threat can experience a real terror in the lion's presence even though the lion does nothing to threaten him.

This, to be sure, does not mean that the possible is a sufficient cause of the actual. A subject's ability to imagine the lion as threatening does not make the lion hungry, any more than my ability to imagine a cube delivers one on my desk—only the iceman does that. More precisely, the idea of transcendence (that there actually is a cube on my desk) is derived, contingently, from the content of perception (I see a cube and am convinced). When Husserl writes that the idea of transcendence is an eidetic correlate of evident experience, he is telling us that, with respect to the reality of the natural world, seeing is believing. Our conception of a real world is not the necessary conclusion of a deductive argument or an intuitively self-evident certainty. Rather, as Husserl said at the start, our experience is such that it compels us to conclude that it is the experience of a real world.

This recognition helps explain the coherence of our experience. It means in the first place, that anything we perceive *as actual* is something we actually *experience* and so is ordered by the possibilities of our experiencing. But, beyond that, it means that even anything we imagine as possible is necessarily something we could possibly *experience* as actual. Our actuality and our possibility alike are rendered coherent by our experiencing. Possibility, after all, no matter how distant or ephemeral, does not spring into being full grown from our imagination. It is evoked—Husserl uses the term "motivated"—by our experiencing. In a world posited as simply existing, apart from the context of experience, we could not speak intelligibly of possibility. There, what would be, would be; no more. It is our experiencing, ordering a world as a coherent whole with its own "logic," which enables us to envision its "logical possibilities." Even my wildest imaginings, finally, are entailed—motivated—by the coherence of actual experience. §47c

§47d

The argument may seem abstract, but the experience which it reflects is not. Most crudely, the glass balanced at the edge of the table is simply that. Only in the context of a consciousness which constitutes the world as a meaningful whole, integrating into it the vibrations caused by passing trucks, centers of gravity, and coefficients of friction, can I imagine the possibility that the glass may fall. The ability to envision such a possibility, notoriously lacking in children, is a function of the ability to integrate experience. The continuity of our worlds, in principle as well as in practice, is not a continuity of facts but of the constituting experience, whether actual or possible. The possibility of experience, rather than its contingent factual counterparts, thus constitutes the primordial subject of rigorous study.

Here, Husserl points out, it is true and trite that our actual experience is limited to the world of our actual experiencing. As a matter of fact, it is. But any alternative worlds we imagine—such as the royal courts in fairy tales told by peasants doomed to penury, the Hollywood vision of America in the Third World, or the worlds of science fiction —are still worlds of possible *experience*. The mythical king and the §48 mythical American are subject beings. The peasant could take their places; he could marry a princess or emigrate. Whatever is experienceable by one ego is, in principle, experienceable by any ego.

Certainly there is no *logical* reason why we could not posit an alternative reality not experienceable by any ego, since the existence of any transcendent object is not a matter of logical necessity but of experience. But, for that very reason, the notion of a nonexperienceable world, whether we conceive of it as a "noumenal" alternative to phenomenal experience or as a distant star, is necessarily empty. Any real world, even a possibly real world, is necessarily an experienceable world, and, as such, ordered by subject experience.

This recognition has a direct practical implication. While the content of particular experiences is contingent and particular, the structure of subject experience as such is universal. Thus while laws and customs may differ, the experience of a rightful due and of injustice is universal. Any world, even that of a different culture, is in principle understandable by any subject and so by any anthropologist, *qua subject,* sharing a common subjectivity—"humanity"—with the humans from whom he is separated by cultural differences. Contrary to the popular misconception, the epistemological puzzle about cross-cultural understanding is not how we can grasp the "mentality" of a culture far removed from ours in space and time. As subject beings dealing with other subject beings, we can, in principle, understand the pattern of their needs, hopes, and fears. The problem is to understand the specific ways in which another culture *acts out,* in particular, the pattern of being-human which, in principle, we understand by sharing it. But, epistemologically speaking, that is only a problem, not a mystery. As the patterns are in principle shared, the particulars, though hitherto unknown to us, are in principle experienceable.

§ 49a   But, as we noted already, while any real world must be experienceable, there need not be a real world to correspond to every experience. Existence, Husserl tells us, is the correlate of certain patterns of experience. Certain coherent sets of experiences, say, subsequent perceptions of a cube on my desk, lead me to conclude that I am dealing with an actual object. That conclusion, however, always remains dubitable. I have been mistaken in the past, and I could be mistaken on a large scale. Or it might be that only scattered traces of a once existing reality remain, just enough to confirm the conviction that the reality still exists. This is in fact a common experience of exiles, who carry with them memories of their homeland and can always find fragmentary bits of news to support what they want to believe, that the home they left is still there, unchanged, a generation later. Again, as in the preceding section, it is *the experience* which is the datum; *the experienced,* conceived as real, is a conclusion based on it and so cannot be used to explain it.

Note that Husserl is not proposing a metaphysical theory but is simply summing up the evidence of ordinary experience when he concludes that setting the real world out of action as a principle of explanation does not affect the basic structure of experience—or, in his words, that the being of consciousness is not affected in its proper existence by nullifying the thing world. Though Husserl does not say so here, this is what makes the naturalistic model of trying to "explain" experience by natural reality ill-suited to the understanding of the reality of our lives. Experience is primary—or, in Husserl's words, lived experience is "absolute"—in the sense that it does not require any actual entity for its existence and so can be studied in its purity. Even though a fully just society may never have existed, we can consider the idea of true justice. It is in fact this ability which makes it possible for us to understand various forms of adjudication as comparable instances, albeit flawed, of justice. Without it, they could appear only as brute facts about this or that society.

§ 49b

§ 49c

This applies equally to the subject matter of all social and human sciences. In all cases, what we are wont to consider "hard, irreducible fact" is actually a conjecture (even if probable beyond a shadow of doubt) based on the growing experiential coherence of our experiences. To assume that such experiences represent a perfect system of deception, staged for our benefit by some Cartesian malicious demon, is again logically possible but practically absurd.

§ 49d

This is a fundamental point. For a century or more, we have tended to conceive the task of science as one of uncovering the "hidden reality" behind a deceptive appearance, in effect elevating the Cartesian demon to the status of a fundamental methodological axiom. At its crudest, this axiom produced the devil theories that interpret history as a Jewish conspiracy or a CIA plot. In a more subtle version, the same axiom is operative in the Marxist contention that the lived experience of our humanity, our quest for truth, freedom, and justice, is an overt reflection of the changing modes and means of production, or in the Freudian contention that it is a mask of our libidinal drives.[14]

In each case, the proponents of such theories claim not only that experience deceives us but also that they have unmasked the malicious demon and are exhibiting the true reality. But paranoia is self-perpetuating. As Bowne saw and pointed out clearly, when we start with distrust, we can never move beyond it.[15] Any reason for trusting will always be subject to suspicion. If we begin with the assumption that reality is a CIA plot, even the most persuasive evidence will appear only as further proof of that agency's demonic cunning. As every marriage counselor knows, it is impossible to prove innocence, which is why Anglo-Saxon jurisprudence insists that innocence must be assumed, guilt proved. This is no less the case in science: to reach the truth, we have to assume the veridicity of experience and look for reasons to doubt it, not the other way around. A century ago, Bowne's insistence on trust as our starting point may have appeared as naive fideism. Today, when Ricoeur echoes it, it appears as our sole hope of escaping from paranoia.[16]

That is the point which Husserl is making throughout, and especially in *I* § 49d. There is nothing naive about it. Husserl recognizes clearly that our experience overwhelmingly supports the contention that consciousness and "reality" are distinct. We may be utterly convinced, and yet err. But he points out no less clearly that, while distinct, the two are not coequal. Consciousness is an absolute—literally, *ab solo*—given. Transcendent reality is given as relative to it.

§ 49e   Thus it is inaccurate to speak of consciousness as being "in" a world. Consciousness—the stream of lived experiences—constitutes a self-contained matrix which includes all its objects as meaningful
§ 49f–g   within it and so cannot be understood in terms of alleged causal influences from the "outside."[17] If anything, we could say that it is the world which is "in" consciousness rather than the other way around. The world, including human subjects as natural beings, appears as real (or imaginary) and meaningful in the context of experience. It is experience which leads us to attribute reality and meaning to (some of) its objects. If we can understand the structure of experience, we can understand its contents. The need for identity, for instance, explains the "territorial imperative," not vice versa.

Should we call Husserl's position a realism or an idealism? Strictly speaking, both terms are misleading. Husserl is not trying to claim that the ultimate nature of reality is material or that it is mental; he seeks to describe critically the actual givens of our experience.

However, it is definitely a denial of the naturalistic claim that we can understand human experience as a reflection of natural reality. What we posit as natural reality is contingent on experience. Husserl is in fact inverting our usual assumption that experience begins with an object which in some sense brings it about; he is pointing out that, in fact as well as in principle, it is the experiencing which is our primordial given, while the object is secondary to it. In ordinary terms, I first *see* a cube, then conclude a cube *is* there.

§ 50a

But Husserl's critical description represents no less a rejection of the subjectivist idealist claim that the order of objects follows the order of thought—colloquially, that thinking makes it so. Such a reading still assumes two distinct orders: one "in" the mind; the other, reflecting it, "out" in the world. In terms of our actual experience, however, both such orders are abstractions.[18] Reality, as we have seen, is not meaningful as such, but only in the context of experience. That context is neither private nor arbitrary. Our experience has its own rules. At the most elementary level, object A is "to the right of" object B only in the experience of subject S. But, given S at location l_1, it is not a matter of personal preference whether A is to the right of B or not. Given Sl_2, the statement ArB is either true or false; it is not arbitrary. Similarly, carbon monoxide is a poison only in the experience of an oxygen-breathing subject; but, in that experience, it *is* a poison. Or, finally, to us an utterly non-Husserlian example, breaking a promise is wrong only in the experience of a conscious subject; but, other things being equal, in that experience it *is* wrong, simply and clearly. It is not arbitrary. The world is what it is only in the context of experience; but, in that context, it is what it is and no other.[19] That is why even an inquiry into social and human phenomena can be a rigorous science rather than an impressionistic collection of individual preferences; but that is also why such an inquiry must focus on the act of experiencing rather than on the object of experience.

These considerations, even if not these specific examples, lead Husserl to his restatement of the phenomenological bracketing, in § 50b, as an *abstention:* abstaining from positing a world, stopping short, so to speak, of the object while focusing on the act. The distinction between the act and its object, to be sure, is legitimate only as a heuristic device. As we have noted earlier, all consciousness is intentional, an experience *of* (an object). But, while going beyond the text, that device may help explain the notion of abstention. In bracket-

§ 50b,c

ing, we focus on the experience from the perspective of the act of experiencing rather than from that of a putative transcendent object alleged to "cause" and "explain" it. Habitually, in interpreting our experience, we pass unnoticing through the act to the object. The subject sees, but pays little attention to his seeing. What he notices is (that he sees) *a cube.* The actual datum is his seeing (a cube), which is the sole warrant for asserting that there is a cube there. But, under ordinary circumstances, we ignore that datum and instead treat the putative object, the cube, as datum, in turn using it to explain our seeing.

In acts of object-perception, this may cause little mischief. But in areas crucial to the human and social sciences the effects are destructive. The subject may, for instance, experience himself as threatened, but ignore the experience, passing through it to posit a threatening object, and then devote his energies to changing the object. Thus a paranoidal subject will seek a community of persons who do not threaten him—in vain, since being-threatened is a mode of experiencing rather than a function of its object. A well-meaning friend might, no less in vain, seek to convince him that the threat is "in his mind," and conclude that the subject needs to be "cured of his mind," by surgery, analysis, or behavior modification. But neither attempt will serve. The threat is there: not in the world, not in the mind, but in *experience.* To understand it, we need to focus not on the subject, not on the world, but on the way [(the subject) *experiences* (the world)].

This is what we do, Husserl now tells us, when we impose the brackets. We are going beyond the pure subject to the *Erlebnis,* the experience, but we are stopping short of positing a transcendent object. Our focus shifts to the primordial act of experiencing, being threatened (or seeing-a-cube), with its intentional correlate, the threat (or the cube) as experience. We are not losing anything by that abstention. Rather, we are gaining all reality, though no longer as a mysterious brute given but as experience and so as intelligible.

§ 51a   This, to be sure, is familiar enough from ordinary reflection. When a subject feels bored while reading a book, he habitually passes through the experience of boredom to the conclusion that the book is boring. Yet a book, of itself, cannot be boring or interesting. Nor can a mind, as such, be qualified as bored. Boredom enters in only as a mode of experience.

This is something even an ordinary reader, in ordinary reflection, will recognize. But when challenged about his assertion that it is the book which is boring, he will normally shift to the question of why *he finds it* boring, speaking no longer of the book but of his preferences and dislikes, once again neatly missing the basic question, why the book is boring, not "as such" but as experience.

As a less trivial example, consider the perception of an evil act, an aggravated assault with a deadly weapon such as six armored divisions. Initially, we perceive such an act as evil. But, "objectively considered," the act quickly reduces to no more than a series of morally neutral events, each in its turn fully explained by antecedent causal conditions. To preserve the moral point of view, we shift to explaining why we, as victims, happen to consider such an act as evil. We might even speak more generally, claiming that all persons, or at least a majority of persons, consider such an act evil. But this again misses the point that certain acts, though morally neutral "objectively," are not simply "considered evil" but, *as experience,* are intrinsically so.

To be sure, the shift from an objective to a subjective standpoint, much acclaimed in existential philosophy and subjectivistic social science, is in itself praiseworthy enough insofar as it breaks the stranglehold of objectivism on our thought. The trouble with it—as with most of the examples we have used—is that it obscures the crucial distinction between the necessary structure of subjectivity and individual subjective preference.[20] That is how far our natural reflection will take us. At best, in our natural reflection we recognize the primacy of transcendental experience, but far more frequently we simply invert our natural standpoint and shift from explaining in terms of "objective" entities to explaining in terms of "subjective" entities, concluding that *de gustibus non est disputandum.*

That is why our habitual reflection, while helpful in breaking the hold of objectivism, is not an adequate basis for social science. A genuine science must do more than simply accumulate statistics about individual likes and dislikes, the way natural science accumulates statistics about what is in fact the case. As *scientia,* a social or a human science needs to turn to the intrinsic structure of experience as such. It needs to ask not only why a given subject considers a particular book boring—or what proportion of subjects do—but what, in principle, constitutes the subject-experience, *boring book;* not only who considers what an evil act, but what in principle is the experience of evil.[21]

Or, summing up the argument thus far: as a matter of fact, the natural world is real. But what we mean by calling it real is that it can be experienced. It is the *common way* we *experience* it—not as "I," as "you," or as "we" in our idiosyncratic particularity, but rather we, each of us, simply as subjects, which we all alike are—that makes it possible for us to speak of a *common* world.

§ 51b   As a postscript, let us consider Husserl's "Note" (§ 51b) concerning the mentalistic inversion of naturalism. In terms of what we have just read, the purpose of that "Note" is clear. Just as a transcendent world cannot be used to "explain" the causal ordering of experience, so a "world-ground" or a God cannot be used to "explain" its teleological ordering. In the first instance (as Hume recognized) it is the order of our experience which leads us to posit causality at all. In the second instance, it is its intelligible teleological structuring which leads us to posit an intelligent, personal world-ground, God. Metaphysically speaking, the two are not symmetrical: God can account for matter, but matter cannot account even for itself. (When the occasion arises, we shall argue that an adequate metaphysics must be theistic.) But from an epistemological standpoint, the two are strictly analogous: in both cases, it is our lived experience which leads us to posit a transcendent reality. Thus our experience, moral and physical, has to be initially intelligible in itself to enable us to recognize an order within it which leads us to posit such a transcendent reality.

Husserl's §§ 52–54:
The Reality of the
Intersubjective World

The crucial point of Husserl's analysis and of our examples gradually emerges as the distinction between two levels of subjectivity, which, following Husserl's usage in *Crisis,* we shall label "natural" and "transcendental."[22] It is the difference between assertions of the type "(For this subject) a thick tripe soup is better than any steak" and assertions of the type "(For this and any subject) being deprived of freedom is destructive." Both deal with "subjective" (really, subject's) experiences. But while one is relative to *this* speaker, the other is not.

This recognition represents a turning point in Husserl's presentation. Throughout the first part of the text, Husserl's chief concern was to reassert the primacy of subject experience in relation to the natural world. His presentation was, basically, a phenomenological challenge to naturalism. The reflections of §§ 50 and 51 introduce a second focus, this time questioning the assumptions of subjectivism. That theme is entirely within the perspective of the subject. Strictly speaking, neither the phenomenon "the book I find boring" nor the phenomenon "intrinsically boring book" is a natural entity. Both are phenomena in experience, but there is a basic difference between them: one is private, the other universal.

The first phenomenon, the "book I find boring," is strictly a private entity, relative to this specific subject and real in the context of his experience alone. The "intrinsically boring book," by contrast, while still an entity conceivable only within the context of subjectivity, is independent of any one subject. For that matter, it is independent even of the sum of all individual subjects; the book everyone finds boring is not the same as the intrinsically boring book.

Less trivially, an experience of which everyone disapproves is not the same as an intrinsically evil experience. Lest our earlier example, aggravated assault, seem controversial, we can use a less problematic one. The experience of pain is one which any particular subject will recognize as evil: pain hurts. Yet, in specific contexts, pain can be good and experienced as such. We need not go so far as the role of pain as stimulus to moral growth: pain can be good as a warning of danger or as the price of avoiding a greater pain. While always a subject experience, pain functions on two levels. One is transcendental, the experience of pain as such, as the experienced negation of being. In that sense, it is intrinsically evil, regardless of what anyone thinks of it. The second is natural, pain as a particular subject's experience. As such, it may be good or bad, depending on the relation of a particular context to the absolute meaning. The expression "It hurts but it is good for me" represents a recognition of two distinct dimensions of subjectivity in ordinary usage.

This is the distinction which concerns Husserl in the second half of the chapter. Understanding presupposes subjectivity; the objective, as such, is intrinsically unintelligible. But scientific understanding, whether in philosophy or in any of the special sciences, presupposes more. In terms of the "natural" subjectivity of "the book I find boring" or "the experience of which everyone disapproves," science could only be a collection of individual impressions, perhaps systematized in the form of generalizations, but not a rigorous explanation of fundamental

§ 52a

principles. In Plato's terms, it would be a *technē,* an art, not *noēsis,* not a *scientia. Scientia* presupposes a transcendental subjectivity—the subjectivity of any subject as such; and so in principle intersubjectively applicable.

§ 52b   Since common sense and the sciences based on it in fact identify subjectivity with private, individual subjectivity, accounting for inter-subjective applicability has traditionally appeared as the greatest obstacle to subject-centered understanding in the sciences. The great appeal of objectivism—the "natural science model"—is that, in spite of the obvious distortion it introduces, it does appear capable of claim-ing interpersonal validity.

Most crudely put, the realistic claim appears obvious: intersubjec-tive statements are possible because two subjects perceive the same object which is there to be perceived. The difficulties with that conception are equally obvious. Quite apart from differences of inter-pretation, two subjects, simply by virtue of spatial perspective, cannot actually *see* the same object. This is what leads common sense to distinguish between the "appearance" which Subject A or Subject B sees and the alleged "reality," itself unseen, said to "cause" Subject A's and Subject B's perception of the thing. Realism, very early in the game, produces the strange view that a common reality, itself actually unseen, underwrites the intersubjective validity of our assertions by "causing" both your and my impression, although those impressions are actually different.

§ 52c,d   This, Husserl argues, is a confusion owing to a failure to grasp the essential meaning of thing-givenness: of the way in which reality pre-sents itself in consciousness as well as of the conception of a thing as such. We have examined it in detail earlier. To speak of anything as real means necessarily to speak of it as available for possible experi-ence. Any such hidden cause of our appearances would be unreal; or it would have to be perceivable by some subject, much as a Freudian analyst claims to be able to "see" the entirely latent true causes of phenomena which appear in the patient's consciousness only as trans-formed by secondary work. But the analyst's perception would once

§ 52e,f   again be a perception from a perspective, raising anew the problem of the common reality. The primordial, unperceived reality posited by physicalistic realism as essentially unperceivable is in principle also un-available for explaining the intersubjective validity of our perception.[23]

§ 52g,h   Husserl proposes to avoid the entire circuitous argument. Let us assume, he tells us, that the perceived thing is always and in principle what the physicist studies. The perceived thing in fact is not identical with the physical thing. The cup as an object of perception is not identical with, say, the assemblage of molecules which becomes my working substitute for it when I am concerned with bonding two of its fragments. But neither is the perceived cup a mere sign or appearance, pointing beyond itself to an alleged physical reality, the set of molecules. The physical thing is not hidden beyond the perceived object; it is, we could say, present *in* it or, perhaps more accurately, if ungrammatically, it is present *as* it. Sensory presence is its only possible presence.

The reality of the cup is, in other words, its reality in ordinary experience. It can be modified, just as the experience can be modified. When a physicist approaches the object with his particular concern— bonding a break—he does in fact constitute the perceived object as a sign motivating his secondary description of the cup in molecular terms. The molecular properties of the cup are clearly transcendent, not present in ordinary experience as appearance. But even here we are not going "beyond" consciousness. Rather, the term "motivation" is again in order.[24] The physicist is led by strictly rational motives to construct certain explanatory models in order to account for the perceived objects (which is what he is studying). The molecular structure is an intentional object; that is how the cup presents itself in the special context of physics. But to posit it as a higher, true reality is a myth.

§ 52i

We can draw an analogous example in the context of social science. For the purposes of describing the social changes that occurred in Europe between the first Russian incursion and the recent stabilization of the Russian empire in central Europe—roughly, between the Congress of Vienna and the Helsinki Conference—it may be useful to describe the way the events of the period fitted together in the experience of the people who lived it in terms of their relation to the means of production, as "classes." A social scientist, like a physicist, may be led by strictly rational motives to construct an explanatory model in terms of "class struggle." But to posit such struggle as a law of history, and class as a higher reality than the actually experiencing "shabby individual," is no more justified by experience than treating molecular structures as reality and tables as "appearance."[25] To deprive individual workers of their human rights in the name of "working-class interest" is a mystification.

To return to Husserl's example, the realist assumption that the

§ 52m

intersubjective validity of experience can be accounted for by some hidden reality said to "cause" the appearances we experience is, Husserl tells us, strictly *absurd,* rationally inconsistent. What physics describes when it speaks, for instance, of subatomic structures are literally "appearances," that is, things *appearing*—though as they appear in the context of that special science. But it would be a mistake to take these appearances as substitutes for the direct lived experiences which lead us to posit them. Causality, finally, is a description of the order of *experienced* objects, not a principle capable of explaining the constitutive experience.

§ 52n   The physicalist language does, to be sure, provide a useful shorthand for the description of our experience. It would be rather awkward to speak of the subject, functioning as an instance of subject-as-such, constituting an intentional context in which the object of experience can be most usefully described in terms of a molecular model. It is far more convenient to say that water "is" H_2O, or even to speak of libidos, classes, and territorial imperatives. But it is not such models, posited as absolute transcendent realities, which constitute human subjectivity. Rather, it is subjectivity-as-such—the necessary structure of subject experience—which enables us to constitute the objects of our experience, in spite of the differences of actual experiences, as a "common reality."

In an elementary example, the statements made at a convention of nuclear physicists are intersubjectively intelligible not because reality "really is" subatomic but because it is so constituted by the shared concern of the participants. Analogously, statements in ordinary discourse are interpersonally intelligible not because your and my experienced reality is the same in all particulars—it is not—but because the experiences of individual subjects are analogously structured in terms of a shared human subjectivity. The disappointment you have suffered may be quite different in its particulars from the one I have known, but I can understand you because the structure of the experience is necessary and common; you can always "fill me in on the details." No amount of details, however, can make me understand an experience which I am not capable of grasping simply as a subject.

§ 52o   This theme, Husserl tells us, needs further development. In his subsequent work, he provides that development: in the analysis of the constitution of the common world in *CM,* in the analysis of the world of lived experience in *Crisis,* as well as in *Ideen II* and *III.*[26]

§ 52p   One of Husserl's offhand remarks at the end of the section deserves special attention. Here Husserl tells us that his observations about the objectivities of traditional realism are equally applicable to axiological or practical objectivities. The terms refer to what we have throughout taken as our primary source of examples, the cultural and ethical products of our individual and social life.

Here we are turning to the distinction between, for instance, the act which all concerned consider evil and the act which is intrinsically evil. A majority vote cannot make a people's quest for identity "racism," any more than worldwide consent can make armed aggression "fraternal aid." The distinction was worked out most clearly by the great Stoic jurists who distinguished the *ius gentium,* a summary statement of the preference of most or all individual subjects of a given nation, and the *ius naturale,* a delineation of the intrinsically necessary conditions of being-a-subject. The rights and obligations of the first have only a limited validity, restricted to the context of the consensus. The latter have a universal validity for all humans, by virtue of their humanity.

In both cases, the intentional objects of which we are speaking, rights bestowed by a particular group on its members and rights pertaining to humans as such, are not transcendent objects, "in the world." They are strictly entities in experience. But in the first case we are dealing with the product of a particular, "natural" subjectivity—as when one group of Rome's subjects recognized a day of rest in every seven as a right. In the second case, we are dealing with rights which are in principle independent of what any group of humans chooses to recognize. Liberty, for instance, is intrinsically a part of being-a-human, as having angles adding to $180°$ is intrinsically a part of being-a-triangle. When a human is deprived of liberty, as by hypnosis or drugs, he is losing not one aspect of himself but his very being as a subject. Liberty is a trait of human experience in principle, of subject being as such.

The problem, however, is that there are and can be no "subjects as such," having "experiences in principle." Subjects are always particular subjects; their experiences are particular, "subjective" experiences. What then is the relation between subjectivity in principle, characteristic of all experience (Husserl's absolute transcendental subjectivity), in which all meaning is constituted, and the actual human subjects? Quite concretely, a subject, I, is both a natural subject—an I which thinks wills, desires, and perceives from a particular perspective—and a transcendental awareness of all this activity. That awareness of all of

§ 53a

§ 53b

my acts is "mine"; it is I who is self-conscious, but it is also I of whom I am conscious in self-consciousness. How can I be both? Or, in traditional terms, how can consciousness be both a subject and, as a natural subject, one of its own objects?

That problem plagues all transcendental philosophies.[27] Less overtly, it is also a perennial problem for social science. What is the relationship between the scientist making a statement about all humans—say, that their behavior is a determined response to a stimulus —and that same scientist as himself a human being?[28]

Though in less specific terms, it is also a continuing problem for social science. What is the relationship between the human in principle and any particular human beings? If we do not recognize the reality of the human-as-such, in principle, we can at most make problematic generalizations, but we can make no universally valid statements about more than one subject. Nor can we then ever make normative statements, such as that men "ought to be" free. On the other hand, if we posit a transcendental subject—the human as such—as constant and absolute, we cannot make our way from it to the particular, changing subject of actual experience. The human, as such, is free; yet almost everywhere humans are in chains.

In speculative terms, the problem may well be insoluble. If the natural and the transcendental ego are conceived as two entities, their definitions will make them in principle incapable of relation. The I who thinks and the I who is aware of the I as thinking become hermetically distinct. That, however, is not the case when we approach the problem from a rigorously experiential standpoint, treating the two conceptions of the ego as two dimensions of lived experience. Here the basic given is the subject as a Person, aware of himself both as persisting through time and as changing, experiencing necessary structures (two and two are four) as well as contingent facts (two apples and two apples are four apples), capable of grasping the idea of joy in principle as well as experiencing joy as a particular inner state.

My "transcendental" awareness of myself and my "natural" awareness of the world are not two entities but two dimensions of my being-a-subject.[29] Availing ourselves of the Scotist term mentioned earlier, we can say they are not *res* but formalities, formally distinct in Scotus's specific sense. They are not distinguished simply "in the mind" of some observer (the "third-man" regress), nor are they distinct in the world as entities. But they are formally distinct, as my distinct ways of being.

This is basically Husserl's approach in § 53b, where he speaks of a "certain participation in transcendence" as well as of being incarnate, and so in the world. Though the passage may sound obscure, the experience it reflects is not. We are in fact capable of thinking in principle, recognizing the necessary structures of consciousness as well as our identity through change, and are capable of *communicating* universal statements, precisely because we are *also* particular, embodied, able to speak.

But consciousness is still consciousness, even when incarnate.   § 53c
Though transcendent objects are given perspectivally, consciousness can still grasp their *eidos* as absolute. In the process of what Husserl will call "pairing"[30] a special mode of apperception takes place: though referring to a transcendent object, which necessarily is not the same when seen from different perspectives by two subjects, both subjects grasp the same basic insight, as when two children, one counting oranges, the other apples, both arrive at the conclusion that $2 + 2 = 4$.

Since both subjects—or both children in our example—are corpo-   § 53d
real beings, the state of consciousness inevitably appears as the state of an ego subject: I think two and two oranges are four oranges; you think two apples and two apples are four apples. It is the ego subject who gives unity, form, and meaning to physical states. Thus we can speak of the world as the *Umwelt* of a particular subject—the life-world of a streetcar conductor or even the life-world of a dog—as the biologist Uexküll in effect does when he speaks of an organism's *Funktionkreis,* the functional cycle defining its environment. Yet because subjectivity has a structure as such, those worlds will be necessarily identical in their eidetic structure. We both will come up with four fruits. Or, while I may experience, in Husserl's example, my joy as an inner state, I am also aware of it as a type of experience *in*   § 53d
principle, applicable, albeit with factual modifications I can determine only empirically, to the experience of any possible subject.

Intersubjective communication, finally, is possible because, and to the extent that, I am capable of grasping my lived experience, not only in its particularity but as having a necessary, transcendental structure, not "objective" yet not arbitrary—and of using it as a key to interpreting the experience of the other. Quite concretely, in experiencing, say, shame, a subject experiences not only this particular situation (say, perceiving an earlier act in terms of a subsequent, broader awareness) but also the structure of subjectivity: the impact on a subject of an experience which he would like to disown but must accept as having been his. Though the empirical content may be quite different in the experience of the other—the things that make you ashamed may be quite different from those that make me ashamed—the principle remains constant. The empirical content of your experience is susceptible only to empirical presentation, but it is intelligible to me because it is ordered by the same necessary structure as mine.

Finally, when ordinary usage resorts to statements such as, "No, it never happened to me, but I can understand how he feels—after all, I'm human too," it acknowledges quite accurately both the necessary structure of being-a-subject as the basis of intersubjective communication and the empirical limitations of its applicability.

§ 54a   That is Husserl's conclusion when he distinguishes between the contingent, relative, "transcendent" psychological experience and the necessary and absolute structure of that experience as transcendental. Even if we leave out of consideration all empirical instances—such as inner imagination—experience remains ordered: joy, fear, and envy still have their logic. Particular empirical contents are meaningful rather than a chaos of impression to the extent that the subject is capable of relating them to what Husserl somewhat grandiosely calls "absolute experience," the structure of being-a-subject as such. Or, reverting for a moment to our earlier examples, as long as social science restricts itself to gathering and generalizing particular individual experiences, it can claim validity only for the subjects examined. It can claim intersubjective validity, a priori, only to the extent to which

§ 54b   it concerns itself with the evident, necessary structures of subjectivity which make such particular experiences intelligible.

§ 55   **Husserl's § 55:**
                                 Realism or Idealism?

Husserl's analysis of intersubjective validity provides us with a model capable of accounting both for the subjectivity of all meaningful experiences and for their intersubjective availability. What he is presenting is neither a subjective idealism nor a traditional realism. The components of our experienced world do not in any sense have a meaning "in themselves," but only in experience. Even an object as humble as a cup is a cup only in the context of experience. It is in the context of a consciousness that the undifferentiated continuum of possible experienceables sorts itself out in terms of objects and their relations.

Yet a cup's being-a-cup rather than a clock or a lamp is by no means a function of the subject's arbitrary preference; it is literally *given* in experience. Analogously, the conception of justice is inseparable from subjectivity; apart from subjects, we could speak at most of relations. Yet justice, just as the cup, is not a matter of individual preference. We might wish to make it so and, on a verbal level, succeed, but in experience it is given by the nonarbitrary structure of being a subject among others. Even if we succeeded in milking the male goat of Kant's famous example, we could not drink the milk from a sieve. Though we may convincingly present autocracy and orthodoxy as a "higher dialectical stage of freedom"—and history bristles with examples—we will not achieve the growth of a free society. Even the concept of the "order of nature" is intelligible only as a description of experience. Apart from that, natural objects simply are. They present themselves as constituting a nature only in the context of experience.

§ 55a

Husserl speaks of this as *Sinngebung,* conventionally translated as the "dispensing of meaning." That translation, however, can be read in subjectivist terms, as the bestowal of meaning by the natural subject, leading to the problematic conclusion that reality exists only as I bestow meaning upon it. But in ordinary usage *Sinn* functions not only in the lofty sense of meaning but also in the workaday sense of plain sense. The common phrase *Das hat keinen Sinn* does not, for the ordinary hearer, have the primary significance of "That dispenses no meaning," but simply "That makes no sense." Thus we can legitimately interpret the assertion *Alle Realität seiend durch "Sinngebung"* (which we cited earlier in the conventional English translation, "All reality exists through the dispensing of meaning") in the sense that our experience presents itself to us as reality to the extent that it *makes sense,* that is, presents itself not simply as a brute given but as a *meaningful* given. Only what *makes sense*—and only *inasmuch as it does*—functions as real in our experience. The reality which, empirically, appears as a sum of particular entities is, in an absolute sense, a unity of meaning, with obvious connotations for the interpretation of social phenomena from the Russian revolution to a patient's personal history.

What Husserl proposes is not a conventional realism, since he

§ 55b

recognizes that *res* are always objects-in-experience. But neither is it a conventional subjective idealism. Husserl's claim is not that reality does not exist or that it exists only "for me" in my imagination. Rather, he is pointing out that it is the presence of subjects—subjects as such, including you and me but not you or me in particular—that gives to whatever there may be the unity and meaning of a *reality*.[31] Far from denying the reality of human and social phenomena, Husserl is pointing out *how* they are real. The only thing he is denying is the assumption that it is nature itself, not an experience, which is in some sense absolute and so explains experience. If we had to pin a label on Husserl's phenomenology, the term we used earlier, "transcendental experientialism," might serve better than either "realism" or "idealism" in their conventional senses.

§ 55c   Husserl's conclusion, that the natural world is constituted in absolute consciousness, does not mean that reality is merely an idea in the mind of God, or that I, closing my eyes to all else, make it up in my mind. Rather, he is pointing out that the contents of our experience acquire the status and force of "reality" to the extent that they present themselves as coherent and meaningful. This they do only in the context of experience—only for *a* subject is A to the right of B or an act just or unjust. In this sense, reality, including the natural world, is constituted in consciousness. However, the constitutive consciousness is not my particular experience as an individual subject but my experience as an instance of experience as such; for any experiencing subject occupying my position, A is to the right of B, act X is unjust. Reality is not constituted in consciousness as individual and particular but in consciousness as such, *ab solo,* or absolute. Reality is not in the world or in the mind—it is in experience.

With that we can return to our original question. An experientially conceived science, even at its most radical, rigorously bracketing the natural world as a principle of explanation, does have a subject matter: the world, though now as human experience. We can answer our second question as well. That subject matter is not "subjective" in the sense of being arbitrary, relative to particular individual preference, because in principle—though not in particular instantiation—neither is experience. A rigorous human or social science is possible as a study of the necessary structures of our being-as-humans.

Reflection, Intentionality, Constitution

5

With the transcendental turn which we discussed in chapter 4, Husserl's presentation of the idea of phenomenology is essentially complete, as Husserl notes in § 76d.[1] The basic insight has been presented: it is necessary to ground knowledge in the essential structures of experience—or, more precisely, of conscious subject being—brought to the primordial givenness which Husserl calls *Evidenz*.[2] The task now is actually to *do* phenomenology.

Much of the material between the preliminary conclusion in *I* § 76d and the final closing of the presentation in § 96c is in fact programmatic, outlining several areas of inquiry which Husserl was to explore in separate volumes.[3] However, there are also sections devoted to clarification of material already covered. Husserl foresaw as much in *I* § 55, though he did not, at the time, seem to anticipate how complex that clarification would prove to be. In subsequent years, he would write two more Introductions to phenomenology, *CM* and *C,* as well as devoting the latter half of *FTL* to an elaboration of the themes of *I*. We would distort the basic insight we seek to grasp if we attempted to cover the full extent of the debate of clarification which followed the publication of *I,* but we would do Husserl less than justice if we passed over those aspects of his presentation.

For instance, given the basic insight of grounding knowledge in transcendental *Evidenz,* what would be the ontological assumptions and implications of such an approach (see chapter 8, below)? What would be the relationship of philosophy so conceived to more traditional modes of philosophizing (below, chapter 7)? For that matter, how would we actually go about the task of seeing the primordial givenness that Husserl calls *Evidenz* (below, chapter 6)? And, most immediately, what is the effect of reflection on the supposed immediacy of that *Evidenz* (present chapter)?

That last problem, scarcely noted in *Ideas I,* was to prove most vexing. Judging by the minimal space and consideration devoted to it, Husserl, in the flash of insight which led to the writing of *I,* did not consider reflection inherently problematic. Yet even on a naive, uncritical level something does seem amiss. On the one hand, Husserl's entire project stresses the primordial givenness of lived experience. On the other hand, he devotes a whole volume (with more to come) to a highly complex analysis of that experience. His own critique of the naive theorizing of our common sense seems to suggest that, apart from such a reflective critique, the immediacy of our lived experience is of little cognitive value. But if such a critique is needed, how can the results of phenomenological reflection still claim immediacy?

I am utterly convinced, with Husserl, that reflection and *Evidenz* are not contradictory but in fact entail each other. Only critical reflection brings to clear focus the immediate givenness of lived experience, which would otherwise be obscured by contingent instantiation. Conversely, immediacy *is* awareness: reflection, I would say, is intrinsic to it. Husserl, in his unwavering commitment to the univocity and accessibility of truth in an age far too ready to relativize truth and untruth, good and evil, bears witness to the noblest achievement of Western consciousness, the conviction that Truth is Truth and Good is Good, though the worlds fall asunder.

Yet once the question is raised, it cannot be ignored. And raised it was, not only by the empiricist skepsis which denies the reality of essence but also by the mystical skepsis which claims that the clearly grasped truth is an articulation—and so also a distortion—of a primordial, prearticulate reality. Husserl's brilliant pupil, Martin Heidegger, presented a persuasive statement of that latter, far subtler skepsis. So did Heidegger's contemporary, Karl Jaspers, for whom philosophy speaks in symbols and issues in a "philosophical faith" rather than a *strenge Wissenschaft.* Even Jan Patočka, who Husserl had hoped would edit his unpublished writings, does not remain immune to it.[4]

Husserl, in his later writings, does respond to that form of skepsis. His *FTL,* for instance, opens with an etymological analysis of the terms *logos* and *legein* (§ 1), in an obvious reference to Heidegger's analysis in *Being and Time.* Husserl's followers—Eugen Fink, Ludwig Landgrebe, Aron Gurwitsch, and Dorion Cairns (to mention only a few)—remained faithful to his conviction that reality is experience, not some putative protoreality, that the truth is overt, not latent, and that it is to be grasped in evident givenness, not hinted at in oblique poetic reference.[5]

A survey of that debate, at this stage and in this volume, would defeat our purpose. We have set out to grasp, in the clarity of evident givenness, Husserl's basic insight. That must remain our first concern. At least some of the criticism directed at Husserl from the standpoint of both empirical and mystical skepsis might reflect a less than clear grasp of his insight. Before we can criticize or defend that insight, we must first grasp it clearly.

For that reason, we shall continue to follow the approach we have used thus far, guided by Husserl's methodological strictures. We shall first focus on the reality of evident givenness in lived experience at its most ordinary. Then, using relevant texts (again, except in the footnotes, from *Ideas I*), we shall focus on the aspects of that experience which Husserl seeks to bring out—reflection (§§ 77–79), the intentionality and constitutive function of human acts (§§ 84–86), and the relation between such acts and their contents (*noēsis* and *noēma,* §§ 87–96).

The World We Find, the World We Make

In the context of ordinary experience and usage, reflection appears profoundly suspect. Terms like "spontaneous," "sincere," "unpremeditated," and "reflecting" carry positive intuitive connotations. Common sense has always been convinced that there is truth in wine, in the mouths of babes, and in the simplicity of rustics. Even Husserl's own distrust of theory and repeated emphasis on faithful articulation of the clearly given bear the mark of the antispeculative bias of our ordinary experience.

That bias is more than the understandable caution of beings capable of deception and self-deception. It has a very real experiential basis as well. All of us are familiar with the experience of changing our behavior while under observation or even self-observation. At the most innocuous level, we know that even a naturally graceful person becomes clumsy and awkward when he becomes aware of a camera or a microphone aimed at him. Anthropologists despair over the effect of their presence on their subjects. Far less innocuously, we have all watched ourselves acting out roles that felt strained and alien to us because we sensed or just imagined someone watching, and wondered how much of what we do and are is real and how much playacting.[6]

It is not a difficult step from such experiences to the deep-rooted suspicion that each of us really carries within himself two selves: one that is pure, spontaneous, and free, though also unknown; the other one radically altered by awareness. The romantic quest for the true self, motivated by the suspicion that what I am aware of is *eo ipso* distorted, is understandable. It is also self-defeating. Each deeper layer the subject uncovers within himself raises the suspicion that it, too, is distorted by consciousness. Art as a happening, politics as spontaneity, or philosophy as poetry represent the *reductiones ad absurdum* of the romantic quest.

The notion of a spontaneous, "true" self and a distorted, "affected" mask imposed by consciousness may be intuitively appealing, but how much consciousness can we remove and still retain a human identity in any significant sense? The extreme case would be a human under hypnosis, under narcosis, or, perhaps, in a coma. Here all vestiges of consciousness are removed. Yet we would hardly consider such experience, if we could still speak of experience at all, as "authentically" human. What endows a person with a personal identity is precisely that he knows what he is doing, he is aware of his acts, he is capable of identifying them as his own and of bearing responsibility for them. Even spontaneity is human only when it is conscious.

Confronted with that difficulty, common sense gropes for another distinction. Habitually, it distinguishes the unproblematic, happy consciousness which popular mythology attributes to animals, poets, fools, and "savages," once quaintly called the *Naturvölker,* from the contorted consciousness said to have been corrupted by civilization. Such innocent consciousness is then said to be a spontaneous reflection of the lived moment, uncomplicated by memory and anticipation.

Yet even if the mythical innocents told no myths and dreamt no dreams, that distinction would not do. Consciousness is never innocent of temporality: it bears time within itself. As the discus thrower swings through the practiced arc, he is not, at midpoint, aware simply of holding the discus in an extended arm. Even in the most innocent, direct awareness he is aware of throwing: of the discus as "just now" (really a split second ago) having weighed his arm behind his back, and "presently" (really in a split second) about to leave it, sailing off down the range. That is not a matter of any tortured, corrupt recollection or anticipation, but a direct, present awareness which yet bears a past and a future within itself. Even at its most innocent, consciousness raises the human above the moment.

Still, the gnawing sense of a difference between being and knowing lingers, driving common sense to yet another distinction, this time between the allegedly innocent data of the senses and the gnoscent— and so no longer "spontaneous"—unities of meaning. We have all heard some variation of that argument. I think I see a Christmas tree— but do I really? Or do I see green, sparkling, prickly, scented, and "interpret" it as a Christmas tree, as when I read the shapes of dogs and people into the hairline cracks in the plaster on the ceiling? Is there really a Christmas tree?

That argument is not altogether groundless. Certainly, the datum of my experience is a Christmas tree. That is what I "see," what I respond to; that is what functions as the given in my awareness. But it is not my senses which, so to speak, deliver a Christmas tree to me. When my consciousness has been paralyzed by a sharp blow on the head or an emotional trauma, leaving my senses to their own devices, they indeed deliver only a swirling melee of colors, shapes, and sounds. Could it be that a blow on the head—physical, chemical, or emotional—restores the innocent consciousness and reveals "true" reality?

A number of young artists have explored that possibility, using "happening" as a method. Along similar lines, drugs that paralyze our ability to perceive actively have been mislabeled consciousness-"expanding," because, while delivering less meaning, they deliver ever so many more colors. But such innocent consciousness is anything but expanded. It is a paralyzed consciousness, less than human, less even than animal consciousness. It is a consciousness reduced to the level of a camera uncomprehendingly recording colors, sounds, and shapes. What distinguishes human consciousness is precisely its ability to act, to perceive the melee of sense data actively as units of meaning. The most we can ever claim for the shock which paralyzes our ability to perceive actively is that it disrupts our habitual ways of perceiving. If we are fortunate enough to survive the shock, it offers us the possibility to start afresh, though, as the experience of revolutions, nervous breakdowns, and divorces testifies, in so mauled and impoverished a state that even minimal survival seems a major achievement.

Passive reception, whether innocent or not, is simply not human. Human consciousness is an act, seizing and molding the data of the senses, creating meaning in the act of being. The phrase may sound lofty, but the reality it describes is commonsensical. Meaninglessness is a product of idleness or frustration. When we are bored or helpless, have nothing to do or are not able to do anything, our universe appears meaningless. Drugs or blows on the head, which at least introduce new colors or let us see stars, may then seem to "expand" our consciousness. But when we are busy, have much to do, and want to achieve much, the universe becomes meaningful. A child's anticipation awakens me and enables me to see a Christmas tree in the swirl of green, silver, and gold.

To understand a person's world, finally, it is not enough to know its components. More than anything else, we need to understand the thrust of his acts, what it is he seeks to do with his world. What he reports seeing, as Dr. Rorschach noted, is a useful index to what he is: how his experience fits together or, more precisely, how he fits his experience together. The key to understanding human acts is to understand their thrust, the way the subject grasps and molds his experience. Humans *make a world,* though they may *find* sense data.

But then, what of the Christmas tree I see? Is it real or isn't it? Of course it is real, though, in another sense, it also is not. It is real in perhaps the basic sense of functioning coherently and meaningfully in the context of experience and making sense data intelligible. It does, however, differ from the raw data of the senses, which alone remain when a blow on the head paralyzes my ability to perceive actively. The Christmas tree is real in the context of my active experiencing. But, unlike my act of perceiving, the Christmas tree is also distinct from my experiencing. It is not simply something I am thinking; it acquires a certain autonomy. The thrust of my experiencing seems real, primary, as do its sensory data. Its actual content, the Christmas tree, is different: it is something which I have constituted as real in the act of experiencing and which, in turn, becomes the primary given of my experience.

In that sense, reflection is crucial not only to human experiencing (by raising it above passive reception of the melee of sense data to coherence and meaning) but also to the world that we experience. That is not a world we find; it is a world we make. The romantic attempt to reach beyond it to a more primitive, unshaped reality is self-defeating. It cannot uncover "the real world." It can only destroy the one real world there is, the world we mold by our experience, and reduce us to the poverty of raw material and raw act. Destruction, finally, is never a creative act, because reflection in the broadest sense does not distort a pure reality but makes it. Very metaphorically stated, reality is not a peach which under a coat of skin and soft flesh hides a true, hard core. It is an onion, made up of, rather than hidden by, its skins. If we peel long enough, we will not reach the true, hard core. Instead, we will end up weeping over a meaningless handful of onion skins.

That metaphor, admittedly, is extremely loose, and the recognition it sums up is no more than an outline, roughly sketched on an entirely common-sense level. We could, however, develop a rigorous, careful presentation—as we shall see that Husserl does—and show, flawlessly, that reflection is not a contingent distortion of lived experience but rather the way in which we, as humans, necessarily live it. The persistent skeptical doubt, the perennial suspicion that we are deceiving ourselves or that we are being deceived by a malicious or a benevolent demon, is wholly without any epistemological foundation.

And yet the suspicion persists, and will do so even after Husserl presents his analysis. As the Personalists were fond of pointing out, scandalizing their uncomprehending readers a century later, certainty, even after the most rigorous, irrefutable argument, remains an act of faith.[7] The doubt persists, fed not by flaws in the argument but by the inescapable experience of a radical difference between experience as lived and experience as self-consciously acted out. There is an inescapable difference between doing something single-heartedly, fully, and doing it in the cold light of reflection. As we have seen, reflection does not have to distort, but too often it does. Philosophers may present their arguments, but common sense still knows that.

Common sense, however, fails to note that what it senses is a matter not of reflection but of the will. The undercutting effect which common sense ascribes to self-consciousness reflects a divided will. Quite concretely, when I am engaged in an act in which I am completely confident and wholeheartedly committed, whether cooking a goulash or growing a garden, being conscious of what I am doing does not undercut my activity. Quite the contrary; it enables me to function more effectively. The undercutting effect does not accompany self-consciousness necessarily but only in those cases when my confidence or my commitment to a course of action is less than wholehearted, when there are reasons to hesitate. In such a situation it is indeed the case that I can function effectively only as long as I do not become self-conscious. Preoccupation effectively prevents my doubts from surfacing. Reflection, introducing a cognitive distance between myself and my act, makes me free and so also human, but by the same token it opens the way for doubt and reveals the cracks in my resolution and competence. The romantic escape from doubt to "authenticity" or true faith is possible only as an escape from awareness and so from responsibility—and from freedom.

At this point we could introduce a truism familiar to common sense, that the person of clean conscience need not fear self-consciousness. That is true enough, and, under a thousand trivial circumstances, also well enough. A competent dancer will not be handicapped by becoming aware of—say, demonstrating—what she is doing. Abandon is necessary only as a substitute for competence. Nor need a competent philosopher hesitate to examine his thought critically. Fanaticism is the defense mechanism of doubt. Self-consciousness is freedom; we need fear either one only to the extent to which we are less than confident of what we are doing.

But, while true and often adequate, in a profound sense that is also a truism. Here Paul Ricoeur is more relevant than Edmund Husserl. As Ricoeur recognizes, a pure conscience, the single-hearted affirmation which is proof against self doubt, is not available, except as destructive dogmatism, to humans whose lives include evil as well as good, in a world whose affirmation means also affirmation of suffering and destruction. As humans, sharing a human world, we may claim innocence in detail, but globally we are never so innocent as to be proof against doubt. Reflection *need not* distort, but it can and in fact often does, not for epistemological but for ethical reasons.

Such considerations, however, far exceed the limits of our inquiry. Our task is epistemological, to understand human knowledge in its essential structure. We shall therefore leave the ethical question of the distorting effect of the flaw and the hope in Paul Ricoeur's competent hands[8] and return to strictly epistemological considerations—and to Edmund Husserl's text.

Husserl's §§ 77–79:
Awareness and Reflection

§§ 77–79

The problem of reflection, if indeed it is a problem, remains unacknowledged in Husserl's initial presentation of phenomenology, and for a good reason. If by "reflection" we were to mean a second-order operation, a judgment about the contents of consciousness, reflection would be problematic, since it could not claim the immediacy central to phenomenology. But it would also be irrelevant to us, since phenomenology deals with primordial awareness rather than with judgments about it.

We can make reflection relevant by using the term in a weak sense to indicate simply conscious awareness. In that sense, reflection could be said to be absent, for instance, in preoccupation, when the subject stares before him, unseeing. It would be present the moment he sees, or, more exactly, becomes aware of seeing. But, in that sense, reflection is also nonproblematic, since it implies no judgment or speculative manipulation of contents and comes to mean simply awareness.

§ 77a

Yet, as Husserl notes, given the usual connotations, describing awareness as reflection does seem to open the way for skepticism. Going beyond Husserl's present text, we can see why. Even in the weak sense, reflection, unlike other modes of presentation, is, so to speak, "detachable." Within the range of direct presentation of lived experience we can distinguish three modes of presentation. One of these, bodily awareness, Husserl does not note until the subsequent volumes of *Ideen*.[9] First, I can, for instance, experience fatigue without being conscious of it. Sheer physical fatigue may affect my performance (in that sense, I am experiencing it) even though I am too excited to notice. Second, I may be aware of fatigue in the margins of my consciousness, but be so preoccupied with the task at hand rather than with my bodily state that, while marginally aware that I am tired, I am not thematically conscious of it. Finally, I can become directly and explicitly aware of being tired. All else recedes from my mind; my overwhelming, preoccupying awareness becomes one of "Oh, I am so tired."

§ 77b

In all three cases, we are dealing with direct experience, not with judgments about it. The mode of presentation varies, but the fact of presentation does not: the experience is simply there. The third mode, which we would normally designate as reflective awareness, is different only in the sense that here we can draw a line between experience and the awareness of experience. The awareness, so to speak, becomes detachable, available for thought and articulation. When we think or speak of experience, it is always experience presented in that mode. Only in that mode can a subject grasp another's experience. Though I grasp that you are tired, my body does not register fatigue, nor am I aware of it in the margins of my consciousness. It is this detachability of experience presented in the mode of reflection that gives rise to the skeptical doubt. To counter that doubt, we have to show that reflection, though detachable, remains a mode of presentation of the given, not an interpretation or a judgment.[10]

§ 77c
Husserl approaches the task by summing up the way reflection appears in ordinary experience. His starting point is the obvious recognition that, though each subject does in fact live his experiences and so "knows" them, it takes an act of paying attention—Husserl speaks of "directing one's glance"—to become aware of them. The subject may have suffered an injury but be too preoccupied with scoring a goal to "notice" it. When he does notice it, it may be in the sense of becoming aware that he is feeling *pain* rather than pleasure, or that he is *feeling* pain rather than imagining it. The awareness does not change the experience—the pain in his legs reduces the force of his kick even when he is not aware of it—but the awareness does make the pain conscious and available to the subject.

§ 77d,e
That is how reflection appears in ordinary experience: the subject notices what he is doing. He is not making a judgment about it, speculating on it, or imagining it. Nor is he recollecting or anticipating it. Anticipation or recollection, even when it is not speculation but rigorous *re*-collection and *re*-presentation of what Luipold von Ranke described as *wie es eigentlich gewesen war,* is still a re-creation rather than an immediate presentation. But presentation in conscious awareness—reflection—unlike other modes of presentation, is not restricted to a razor-edged moment, since our moments are themselves not razor-edged. The discus thrower of our earlier example, halfway between the moment he started to swing his arm and the moment when the discus will leave his hand, is not holding a discus in an outstretched hand. He *is throwing*. As we live it, the posture we can

freeze on high-speed film retains within it the momentum of the swing and the projection of the arc to be described. The subject does not actively "remember" or "anticipate." Concurrently, he is aware of the unitary present act of throwing, of which the just-past and the about-to-be—what Husserl calls "retention" and "protention"—are an intrinsic part. Reflection does not have to add a temporal thickness. That is already there, in the act. Metaphorically, reflection does no more than turn on the light, bringing the act to awareness, and what it reveals is not a razor-edged moment but an ongoing act.[11]

Imposing the phenomenological brackets confirms this basic recognition. The brackets, Husserl stresses, do not change the experience but shift our focus. While in ordinary reflection we tend to be preoccupied with what the lights reveal, within brackets we are asking what, in principle, takes place as the lights go on. Husserl uses the experience of joy, in a typical contrast with his existentialist successors, who invariably choose as their examples experiences of hate or shame. We shall use the neutral experience of typing.   § 78g,h

First of all, as ordinary experience already suggested, when I become aware that I am typing I do not have the sense of thereby initiating that activity. Rather, I become aware that I am in the process of typing. Reflection reveals it, brings it to light; it does not create it. Second, I can then bring to awareness earlier stages, retained though not reflected upon in consciousness. I become aware of having been typing for some time. Finally, I can even compare my awareness with the simple experience, as when I compare the number of strikeovers I make when I am preoccupied with the text and when I carefully contemplate where to set my fingers.

Throughout, however, eidetic analysis confirms ordinary awareness. Reflection is not a matter of judgment about experience, but rather a presentation of the stream of experience, as fact and *eidos,* in consciousness. Thus it does not introduce a skeptical distance between awareness and experience. Rather, as Husserl notes in the next section, it is consciousness' own method of knowing consciousness or, less loftily, the way we know what we are doing.   § 77j   § 78a

Reflective illumination thus is a mode of presentation. Such modal difference, to be sure, is not insignificant. Though the structure of fear is the same whether the fear is lived, remembered, or imagined, we would far rather imagine than remember fear, and would rather remember than live it. But the phenomenon of fear, whether remem-   § 78b,c bered, imagined, or presently given in awareness, remains constant. Throughout, a mode is always a mode of presentation *of a basic datum,* here fear as such, unreflectively lived.

§ 78d   Conversely, every experience can be presented in different modes. Fear can be lived, remembered, anticipated. Because they present a datum, modal presentations have a cognitive value. Because they present it in a given mode, they require study. We need to understand the rules of modal variations: what happens to an experience when it is reflected upon, what happens when it is remembered, and what happens when it is anticipated.

§ 78f,h   In principle, what happens is that the experience is re-presented— perhaps simultaneously—in an ideal parallel. As the subject lives it, an experience is a flowing acting-out of a basic type of experience, such as typing or making coffee. As he is aware of it, it is still the same type of experience, but in that mode of presentation it can be repeated, held still, considered from different viewpoints, as a particular experience or type of experience, or even considered in a different context, such as that of moral evaluation. Reflective awareness makes knowledge possible, not as mere recording but as active understanding.

§ 78i,j   But, for all that, it is still the same experience. Or, more precisely, what I encounter in reflection is not a distinct entity but the lived experience *as presented* in awareness. The fatigue of which I am aware is the same as the fatigue which slows my typing; it is only present in a different mode. The statements we make about the experience in knowing it are statements not simply about "our idea of . . ." but about the experience itself. It is the pain that weakens my kick, not just my awareness of the pain (though the latter could also do so). The skeptical distance is not there because there are not two realities, experience as lived and experience as caught in reflection. Rather, lived experience presents itself to us, necessarily rather than contingently, in reflection. That is not a defect of our way of knowing, nor are its results defective. It is the appropriate mode of knowing for a being whose lived experience is characterized precisely by the fact that he is aware of living it. Experience which escapes awareness is not "pure"; it is prehuman, less than human. Human experience is reflective experience.

§ 78k,l   In turn, our reflective experience itself teaches us that its meaning and cognitive validity, even in rigorous phenomenological brackets, are not those of self-revelation but of seeing something. Perception, or, most primitively, *seeing,* is the basic model. That seeing, however, is not a momentary passive mirroring; it is an active grasp of lived experience as a meaningful, structured whole.

Or, summing up the whole painstaking analysis, we can say that to see something necessarily means also to be aware of seeing it. When we face something, open-eyed but completely preoccupied, "unseeing," we cannot be said to see. We see when we are aware of seeing. But it is the seen, not the seeing, that we see. As against the two-tiered model of reality, said to consist of the "authentic," unseen reality and its distorted but accessible double in theory, Husserl is presenting a unitary model of reality as experience, capable of being presented in various experiential modes, as fact or essence, as presence or imagination.

More basically still, we can say that, as against the romantic opposition of a pale but potent theory and a full-blooded but unreflecting praxis (reflection upon lived experience and the living of that experience, respectively), Husserl is in effect pointing out that in human experience the unity of theory and praxis is a given, not a task. Elaborate attempts to "reunite" theory and praxis testify to an erroneous initial perception. Clearly grasped, experience is essentially present to us in reflection, and reflection is essentially a presentation of lived experience. Reflection does not separate us from experience but presents experience for cognition. That is why, ultimately, the measure of truth of our reflection is how it articulates the lived experience. Clear and indubitable articulation—metaphorically speaking, clear *seeing,* not simply of fragments but of the lived experience in its unity and meaning—is both the way to the truth and the measure of it.

This far too concise presentation retains only an outline of Husserl's text, but what it leaves out are supporting perceptions, not arguments. Husserl does not "argue"; he *points,* carefully, patiently, step by step, to his reader's own experience.[12] Each step is unspectacular in itself. There, see? It has been there all along; just look. Yet the result is rather overwhelming. Against the deep-seated romantic dogma that the thinking man is a depraved animal and that authenticity is to be found in prereflective spontaneity, Husserl is pointing out that the prereflective being, acting out his impulses spontaneously and without awareness, is less than human. The human reaches his full humanity in living his experience in awareness. Against the cults of the primitive, the "spontaneous," the "innocent," Husserl is reaffirming the

Socratic ideal of clear, undistorted self-awareness. His work articulates the genius of Western rationalism, from Socrates through the Stoics, the Enlightenment, and the Renaissance, which he himself summarized at the end of his life against the eruption of the irrational that was embodied, in his day, by the passionate romanticism of the Nazi revolution.[13]

In the argument we have just examined, it was the romantic suspicion that reflection somehow loses the immediacy and purity of lived experience which Husserl had to answer in his investigation of reflection. But an opposite, positivist rather than romantic, critique of Husserl's presentation is also possible, and Husserl turns to it in his next section.

§ 79a–e   In our time, that argument is familiar in a behaviorist form. Basically, it claims that lived experience is in principle knowable only as it is behaviorally manifested because, as presented in reflective awareness (the "self-observation" of the text), it is too subjective to have any cognitive value.

Since Husserl is dealing with pure phenomenology rather than with its applications in human or social sciences, he could, as he points out, simply sidestep that objection. Self-awareness may be of only limited value to an empirical science, say, psychology, which is concerned with establishing the facts of a given case. A patient's experience is a notoriously unreliable guide to facts. Phenomenology, however, is not concerned with the contingent facts but with the necessary structures of experience and so is not affected by the empirical inadequacies of self-observation. A clear, undistorted awareness of experience will serve, whether or not that awareness is factually accurate. Othello exhibits the structure of jealousy even though he is dead wrong about Desdemona.[14]

§ 79f–i   But while that avoids the objection, it does not meet the deep point of skepticism, that reality in itself may be wholly different from the way it appears in our experience. If that were the case, humanistic understanding of lived experience would be in principle impossible. We should be restricted to the alternatives of behavioral description and romantic poetry, each dealing with entirely separate realities.

That skeptical suspicion is not simply the product of methodological speculation; it reflects lived experience. If consciousness—reflection—transformed an act into something altogether different, knowledge would be impossible. If, for instance, an act of generosity (say, giving a penny to a starving eight-year-old, in a thin cotton dress, selling shoelaces on a bridge on a stormy winter night) necessarily becomes an act of vainglory when I become aware of it (I impress my companion: she knows I did not need shoelaces), I could never know what my act really was before I became aware of it. If reflective consciousness were necessarily a false consciousness, knowledge could only be speculation.

Against that doubt it is not enough to reiterate that we are morally certain we know what we are doing. Skepticism doubts precisely the reliability of such certainty. Husserl's argument takes a different form: the skeptical doubt about the validity of experience presupposes that validity. If the skeptic claims that all consciousness is false, he must include himself, and thus his claim becomes groundless. If, however, he claims merely that *some* consciousness is false—so that the evidence he himself presents is veridical—he is claiming only that we have not looked hard enough or clearly enough, while he has. That may well be true, but its implication is not skepsis about the cognitive validity of perception, only the need to look again, better and more clearly. §79j–l

Husserl welcomes that argument. Once the skeptic admits, even if only in principle, by claiming it for himself, the validity of our awareness of our experience—or "reflection" or "basic presentive insight" —then Husserl's proposal to sharpen this insight and base knowledge on it is very much in order. The phenomena of such insight, our basic awareness present in reflection, constitute the purest givens we have. Or, reiterating the argument of the entire section, reflection is not a barrier between our lived experience and our knowledge. It is the way in which lived experience is directly present in our consciousness: we *see,* we *are aware.* §79m–o

That "seeing" is not simply a metaphor. In the last instance, there is no datum more basic: I see, whether it is the candle beside me or the necessary relationship of the opposite angles of a parallelogram. If we disagree, what we need is not to stop looking but to look again. And of the two examples, it is the latter that is fundamental: only as I grasp a principle can I understand particulars as anything more than a buzzing, booming confusion. §79p–t

Husserl's claims about seeing—*Evidenz*—are not just poetic license. Whether we speak of knowing that vitamin C is good for our health or that unprovoked injury demands compensation, we are dealing with claims that must ultimately be based on *seeing*. There is no cognitive court of appeal more basic than that: either you see or you do not. If someone claims that he "just doesn't see that," there is no recourse but to ask him to look again. All our arguments, examples, elaborations are, at the last instance, devices to *help him see*—or to help us see that we were mistaken.

That is as true of seeing ideas as of seeing empirical data. Yet the two are not strictly equivalent. As Husserl points out in *I* § 79q, our ability to *see* ideas is the basis for any ability to see particulars. Lest his claim seem exaggerated, consider the example of empirical medicine. In order to see whether vitamin C is helpful or harmful to our health, we have to have a vision of what it would mean to be healthy. Physical medicine was able to progress because it operated with at least an uncritical, intuitive conception of health: being able to laugh, work, sleep, live. It found itself stymied by life-support technology because this naive idea of health is not nearly precise enough to answer the dark question whether it might be the healthy thing to do to die in one's time. Similarly, if we are at a loss whether the practice of psychoanalysis has wrought more good or more ill, it is because we have no clear vision of what mental health would mean.

Three millennia ago, when Plato told us that all knowledge is but opinion if it is not anchored to a clear vision of the Good, the claim may have seemed far-fetched. Since then, we have witnessed so much destruction wrought in the name of progress by humans of good will. When, after the investigations of the preceding chapters, Husserl tells us that the knowledge of the possible is more basic than the knowledge of the actual, it no longer seems far-fetched. If we could not hope to *see* the point, there would be little point in looking.

§§ 84–86   ### Husserl's §§ 84–86:
                                      ### Intentionality and Constitution

Husserl's analysis of reflective awareness answers the question which common sense poses about the relation between experience and awareness. Reflection, in the sense of conscious awareness of lived experience, is not an extrinsic distortion but intrinsically the way we live that experience, and the reason why we live it as a meaningful whole rather than as chaotic, atomic moments. A human is not a being who is also or subsequently conscious; he is, in principle, a conscious being.

The persistence of the question, however, suggests a deeper problem, not in theory but in experience, which common sense formulates as the contrast between the austerity of knowledge and the immediacy and profusion of experience. Lived experience is rich and miserable with the full richness and profusion of the world. Can a science based on the necessary transcendental structure of subjectivity claim to be speaking about "real life" in a "real world"?

We have the grounds for an answer in our early recognition that our life and world are not "rich and real" in themselves, somewhere beyond our experience, but in it and for it. Reconstructed apart from the subject, the world becomes as empty and meaningless as the whitewashed house with low beams and a deep fireplace without the woman for whom I built it. Less poetically, the world is rich in a subject's experience, and that experience structures it as such.[15]

This is what Husserl seeks to clarify with his conception of inten-   § 84a–d
tionality. Unfortunately, that term is hardly self-explanatory, and the definition which Husserl provides in § 84c is less than helpful. Oft cited, it defines intentionality as the characteristic of experience of being an experience *of* something. Or, in ordinary usage, the term "intentionality" points out that when I see, I see *something,* and when there is nothing to be seen, I do not see. Psychic acts, cognition, conation, and affectivity have an object. True enough, but hardly earth-shaking news.

The significance of the term in Husserl's work, however, is not simply *that* experience has an object, but, so to speak, *how* it has an object. In an earlier work, Husserl had described intentionality as the "act-character" of perception.[16] Perceiving, that is, is not a passion, something that happens to the subject, but something a subject *does* to and with the world.[17] To understand it, we cannot follow a model of a physical relation, such as the reflection of an object in a mirror or the impression of a signet ring on a wax tablet. Rather, we need a model from a human activity which is guided by an intention rather than determined by mechanical causality—for instance, a potter molding clay. Consciousness, here perceiving, is not a mysterious inner state, at best passively affected by the presence of external objects. It is a way of being in and coping with the world, *having a world* in an active sense. Conversely, the world is not an object passively reflected in the mirror of consciousness; it is something that arises in the context of the subject's active perceiving.[18] Stones there may *be*—but we make *a world* as an intelligible unity of meaning. That is why, when dealing with the necessary structures of transcendental subjectivity, we are not avoiding the "real" world but dealing with its innermost essence. To be realistic, a science of human or social phenomena must be "idealistic" in Husserl's sense—dealing with experienced reality rather than with reality posited as a set of objectively existing entities.

We have touched on all of this before, but we have yet to examine it in detail, and that is what Husserl does in §§ 85–86. Intentionality, he tells us here, is the universal medium of our experience. That is, experience, even if not specifically intentional itself, is lived in the context of and mediated by the act-character of being-human, is structured as such, and is so to be understood. Efficient causal explanations are always secondary. They are possible because the reality they explain is not random but primordially intelligible in terms of the teleology—the intentionality or the act-character—of experience.

§ 85b–d But while this is true of experience taken as a whole, in analyzing our actual experiencing we need to distinguish two distinct dimensions. To indicate one of these, Husserl reintroduces another term from *Logical Investigations,* "primary contents." This term points to what we could call the *hylē,* the raw material of experiencing, such as the experience of color, feeling, sound, or pain, taken in isolation. Such experiences, given marginally in the context of experience, are not of themselves intentional, but they occur and become intelligible in another, specifically intentional, dimension of experience. The subject sees a Christmas tree—that is the basic given, intelligible even with wide variation of hyletic data. Within that experience, though, the subject can subsequently isolate pure hyletic data: the "primary contents" of green, glittering, prickly, scented.[19]

The older term, "primary contents," is somewhat unfortunate since, in actual experiencing, it is the intentional experiencing which is primary. The *hylē*—green, prickly—is not something with which we would start but something *into which* we could analyze the perception. To indicate the primacy of the intentional object, Husserl introduces,
§ 85e–i briefly, the term *morphē* to indicate the form as distinct from the hyletic content of the experience. The term soon disappears from the text, displaced by the more accurate *noēsis.* But the concept remains crucial. It points out that experience is rendered intelligible not simply by consciousness in a passive sense but specifically by the intentionality, the act-character, of consciousness. It is not simply the passive presence of an object in a subject's field of vision but his *act* of per-

ceiving, in a strong sense, that constitutes the perceived as intelligible.

In part, what Husserl describes here is familiar enough—we have to note to see, and can overlook what we do not consider worth seeing. In part, it is something we have already noted, that what we see is intrinsically *the seen*. It is not the case that in perceiving we superimpose a "subjective" layer on an "objective" layer of fact. Rather, the object of our experience is intrinsically the seen, the judged, the valued.[20]

But, while somewhat obvious in itself, this recognition leads us to a new level of subjectivity. The first level is one Husserl has recognized from the start: what is, is intelligible only for the subject. Quite simply, what I describe as hail beating down prairie grass is nothing and means nothing in a world devoid of subjects. Only for a subject does it become experience. That subject, however, could be basically passive, like a traveler looking out of the dome of a railway car and simply acknowledging the spectacle, or the uncomprehending Martian whom some theorists take for the ideal sociologist. The experience of such a subject remains entirely hyletic, recording primary data, understanding nothing, reducing experience to meaninglessness.

Contrast it, however, with the perception of a prairie Indian who depends on the prairie grasses for his livelihood. The reality he sees is a meaningful whole, a destruction of food which spells a hungry winter. His perception is clearly intentional, partaking of an act-character: its hyletic contents are structured as coherent and meaningful. The presence of the Indian, not his preferences, not what he thinks or "feels," but his very presence, constitutes the experience as a meaningful whole.

Such constitution is the crucial characteristic of subjectivity. Husserl here speaks of the problems of constitution as "functional," in the sense of problems arising from the active presence of intentional consciousness, the way it *works* on its context.[21] That term, too, rapidly disappears from Husserl's writing, displaced by the term "constitution," but the concept remains crucial. Consciousness does not simply record; it is an act of rendering rational, constituting hyletic data as intelligible wholes. The contents of subject experience are intelligible as constituted. The crucial question for any human or social science is not what the subject experiences but rather how he constitutes that experience as a meaningful whole. Or, crudely, to understand a revolution we need to ask not about the condition of the

§ 86a–f

Russian peasants in 1917 but rather about their understanding of that condition. Disciplines such as sociology of knowledge or ethno-methodology do not deal with "subjective aspects" of social reality but rather with social reality itself, in its noetic (morphic) aspect.

Husserl's recognition of the constitutive function of intentional consciousness explains what we have noted all along: the ultimately teleological structure of intelligibility. In effect, it inverts the basic assumption of modern science, that the subject introduces a note of private purpose into a reality structured by efficient causality. Rather, it is the scientist who (incidentally, for good reason and to good effect) introduces efficient causal explanation into what is essentially and primordially a teleologically ordered reality.

That assumption itself needs to be understood teleologically, as defining a model of intelligibility. For a series of reasons—not causes, note, but reasons—Western science in recent centuries has defined its task as one of providing a causal description of a material universe. From this definition follow conceptions of what is to be regarded as real and what as derivative, what as good and what as bad, what as true and what as false, and, finally, what as successful and what as unsuccessful. The alleged success of modern science is success in terms of its own criteria.[22] But we might legitimately ask whether there is not something strange about a group of flammable human beings who learn how to construct nuclear weapons while remaining entirely at a loss as to when and where to detonate them—and call it "success."

§ 86e   The assumption that the first ability falls within the purview of science and so constitutes progress, while the second represents a purely private, subjective concern, is not a "scientific" conclusion but rather one particular ordering of human priorities, and a rather questionable one at that. Before we progress to the point of incinerating ourselves, we need to reopen the question of our priorities—of the basic principles in which we constitute the reality which our sciences so efficiently describe.

The significance of transcendental phenomenology is that it offers us the tools for a rigorous examination of the constitution of meaning. Phenomenology can, to be sure, also concern itself with what Husserl calls "hyletic" phenomenology, the study of "appearances," or the ways in which consciousness experiences hyletic data. Yet such a "hyletics" remains subordinate to transcendental phenomenology, much as hyletic data are intelligible only in a noetic context.[23] The primary topic remains transcendental phenomenology.

With respect to our particular field of concern, the "noetic" study of how humans constitute their experience as meaningful, in terms of, for instance, the experiences of justice and injustice, provides a context both for a "hyletics" of the feelings of just and unjust and for an empirical inquiry into privileges and obligations acknowledged by a particular culture. Both such studies are clearly important as providing us with instances, but those instances become the building blocks of understanding only when we see them from a transcendental phenomenological viewpoint as instances of the functional process of constituting the idea of justice. It is the intentional presence of the subject, constituting reality as intelligible, which makes a radically experiential grounding of the sciences possible. In terms of our initial concern, it is also the reason why a rigorous study of the structures of transcendental subjectivity is, at the same time, the most basic and immediate study of human experience.

Husserl's §§ 87–96:
The Noema:
Reality As Constituted

§§ 87–96

With the recognition of transcendental constitution as the key to the experiential grounding of knowledge we have come within one step of answering our initial question. That one step is a recognition that *esse,* while intelligible as *percipi,* confronts us also as *esse.* What is is not only perceived; it also just *is:* it has a recalcitrant givenness of its own. This is a generic problem for all transcendental philosophy, but it becomes most evident in the social and human sciences, whose object, social phenomena, is most clearly both intentional and nonarbitrary.

The problem is, roughly, that, for good and sufficient reasons, humanistically oriented research must focus on the understanding of human acts, while, for instance, the social sciences, for equally good reasons, must devote most of their attention not to acts but to their products. Though human acts are the constitutive reality, most of our lives are spent coping with the constituted social reality that such acts produce. For instance, the key to understanding jurisprudence may be the primordial perceptions of right and wrong in which humans constitute a conception of justice. Except in rare moments of major social upheaval, however, the givens of our experience are well-stabilized legal codes.

So far, we have tried to avoid all reference to the constituted rather than constituting reality. We were not always successful, and whenever we failed, our examples became misleading. Whenever we refer to constituted reality, it becomes extremely difficult to retain a phenomenological viewpoint and correspondingly easy to slip, with disastrous results, into a phenomenological naturalism, treating constituted reality not as the expression of human acts but as a quasi-substantive nature or "being" of its own. Heidegger's lapse into phenomenological anthropology in *Being and Time* provides perhaps the most conspicuous example of that danger.[24]

§ 87   Whenever we lose clear sight of our phenomenological brackets, we lose the distinction between eidetic necessity (for instance, the question of how human consciousness, in principle, constitutes the idea of right and wrong) and contingent particularity (for instance, what acts subjects within a particular subculture consider right or wrong). Such a confusion discredits phenomenology by claiming necessity for what is merely contingent and makes even an ethical or historical relativism appear plausible. For that reason, we have sought to remain strictly within the transcendental viewpoint, dealing not with the constituted reality but with the constitutive structure of experience.

§ 88   Yet the purpose of human and social sciences, as well as the ultimate justification of our philosophical inquiry, is precisely to understand that constituted social reality. We need to understand not only the way humans judge wanton killing but also the institutionalized product, the judgment that "murder is wrong." We need to understand not only the way humans experience affinity for their fellows who share certain basic experiences but also the constituted cultural product, the "nation" or "class." We need urgently to learn to deal with constituted reality without relapsing into a naive naturalism or, more likely, into the psychologism or anthropologism which attributes to the products of consciousness a quasi-objective reality. We need to deal with the products of human acts as constituted, yet as radically contingent on (transcendental) subjectivity.

In the first volume of *Ideas,* Husserl is not concerned specifically with the social sciences. However, the problem they illustrate is a generic problem of consciousness, in which the primordial awareness is the act of consciousness but the thematic object is its intentional (not "objective") object. For instance, let the primordial awareness be "seeing an inscription." We may focus on that act, but most of the time our concern will be with the inscription we saw, and quite legitimately so. Yet the "seen-inscription" is not a physical entity. It figures as an inscription only in the experience of a seeing (and literate) subject. The subject did not "make it up," yet it is radically contingent on him, as the reality constituted by his intentional act, just as a "seen cup" or a "beloved homeland."

To distinguish the object as intentional from the putative entity abstracted from the lived experience by the natural standpoint and science, Husserl introduces the term "noema."[25] The term becomes as crucial as the concept. We will do well to follow Husserl's exposition closely.

Husserl starts out by calling our attention to the basic distinction   § 88a
between the act of experiencing and its "intentional correlate"—that which is constituted in the experience. There is, for instance, a difference between the act of adding all rational numbers from 1 through 5 and the product of that act, the equation $1 + 2 + 3 + 4 + 5 = 15$. Similarly, there is a difference between judging a particular action to be wrong and the judgment "That is wrong"; or, most obviously, between marrying and marriage. In all these cases, we are dealing with   § 88b
experience rather than objects on both sides of the distinction: for instance, with the experience of marrying and the experience of being married. Yet the two sides of the distinction are, in each case, as different as an act and a fact.

Consistent with his earlier terminology, Husserl designates the first side in each case as the "noesis," or the "noetic phase" of the experience. It is the experience as meaning-giving or, more strictly, as constitut*ing* its data as meaningful. For the second, hitherto unexamined side of the distinction, Husserl chooses the corresponding term, "noema," or "noematic phase" of the experience. This is the experience as meaningful or, strictly, as constitut*ed* as meaningful in the act.[26]

It is not altogether inaccurate to describe the noema as performing,   § 88c
within phenomenological brackets, a function analogous to that performed by the natural object in the natural standpoint. But there is a crucial difference. The natural standpoint presents its object as essentially autonomous and only accidentally ingressing into experience.

Within phenomenological brackets, that is, within a rigorously experiential perspective, the object, designated as noema, stands out as essentially constituted by the intentionality of the experience.

Husserl's examples include the noema "the pleasing." "The pleasing" is not an object which (also) pleases, but what we earlier called an "object-in-experience," the pleasing as such. The difference is one between the perspective of the natural standpoint and the actual experiencing uncovered by bracketing. The former conceives the object apart from the experience, as neutrally existing, endowed with certain qualities and, accidentally, pleasing me. In the latter, "the pleasing" emerges as the basic reality, constituted by the intentionality of perception.[27]

The distinction is subtle but not obscure. As I dive precipitously for a dime-store ring which my daughter, then aged two, gave me in another life a quarter century ago, I do not experience myself as anxiously rescuing a tin trinket to which I attach considerable sentimental value. That may be the account I give in retrospect, but the lived experience is one of *my precious ring* rolling toward the sewer. The lived reality is not ring + sentimental value but rather the noema, constituted in experience: this precious ring. The object of experience is numerically identical in both cases, but in dealing with it as a noema we deal with it, as Husserl puts it, in quotes, in terms of the being it has in the context of experience.

§ 88h   The radical experiential turn represented by phenomenology consists precisely in turning from objects as abstractly reconstructed to objects as noemata, that is, as actually presenting themselves in the context of experience. The point of intentionality is not simply that every experience has an object but that every object is the object of experience. What is "actually presented"—say, a tin ring—is no more than a nucleus of the full noema, the entire complex of meanings which constitutes the object of my experience, that which I experience and to which I respond.[28] But while such an analysis of the noema is possible, it is crucial to note that, as a matter of actual experiencing, the operative—"real"—objects of our experience are not such thing-nuclei but rather full noemata, full meaning complexes.

§ 90c–g   Having made the distinction between the noematic nucleus and the full noema, Husserl sounds a warning. The noema is not an object but the presence of an object, the way it is present in experience. Thus Husserl warns us against speaking of "intentional objects," as if the world were peopled by two kinds of entities, natural objects that really exist and intentional objects that we create or project in intentional acts. Not so: there is no two-tiered reality. The noema is not a secondary "intentional object"; rather, it is a real object that is present in an experience as the object of an intentional act. Similarly, the natural object is not a different entity but rather the same object, now considered abstractly, in a theoretical "natural" context. The noema is not an immanent double of the natural object but rather the one object of intentional experience.[29] In terms of Husserl's example, the reality is the meaning complex, this tree-in-bloom-pleasing-to-me. The natural standpoint in effect suspends the intentional context and presents us with one of its hyletic components, actual but always less than the full experienced reality.

Husserl's concern is familiar: to enable us to deal not only with constituting reality but also with constituted reality without lapsing into a prephenomenological naturalism. He complicates his presentation, especially for an English reader, by introducing the terms *reel* and *irreel,* in what may appear as almost the physicalist sense of what is and isn't "there" in the world. Since we have been using the term "real" throughout in an experiential sense, the usage is startling. However, the point is to emphasize that the noema is radically contingent on the experience that constitutes it.

To do this, Husserl calls our attention to the three phases or components of experience which we have examined.[30] One is the hyletic phase, the passive recording of sheer sense data. This, Husserl points out, is a "real" phase: it is there, given rather than constituted, albeit given within the context of our experiencing. The second is the noetic phase, the actual intentional act. This, too, is a "real" phase, an intrinsic part of our lived experience. It is, to be sure, something I do rather than something there is, but it is something I do necessarily. Without the noetic phase, (the intentional act of a subject,) we can in no sense speak of an experience. To these two phases, given in experience, Husserl contrasts the primordial noematic phase, constituted by experiencing rather than "given" within it. The analogy that suggests itself is that of two electrodes, the act of charging them with electric current, and the arc of light this produces. The noema, like the arc, is "irreel" in the sense that it is a constituted rather than a given reality, a product of the constitutive act of experiencing.

But while "irreel" in that precise ontological sense, the noema, like

(§ 97)

the arc, is still emphatically *real* in an experiential sense. As we have stressed all along, the "realities" of my experience, in terms of which I respond and build my life, are precisely the "irreal" meaning-complexes which, with Husserl, we have designated as noemata. In terms of our initial example, the reality I know is the Christmas tree; that is what I encounter, what I respond to. It is not a natural but an experiential reality: reality in experience. This, to be sure, makes it no less real, but it does explain why, to understand it, I must incorporate it in the context of experience rather than in the context of abstractly reconstructed "nature" or a no less abstractly reconstructed order of ideas.

§§ 91–95   We could go on to cite other examples, and, in effect, that is what Husserl does in the closing paragraphs of his presentation of the project of phenomenology. The point he stresses is that the basic pattern of noetic and noematic phases, exemplified in acts of cognition by the experienced reality constituted in the rationalization of hyletic data in the intentional act—and endowing experienced reality with its intentional meaning-structure—repeats itself in all human acts. We can draw the same distinction between the constitutive act of experiencing and the constituted reality in whose context we live not only in acts of knowing but also in acts of judgment and acts of willing and feeling.[31] Thus, for instance, it is in the act of valuing that we constitute the reality of "the valuable,"[32] while in the act of resolving ourselves we constitute the noematic corollary, the resolve. But, throughout, the same principle holds. The reality of our experience is not a "brute," hyletic reality, nor is it a set of pure ideas contingently acted out in the world. Rather, it is constituted reality, intelligible not on analogy with natural objects but on analogy with human acts. To return to our initial example, if a human or a social science wishes to be "hard-nosed," "tough-minded," or, in any other synonym, realistic, it must build on an idealist epistemological foundation, because the hard realities of human existence are not the "real entities" with which the naturalists furnish their universe but rather the "ideal" constructs, the noemata constituted as the intentional correlates of human acts. The world may often seem less than human, but it is a human world.

§ 96   With that recognition, Husserl brings his presentation to a close. There are still problems of clarification, and there remains the actual work of phenomenology—recasting our knowledge from the ground up, starting this time with the transcendental subject whose presence constitutes experience as intelligible instead of "explaining" the subject away as the product of a world. That task is by no means easy; phenomenology is no magic wand. Any attempt to pursue a facile, impressionistic recounting of individual preference in lieu of the rigorous search for the evidently given can find no warrant in Husserl's work.

And yet, as Husserl notes, in one sense the presentation is complete. It has given us a perspective and a method. The perspective is that of a radical experientialism, the method that of clear, rigorous articulation of lived experience. To that method we must now turn.

Method in Phenomenology

If we understand the concept of method properly, we can consider the entire project of phenomenology as an essay on method.[1] Husserl is presenting not so much a philosophy as a way of philosophizing. His central concepts—*Evidenz,* intentionality, constitution, even the very notion of *Fundierung,* "the grounding of knowledge"—thematize the structure rather than the content of knowing. Similarly, his crucial step, the basic shift of focus represented by the phenomenological bracketing, is a methodological rather than a substantive one. Nor is there a lack of references to phenomenology as method in Husserl's texts.

Yet, for all that, we would be well advised to exercise extreme caution in speaking of "the phenomenological method." In our ordinary usage "a new method" suggests a set of clever new techniques for doing the same old thing, whether extracting oil from shale or teaching children arithmetic. In that sense, the term is utterly inappropriate. Phenomenology does not claim to offer any bright new techniques. Its basic tool, *seeing and grasping clearly,* is a very old tool indeed. Nor does phenomenology claim to do the same old thing with it. Instead of constructing yet another theory about the experience we take for granted, it proposes to focus on just that experience, to see and grasp it afresh.

But "method" can also mean something quite different—a stance and a perspective, as it does when we speak of the scientific or the dialectical method. In that sense, the whole project of phenomenology is basically methodological. It proposes a fundamental cognitive reorientation: the perspective of subject experience.

If, within that basic orientation, we wanted to single out some aspects as specifically "methodological" in a narrow sense, then the attempt to *see and grasp clearly* would be that "method." Given the basic stance of phenomenology, its explicitly methodological considerations would entail a phenomenology of phenomenology (of clear seeing) itself.

That is what in fact concerns Husserl in the sole chapter of *Ideas I* which is explicitly devoted to methodology. To follow his investigations, we shall first try to see clearly just what is involved in the whole conception of a method. Then we shall examine the three topics in this area to which Husserl addresses himself: the self-reference of phenomenology (§§ 63–65), the phenomenology of "seeing" as a method (§§ 60–70), and, finally, the nature of phenomenology as a descriptive eidetic sicence (§§ 71–75).

Problems of Method

In spite of attempts to isolate a set of techniques and procedures which could be designated as phenomenological, the basic methodological impact of phenomenology has been that of a perspective rather than of a "method" in a narrow sense. A method, conceived as a prescriptive "how-to," is crucial in crafts like pottery or filigree. There the skills, tools, and techniques are decisive, defining fields of endeavor. In the arts, the tools, techniques, and procedures become distinctly secondary, subordinated to the artist's conception of his work. In a science, the method, in the sense of tools, techniques, and procedures, is wholly contingent on the task at hand. The vaunted "Five Step Scientific Method," if taken seriously, would become either a vague truism or a constrictive dogma.

So, for that matter, would any analogous "Five $(+/-)$ Step Phenomenological Method." Humankind has long since discovered that the way to reach reliable knowledge is to gather relevant information, see how it fits together, and determine whether the conclusion will hold up in future experiences. Even medieval theologians followed that procedure. Their "method" in deciding, say, a controversial point of the Scriptures did not differ from that of a natural scientist in the heyday of The Scientific Method at the turn of the century. What differed was their metatheory: what they considered real and what they considered explanation. If we assumed with them that what is relevant is God's revealed will, that what is real is the drama of human salvation, and that to explain means to incorporate into that scheme, then the Five Step Scientific Method would produce a passable article for any *Summa Theologiae.*

The revolutionary impact of modern science was not methodological but metatheoretical. What it presented was a perspective, a set of metaphysical and existential priorities. Basic to this was the conviction that reality is material and only contingently reflected in human consciousness, that it is to be conceived as a mechanical rather than a teleological system, and, somewhat inconsistently, that the most important task is to produce a model of that system which would permit an efficient manipulation of its contingencies for human purposes. The "method" of the natural sciences, in the narrow sense of laboratory procedures, controlled experiments, and, oh, yes, The Scientific Method—not to mention the Canons of Induction—was not a starting point but the product: an understandable adaptation of the obvious ways of gaining reliable knowledge to the new naturalistic and materialistic metaphysical framework.

Similarly, the challenge of phenomenology is not primarily methodological in the narrow sense of techniques and gimmicks. To reduce basic conceptions like phenomenological bracketing to the level of a gimmick distorts its significance no less than reducing the perspective of the natural sciences to a Five Step Method. Rather, phenomenology presents the challenge of an alternative metatheoretical framework. *The crucial phenomenological recognition is that reality is not material or mental but* experiential, *the reality of human praxis whose ultimate structuring is intentional and teleological. Thus, what we need to explain are not objects but experiences; and to explain means to grasp the intentional structure of an experience in principle, as a necessary pattern of subject experience,* and only secondarily, within a particular perspective, to find a cause.

Within this basic perspective the perennial pattern of the quest for truth remains constant, although the emphasis shifts from speculative construction to the initial process, the *seeing.* Even this shift may be compensatory, necessary less because of the intrinsic nature of experience than because of our habits of mis-seeing. But, within its limits, it is crucial. Seeing clearly—and grasping clearly what "seeing clearly" would mean—may well be the most important single component in the actual doing of phenomenology.

Unfortunately, when applied to the clear apprehension of essences, it is also the component which raises the greatest intuitive difficulties for a common sense conditioned by three centuries of naturalism. Seeing, in ordinary usage, has become synonymous with sense perception. While we do use expressions such as "I see what you mean," we take them to indicate a personal comprehension rather than a presentive apprehension.[2] If, as Husserl does throughout, we were to take such "seeing" as providing information about something seen (for instance, "I see that repaying an injury is a prima facie obligation"), common sense would revolt. Such seeing seems too subjective, too private, and too unverifiable to be accorded cognitive validity.

And yet, as we have noted before, seeing in this sense does not differ in those respects from sense perception. A subject seeing a lamp may be as much mistaken as a subject "seeing" a principle, and, like him, has no way of verifying his seeing except by looking again and again, by comparing his perceptions with those of another subject or examining their coherence with other perceptions. Knowing has no more primordial basis than what we have been calling "seeing": the direct apprehension in evident givenness, whether of a particular or of a principle. No matter how elaborate our procedures for the clarification of content and coherence, no matter how circuitous our speculation and our play with lenses, symbols, and mirrors, in the first and last instance there is one crucial difference: either I "see" it or I just don't.[3]

In our ordinary usage, while using the one term, "seeing," we do recognize a range of differences in the ways we "see" a particular—what Husserl called a "fact"—and "seeing" in the sense of seeing the principle or the point of something (Husserl's *Wesen,* or eidos). A careful analysis will bring out even more differences among the various senses of "seeing." But, even on the most ordinary level, one difference stands out. "Seeing" a fact—or even an endless number of facts, ordered with all the sophistication of a master statistician armed with a battery of computers—can tell us only that something in fact *is* so. By contrast, "seeing" in the sense of grasping a principle tells us that something *must* be so, that it is so *necessarily.*

That again is something which, on the level of ordinary conversation, we are likely to deny in theory and treat as evident in practice. I see a chair: that is a fact, but it could be otherwise. Statements of fact are always contingent on a fact, and facts are infinitely variable. But when I grasp a principle, such as the relationship between the opposite angles of a parallelogram or between an unprovoked injury and the obligation to make amends, I grasp it as a necessary relationship, in principle, even if the parallelograms I trace in the sand are crooked and the humans in their dealings with each other even more so. Contrary to our habitual assumptions, it is statements of fact that are always "merely relative." Only statements of principle, whether formal or moral, can claim certainty *ab solo*.[4]

Husserl's insistence on the apodictic certainty of clear perception of principles figures prominently in much of his work, especially in *CM* and *FTL*.[5] While it may seem startling in an age habituated to uncritical naturalism, it is evidently legitimate in dealing with the formal sciences or with the immanent structures of consciousness, as, for instance, Husserl does in *The Phenomenology of Internal Time-Consciousness*. Its applicability to the human and social sciences, however, requires elaboration. Here, after all, we are dealing for the most part with facts or with what Husserl had earlier called "transcendent" essences, the patterns of contingent events, for which it would seem difficult to claim eidetic necessity. While in *Ideas I* this was not Husserl's primary consideration—his concern was the analysis of the essential structure of consciousness as such—he clearly did not regard his findings as inapplicable to social and human phenomena. Works like *Ideen II, Phänomenologische Psychologie,* and *Crisis* attest as much. Many scholars who continued his work—Gurwitsch, Schutz, Garfunkel, and a host of others—did in fact so apply Husserl's insight.

In such application, phenomenology becomes explicitly a method, and does so on three levels, each with its own specifications. Perhaps the most common (and rather less than Husserlian) use of phenomenology in the social sciences takes phenomenology to mean simply a perceptive structural observation of a particular event in order to generate a hypothesis covering all events of that particular type. In effect, it is a substitution of a clear grasp for induction. Such a use is, of course, entirely legitimate and all to the good. Phenomenology aside, even while claiming induction we do, as a matter of fact, arrive at our hypotheses at least as often by a structural analysis of a typical instance as by generalizing common traits of a class of phenomena.

Induction would still remain an unreliable tool, even if we could avoid being convinced by Karl Popper's critique of it. Anything that might reinforce it as a source of hypotheses can only be heartily welcome.[6]

But, while welcome, such a use of phenomenology remains marginal at most. It leaves unfulfilled phenomenology's most basic promise, that of a model for understanding human and social phenomena on the basis of human acts, in terms of their lived intentional structuring, rather than explaining them away in terms of alleged "causes." Such an alternative model of understanding is badly needed, not only on philosophical but also on practical grounds. When sociologists explain delinquent behavior as a product of underprivileged environment, they leave society helpless in dealing with the delinquent. What we need is not to explain what "made" him do it but rather to understand what, as he understood his own acts, he *chose to do.* In our terminology, we need to understand what kind of noematic world he constituted about himself so that his behavior appeared appropriate to him. We have to understand his choice. Assigning human acts to material "causes" is a dubious procedure, since objects function as motives not qua material entities but as presented in consciousness as noemata.[7] It also is not overly helpful, for it leaves society no recourse other than behavioral conditioning, which may assure tranquillity but contributes little to the growth of free moral persons.

A humanistic model of understanding would begin by seeing the human not as the *explanandum* but as the *explanans,* and human choice as constitutive rather than constituted, with its context noematic rather than objective. How do humans perceive—and so constitute—particular typical situations, and what makes particular patterns of behavior appear appropriate? That is a phenomenological inquiry in a far broader sense than the generation of hypotheses for causal explanation by structural analysis of typical instances. Its entire framework is phenomenological; its tools are intention and constitutional analysis. It can understand the human and his world rather than "explain" him away as a subjectively incomprehensible product of a physical context (which itself is intelligible not per se but as constituted by the intentional orientation of the natural sciences).[8]

The greatest significance of phenomenology for the human and social sciences might, however, lie in a third, even less recognized, application, that of providing a basis for normative judgments. This is a task which our present social sciences can neither avoid nor under-take. They cannot avoid it, for even the most routine psychotherapy tacitly assumes a normative ideal of mental health and even the most value-free behavioral modification assumes a normative ideal of de-sirable behavior. Yet the prevailing naturalistic metaphysics and em-pirical methodology of most human and social sciences are in principle incompatible with the making of normative judgments. As a result, such normative judgments are not so much made as allowed to happen, absorbed from a prevailing climate of opinion or an individual scientist's needs and preferences, with the best intentions but not always the best results.

Uncovering the necessary value structure of subject experience may prove the most significant application of phenomenology. We have already cited examples from it, as we considered the normative value of freedom. Such an application, to be sure, is no longer absolutely presuppositionless, even though its presupposition is subject to phe-nomenological critique. It does assume a fundamental decision about the purpose of being-human, in our case the Western assumption that the purpose of being-human is not merely to be born, to reproduce, and to die on some battlefield of the mighty but to realize human value or, in the quaintly Victorian terminology of the Personalists, "the growth of moral persons."[9]

Husserl himself does not *make* that assumption; he lives it in all his thought and work. Explicitly in his perspective on the history of Western thought in *Crisis,* and implicitly throughout, he embodies the Western humanistic commitment to the reality, value, and veridicity of individual experience.[10] In turn, the lived reality to which Husserl's investigations call our attention sustains that basic conviction.

When, within such a perspective, phenomenology is applied to the task of making normative judgments, the enterprise becomes fully phenomenological: a descriptive science of the essential structures of being-human. It is no longer concerned with facts, as in the first application, or even with transcendent essences, as in the second. Now its focus shifts to strictly necessary, eidetically pure structures of being human. What, for instance, would mental health mean? We are not asking what it has meant or been taken to mean, nor what the characteristics are of individuals regarded as healthy, but rather, in principle, given the necessary structure of being-a-subject, what it must mean. Or, analogously, what must freedom mean and what, in principle, are the necessary norms for the relationship of individual and society in dealing with subject beings? Or, ultimately, the self-reflective questions: what is the nature of being-a-subject and what are its implications, necessarily, in principle, for our basic assumption of the reality and value of the human individual? Here, at last, we return to the ideal of apodictic necessity even in a human and social application of phenomenology.

This, admittedly, is a difficult area in which it is desperately easy to lapse into anthropologism or psychologism, attributing the apodictic validity of necessary structures to the contingent, transcendent structures of a particular community. Martin Heidegger's rectoral address, Max Scheler's youthful mistake, *The Spirit of War and Germany's War,* and Sartre's eulogy, "The Communists and Peace," published at the peak of Stalin's terror, can serve as a warning.[11] Yet it is also the most urgent area of inquiry in a world in which humankind has acquired the technological capability of carrying out its mistakes on a global scale. Here we have little more than the barest beginnings, but the question is clear and pressing: what is the meaning of being-human?

Such considerations, however, belong to a different chapter and a different volume. Our present concern is methodological, and so are the questions which these considerations raise. Can phenomenology speak of itself? What does it mean to "see" eidetic structures? And what would it mean to speak of a descriptive eidetic science? These we must now examine, once again with Husserl's guidance.

Husserl's §§ 63–65: The Self-reference of Phenomenology

$\S\S$ 63–65

Husserl's vigorous affirmation of the importance of method in phenomenology, presented most emphatically in § 63—and virtually nowhere else in the book—seems, at first blush, rather less than credible. For all its vaunted importance, the phenomenological "method" does not make its appearance until after the shooting is over, after Husserl has presented the whole project.[12] Even then, the strictly methodological sections are brief and offer little in the way of techniques and procedures suitable for a hypothetical laboratory section of a phenomenology course.

We have already noted the reason. As with every genuine science, the true methodological impact of phenomenology lies in the perspective rather than in the procedures it offers. But, for all that, it would be unwise to dismiss Husserl's praise of method lightly. The crucial point of Husserl's methodological considerations might well be not what he says explicitly about method but what he says about phenomenology in the process.

§ 63b,c   Perhaps the most important point is the utter novelty of the phenomenological perspective. What in the world would a sociologist, preparing a grant application for a phenomenological research project, actually *do?* There are no precedents on file, no established landmarks in terms of problems or data. The entire area of lived experience and its immanent structures is unfamiliar both in outline and content. A prospective researcher has literally nothing to fall back on. He can and must cling to his "method," to the basic project of faithful description of the clearly seen. Not only phenomenology as a discipline but its entire field, lived experience as an object of conscious inquiry, is entirely unfamiliar to us.

A historian of Western thought might, to be sure, gainsay the strict factual accuracy of Husserl's claim, pointing to antecedents in writers like St. Augustine and the Subtle Doctor, Johannes Duns Scotus. But such objections, though often true, are beside the point. The phenomenological perspective remains utterly, startlingly unfamiliar because, though we might find it in earlier writers, we are still thoroughly habituated to interpreting and reading our history, including our proto-phenomenological ancestors, in entirely objectivistic, nonexperiential terms. We do habitually treat as "reality" not the lived experience but rather the putative "objective" entities we abstract from it. As we have already noted, our habitual counter is not the ashtray-experience but an entity about which we assume that somehow, even quite apart from our experience, it "really is" an ashtray. Analogously and less innocuously, we habitually treat as real not the lived experience of value but rather its contingent instantiations, creating for ourselves an illusion of "cultural relativity" because the same value-experience may in fact be embodied in different valued-objects in different cultures. Or, again, the ineptitude of our social responses is often the result of responding not to lived experience but to its contingent expression, treated as a reality, as when we equate a home with a house or a marriage with shared living arrangements. A radically experiential response, seeing the world in terms of basic patterns of experience rather than in terms of predetermined "objects," has become so unfamiliar to us as to require a concentrated effort.[13]

When we break our naturalistic habit, we are confronted with a world which is intimately familiar in terms of what, with Merleau-Ponty, we have called (n. 9, p. 215) "practognosis," the experiential familiarity, but which is reflectively utterly foreign to us. For that reason, considerations of method do become crucial, not in the sense of following a set of familiar techniques—we have none—but in the sense of holding on clearly to the perspectival recognitions which present the new context to us. We must remain ever on guard against the temptation to slip back from a radically experiential perspective into the familiar patterns of objectified thought. The value of phenomenology is its role as a "first philosophy," in the radical sense of providing philosophy and science alike with a clear grasp of the lived experience on which all knowledge is based and from which all science is built. It cannot look to them for help. Hence the importance of method, not in the sense of techniques but in the sense of a self-conscious insistence on a radically experiential viewpoint. §63c §63d §63e,f

It is in this sense that Husserl insists, throughout his work, that phenomenology must be a "presuppositionless" discipline. Not that it presupposes nothing; evidently it presupposes, minimally, experience structured by a subject intending an object. Rather, it must make no presuppositions about the ontological or logical status of the various segments of the phenomenal field. It cannot start with any canons or criteria as to what should count as experience, what as illusion, what as reality, what as appearance. Rather, it must accept as its primordial starting point whatever gives itself in experience, as it gives itself, and only as such.[14] Phenomenology is obviously not presuppositionless in the sense of not presupposing experience, but it is so in the sense of *making no presuppositions* about experience.

This is what leads Husserl to raise the question of the relationship of the phenomenologist to his work. Phenomenology may presuppose no perspective, but the phenomenologist is human, with a perspective of his own. A little earlier, in a section we did not examine in detail, Husserl pointed out as much himself.[15] In grasping the stream of experience as a coherent unity (he uses the term "Idea" in an admittedly Kantian sense) every subject operates within a different horizon; or, simply, even though two humans consider the same experience, §64a,b they do it against the background of vastly different memories, concerns, and anticipations, so that one person's meat may be another's poison. No two perceptions can ever be fully identical, nor can two streams of experience be fully identical. In other words, each of us, including the phenomenologist, starts out within "his own perspective."

§ 64c   The difference, which makes phenomenology possible, is that each of us begins not only with his own perspective as a *particular* person—what we earlier called a natural subject. We also share a fundamental generic "perspective" purely as *subjects* of our experience. Phenomenology deals with the particular contents of a particular subject's experience only *per accidens,* as an instantiation of the structure of subject experience as such. The phenomenologist's private, individual experience has no privileged status; it becomes only an instance of subject experience as such.

Husserl dismisses the point as obvious, pointing to the analogy with the mathematician who, qua mathematician, also functions unproblematically as a transcendental rather than a natural subject in relation to his work. The point, however, is worth stressing because the commonest misinterpretation of phenomenology is precisely one which substitutes "personal" experience, in the sense of private, individual experience in its particularity, for the Person-perspective in the phenomenological sense, that is, experience viewed as in principle subject experience. On the basis of such a misinterpretation, the individual, private experiences of a particular subject acquire a privileged explanatory role. However, focusing on strictly "mine," private experience—often even objectivistically conceived—is not phenomenology; it is the crudest subjectivism, pretentiously attributing absolute validity to private preferences. The point of phenomenology is precisely the opposite: not absolutizing a (private) personal perspective but rather bracketing it, together with the depersonalized "objective" perspective, and substituting for both the perspective of subject experience as such.[16] Phenomenology is radically, not superficially, experiential.

§ 65   What is true of the individual phenomenologist is equally true, *mutatis mutandis,* of phenomenology as a whole. Phenomenology, too, must be studied phenomenologically, seen and clearly grasped as a mode of subject being (in this case, that of knowing) in a world: the primordial, purely descriptive study of essential structures of experience within the limits of sheer unmediated awareness, as Husserl describes it in § 65d. Speculations about phenomenology—the mediate inferences and idealizing procedures which Husserl mentions in § 75f—are legitimate and are the rule rather than an exception in works on phenomenology. But they represent a second-order operation. The primary operation on which they build must be a phenomenology of phenomenology: a faithful articulation of the clearly given.[17]

The importance of method in phenomenology is, finally, the importance of rigor and clarity, of unfailing reliance on clear articulation of primordial insight. This involves not gimmicks or techniques but a radically experiential perspective.

Husserl's §§ 66–70: "Seeing" As a Method

§§ 66–70

When Husserl comes to present the method on whose importance he insisted in the preceding sections, he does little more than call our attention to the rules for "seeing" clearly, both in the sense of perceiving particulars and of grasping principles, which we habitually, though rather carelessly, observe in all our experience. The little more that he does do, however, is crucial. He points out that the same basic rules which apply to seeing particulars apply in a strictly analogous way to grasping patterns of meaning. To see, as ordinary usage would put it, what love is all about (i.e., to grasp the *eidos,* love) is in principle strictly analogous to seeing green. That is not just a metaphor. We either *see* the patterns of experience, or else we do not grasp them at all. They cannot be derived speculatively or by the procedure of "induction" with which the positivistic philosophy of science seeks to overcome the nominalism produced by its denial of *Wesenserschauung,* "the grasp of structures." There is no way we can move from the observation of instances of killing to the recognition that murder is wrong. That we must *see,* just as we see that someone has been killed.

This does not, to be sure, mean that such insight is obvious or effortless. Of course it is not, just as ordinary seeing is not. Seeing requires an effort. We can see dimly, obscurely; we can and often do disagree as to what we see and need to look again, carefully, painstakingly, correcting earlier observations, supplementing them with further clarification. But, even when dealing with primary colors, the only corrective for inadequate seeing is clear seeing. Seeing, not speculation, is the ultimate basis of all knowledge, whether of particular entities or of structural principles.[18]

§ 67a–d   Husserl's methodological section emphasizes this. The "method of clarification" is really little more than the procedure we employ in ordinary experience. At first, we frequently see indistinctly, unclearly, and need to focus, as we do habitually with our eyes and consciously with field glasses (Husserl speaks of this as "bringing to normal distance"), until the object emerges clearly, with no obscurities, no blurred edges. The same is true for an *eidos*. When "looking over" an idea, whether it is a notion that crosses our minds, a suggestion that someone makes, or even a vague "feeling," we focus on it, move it farther and closer, look again and again, until its meaning stands out clearly, with no blurred edges, no obscurities, no "you know what I mean."

In philosophy, this process has often been interpreted as one of definition, but that claim, if we look at it clearly, proves less than accurate. A definition may be arbitrary; understanding is not. A real definition reflects the process of focusing our eyes or field glasses until the shape or color emerges clearly and unambiguously. We do not start out with a preconception of a color, changing tinted lenses until the given corresponds to it.

§ 67e–g   This does not mean that the evident, the primordial given, is simply the obvious. As we pointed out earlier, the obvious may be no more than a familiar obscurity, as when we repeat, for instance, phrases about "human nature" with confident familiarity, though, if challenged, we discover we have no clear idea of what we mean by them. Evidence demands absolute clarity, not obscure familiarity.

In our ordinary usage, we habitually employ two very different strategies of clarification. One of these basically substitutes elabora-
§ 68   tion for clarification. When challenged to clarify what he means, an ordinary speaker (especially one with literary pretensions) will frequently disdain the laborious task of looking again, analyzing, focusing sharply and precisely. Instead, he will introduce other, usually no less vague, considerations. Thus the challenge to define, for instance, the meaning of courage might produce the claim that other qualities are important as well or that you can't praise a given subject for being or failing to be courageous.

Such elaboration is inevitably circular until we clearly grasp the concept of courage. But, on a less crude level, it does have a definite place in the process of clarification. Meaning is never atomic, independent of context (note § 83d!). The elaboration of a context is a valid contribution to clarification. It is, however, no substitute for it; a "broader picture" can be as vague as the initial point in question. The accumulation of vagueness is neither clarification nor phenomenology but just simple obscurantism. It is not vague "intuition" (in the ordinary English sense) which makes phenomenology, but rather the clear, sharp, and evident grasp of a principle.

We are on far sounder ground when we follow the second strategy of our ordinary usage, that of exemplification and variation. In an ordinary conversation, that strategy is equally common. A speaker challenged to define a term will introduce a series of "examples," specific instances which embody the same basic point though in different factual contexts. Thus the question What is courage? might elicit not a definition but a series of profiles in courage, each different but all sharing that common trait.

The presentation of that series has a double effect. For one, since the factual instantiation is different in each case, it makes the point that the facts are not what is at stake, but rather the principle which all instances share. There is a second effect as well. Since each of the different examples will be more or less familiar to the hearer, the series enables him to see the principle at, metaphorically speaking, different distances, from different angles, until he hits on one from which he can focus clearly and sharply—say, an instance of courage which strikes a chord in his own experience.

It is worth noting that frequently the examples we introduce in the most ordinary conversations will be hypothetical and imaginary rather than factual. Thus to the question What is courage? we might respond with "It is like what X did in Y situation," but, since our experience is limited while our imagination is open-ended, we are more likely to respond with "It is as if . . ." or "Imagine that you would . . ." Were we restricted to our actual experiences, most of us would be hard put to overcome the inherent parochialism of limited factual experience. When children first grapple with the mysteries of mathematics, they in fact find it difficult to distinguish the principle of $1 + 1 = 2$ from the apples which exemplify it, but adults often find it no less difficult to distinguish the principle of equity from the familiar pattern of distribution. If we are able to "get the point" rather than remain bound by the particularity of an instance, it is often because we can imagine

factually different examples—such as courage not only in the face of
an armed enemy but also in the face of the elements, then in the face
of weariness and discouragement, ultimately even in the face of the
demands of our pride.

§ 69   The "method" which Husserl describes brings into thematic focus
these familiar procedures of "coming to see." Its core, as he stressed
throughout, is "seeing": grasping clearly, in sharp focus, as evidently
given. But such "seeing" is seldom instantaneous. As with sense
perception, so in the grasping of a point we first see vaguely, indistinctly. Then we look again and again, varying perspective and distance, focusing on a particular segment, returning to patches of
indistinctness, seeking clarity. As Husserl admits, that clarity might
not embrace all specific components of an experience; given the
contingency of particular instantiation, that might not be possible.
But, for the same reason, neither is it necessary. What is at stake is the
eidetic pattern which fuses those particulars into a meaningful whole.
It is that pattern on which we focus, varying distance, varying perspective, until the *eidos* stands out before us with the necessity of the
eidetic insight which we greet with the exclamation, "Oh, *now* I *see!*"

§ 70   In the process, the possibility of imaginary instantiation which we
noted in our ordinary clarification plays a crucial role. Certainly, as
Husserl notes, actual seeing—which he designates as "outer perception"—has advantages of its own, not the least of which is its availability and relative immunity to distortion. In Husserl's example, when
we reflect on our own anger, it often dissipates, while when we observe,
unnoticed, the acts of an angry man, our observation does not modify
his behavior.

But such "outer perception" is also hopelessly bound to the parochialism of the particular. For the same reason as in ordinary clarification, when it is *the point* rather than the fact of a phenomenon that
we seek to grasp, the ability to vary factual instantiation in imagination
is crucial for isolating the point from the instance. It is in that sense
that imagination assumes a privileged position in relation to factual
perception (§ 70a): it enables us to isolate the principle.

This, as Husserl points out, is true not only of the geometer who
varies the shape of a triangle in his mind while noting the constant
sum of its angles; it is also eminently true of the phenomenologist.
Given Husserl's predilection for the formal sciences, it may seem
startling to hear him say (in § 70e,f) that we learn from the fruits of

the imagination, from history, from the arts, and "especially from poetry." But it should not be surprising. Imagination is not an alternative to lived experience but its extension. It acts out the same patterns of being-subject as lived experience, though in a limitless variety of imaginary instantiations.

Fear or courage that is imagined rather than lived is still fear or courage, but it is clearly separated from the parochialism of the particular. Were our sciences—especially those of the human and of society—restricted to collecting empirical data, we should in principle be incapable of doing more than noting what in fact is the case. If we are able to distinguish between what in fact has been so, what is so necessarily, and what ought to be so, it is precisely because, in what has come to be known as the "method of imaginary variation," we can isolate the principle from specific factual instantiation. In the case of an imaginary triangle, the sum of its angles cannot be a function of the materials of which it is constructed, since these are strictly imaginary. Nor can the principle of equity be a function of vested interest in an imaginary example which we can vary freely while the principle remains constant.[19]

Or, as Husserl tells us in the concluding sentence of § 70, it is *fiction* that supports the knowledge of "eternal verities." In light of what we have just noted, Husserl does not mean to suggest, as we ordinarily assume, that the contingent is given and the perennially valid only fictional. Quite the contrary: it is the eternal that is a given; the contingent both presents and masks it, as particular moral judgments both present and obscure the principle of equity. It is imagination that enables us to isolate the perennial principle from the relativity of the factual. Phenomenology, as Husserl insists throughout, is a matter of "seeing"—of grasping with perfect clarity and necessity, free of any obscurity and uncertainty—and so shares all the characteristics of all seeing. But there is a basic difference. phenomenology is the "seeing" of principles.

Husserl's §§ 71–75:   § 71
A Descriptive Eidetic Science

For the reasons we have just noted, the possibility of a descriptive eidetic science is Husserl's most basic methodological concern. The lingering question is one that has figured in philosophy under the rubric of the possibility of a synthetic a priori. Is it possible to make statements which are not merely statements about themselves but about experience (synthetic) yet which are necessary and not a mere reflection of a contingent state of the universe at a given moment (a priori)? Is it possible, for instance, to make a statement such as "Murder is wrong"? We can, unquestionably, make the descriptive statement that, in a given culture, murder is regarded as wrong or the normative statement that we choose to define murder as wrong. But can we make a rigorously synthetic, a priori statement that "Murder in fact occurs, but, regardless of what all concerned think of it, it is in principle wrong"?

We have already dealt with this question and found, first of all, that common sense definitely regards such statements as legitimate (above, p. 79). We have also noted the grounds on which it so regards them. The objects of experience present themselves not only as fact but also as *eidos,* in principle (§§ 2–3, pp. 13–19, above), and such eidetic patterns are not arbitrary and private but a function of being a subject as such (Husserl's transcendental subjectivity, pp. 94–102, above). Finally, as we have just noted, imagination makes it possible to isolate such patterns from particular instantiations and to grasp them clearly.

§§ 72–74   This recognition, however, has not found clear acceptance in our sciences. So far, mathematics is our only explicitly descriptive eidetic science. Geometry, in particular, is concerned not simply with the derivation of necessary consequences of arbitrary axioms (and so not formal or analytic) but with description, although description of an idealized space, space in principle, rather than of physical space. A theory of conical sections deals with necessary ideal entities, yet it is also about sewing striped lampshades. Phenomenology, as Husserl describes it in § 71, is analogous to it: it is, metaphorically speaking, a "geometry of possible experiences."

Because of his insistence on a clear grasp of the clearly given, Husserl is not content with metaphor. He devotes three sections to an exercise in concrete logic—the classification of sciences—rigorously clarifying the meaning of a concrete and an abstract eidetic science, the meaning of description in phenomenology, and the relation of "descriptive" and "exact" as applied to science. Together with the system of categories generated in the latter part of the first chapter of *I,* he provides us with the conceptual apparatus needed to grasp his concluding description/definition of phenomenology in § 75. Yet, in a sense, the presentation is superfluous, except for the purposes of relating the analysis to the categories of the sciences with which we are familiar. For, ultimately, the meaning of phenomenology lies in experience, the root experience which we have examined throughout the volume.

Thus, as Husserl concludes in the title of § 75, phenomenology is a descriptive study of the necessary structures of pure lived experience.[20] By now, all that is intimately familiar. "A descriptive study," yes— phenomenology does not seek to "explain" a phenomenon by ignoring it and positing a hidden infrastructure or a causal superstructure said to explain it. Rather it seeks to articulate in full clarity the "logic" of the phenomenon itself. "Of the structures"—again, of course, phenomenology is not a quasi-empirical study based on extraempirical sources, making factual claims on the basis of individual feelings ("intuitions" in the ordinary, utterly non-Husserlian sense). It is a faithful articulation of the necessary structures of being-a-subject, clearly grasped. And, finally, "of pure lived experience"—there is no realm of ideal objects duplicating a world of physical objects. Experience, not entities, have structure and meaning, and even particular objects are intelligible within the context of lived experience. The intelligible world is a subject's world—not subjective, private, but a world as the context of internal presence, in principle. It is, in another terminology, intrinsically a Personal world, not "my personal world" but structured as the world of Person, in principle, as such. To study social or human phenomena phenomenologically means to study them as intelligible in such a context, describing them rigorously as actually given.

In that context, one other passage, no more than an aside in the project of phenomenology in *Ideas I*, requires close scrutiny because it is crucial for further growth of phenomenological philosophy. We have alluded to it in footnotes; now we need to focus on it: the aside in § 75f–h dealing with "mediate conclusions" and "idealizing procedures."

The basic reference here is not at all obscure. Throughout *Ideas I*, Husserl has explored and emphasized the possibility of placing philosophy, as well as the special sciences, on a rigorously positive foundation. Here he takes cognizance of a more familiar dimension of philosophy, the systematic speculative attempt to build a compre-

§ 75

§ 75a

§ 75c–e

§ 75f–h

hensive structure on such a positive foundation. Though the inferences and procedures he has in mind here may be more modest, the principle he invokes is comprehensive: it deals with the legitimacy of speculative systematic philosophy as such.

In a crucial, seldom-noted passage, § 69c, Husserl implicitly recognized the need for such an extension of positive philosophy. There, in what may be a rare reference to Freudian psychology, he speaks of a "zone of obscure apprehension," of presentations which, *vermöge psychologischen Hemmungen* ("due to psychological hindrances"), *cannot* cross the threshold of clear consciousness. Once we admit the reality of such un-present presentations, such un-given givens, or such un-conscious "consciousness," the need for philosophical systematics becomes evident. Subsequent investigations in philosophy, as well as in psychology, notably those of Heidegger and Ricoeur, have made it difficult to ignore the reality of such un-presented contents. With the broadening of the concept of the subject from the pure Cogito of *Ideas I,* in Husserl's own constitution of personal being in *Ideen II* and "somatology" in *Ideen III,* in Heidegger's Dasein in *Being and Time,* in Merleau-Ponty's "body subject" or Ricoeur's involuntary dimension of subject being, the zone of obscure presentation ceases to be marginal. Phenomenology must include a hermeneutics and a systematics.

The offhand remark in § 69c and the reference in § 75f–h hardly constitute an exhaustive treatment of the topic, but they do include two crucial assertions. While his own interest and insight focus on positive philosophy, Husserl here recognizes that "mediate conclusions" and "idealizing procedures"—which, whether he was aware of it or not, include hermeneutics and speculative metaphysics—are not explicitly precluded by the project of phenomenology. Jointly, the two references we have cited justify the project which Ricoeur describes as "grafting a hermeneutics" onto phenomenology.

A second assertion, however, is no less crucial. Such procedures, Husserl notes in § 75f, must ultimately be redeemed by the clear grasp of essential structures. The legitimacy of hermeneutics and metaphysics as investigations of the zone of the obscure does not change the ultimate goal of philosophy, which remains clear vision, not metaphoric obscurity. Not that the zone of the obscure can be ultimately reduced to clarity; as Husserl admits in § 69c, it cannot. But it can be included within a clear vision which, as we noted in § 69e, demands a clarity of principle, not necessarily of all components of its contents. Hermeneutics is necessary not as a substitute for phenomenology but as the principle of inclusion which transforms the zone of the obscure from an alien body into an organic component. It is a tool of appropriation of the dimensions of subject being which are not directly accessible to subject consciousness but which, nonetheless, remain components of subject being.[21]

The method of phenomenology, finally, is seeing: the clear apprehension of evident givenness. That method may need to be extended, much as even sense perception needs to be extended by conjecture. But the principle of principles remains: there is no ground more primordial than "seeing," and no elaboration more basic than that.

Phenomenology and Philosophy

7

So far, in our presentation of the project of phenomenology, we have, except in the notes, avoided all but the most fleeting references to traditional philosophy. Given the conclusion of the preceding chapter, we might even claim that that is as it should be. Phenomenology is about "seeing," clear direct apprehension, not about speculation. In a phenomenological study of phenomenology, we need to focus on phenomenology as a datum, in the kind of methodological vacuum which Husserl suggested in *I* § 18, grasping the meaning of the text as it confronts us in the text itself rather than reconstructing it from speculations about the text. Our only other legitimate reference is the lived experience which that text articulates. Our basic methodological principle must be to look at the text and, if it is not clear, ask what *in experience* Husserl is talking about, not what commentators have written about it. Phenomenology is radically prephilosophical, a necessary prolegomenon to any further philosophizing. All speculation about it, we might claim, is in principle irrelevant to it.

In the fervor of his early years, Husserl (as in *I* § 24a) did occasionally claim as much, and so have others, in the name of other radically new insights. But, while understandable, such a radicalism is always somewhat artificial. Try as we will, we cannot recapture the innocence of humans at the dawn of history. We are the heirs of three millennia of philosophical reflection.

As phenomenologists, we may and must bracket the products of those millennia as privileged principles of explanation, but they remain as a datum, deeply ingrained in our language, thought, and even our perception.[1] The project of phenomenology is a profoundly philosophical undertaking. Purist protestations aside, a presentation of it must necessarily include a consideration of its relation to other philosophical perspectives.

Husserl, in time, came to recognize as much himself. In the final years of his life, writing his third Introduction to phenomenology, *Crisis* (especially §§ 16–27), he traced the development of the Western (he would say "European") consciousness and presented phenomenology in the context of transcendental philosophy. But Husserl is not unaware of the philosophical context of his work even in *Ideas I,* in spite of the radicalism of § 24. In his second chapter he relates his project not, to be sure, to the factual history of philosophy but to its fundamental eidetic possibilities, to empiricism and idealism, and contrasts his own radically experiential credo to them. We shall follow him in his critique of naturalism and empiricism (§§ 18–20) and of idealism (§§ 21–23). We shall then examine his own radically experientialist credo (§ 24), which by now should no longer sound startling. In conclusion, we shall make some suggestions about the philosophical status of phenomenology.[2]

Husserl's §§ 18–20:
Phenomenology and Empiricism

When Husserl sets out to define the relationship of his project of phenomenology to traditional empiricism, he sets an almost pugnacious tone. The reason may be not only the radicalism of a man presenting a new insight but also the need to distinguish its novelty. Husserl's kinship to empiricism and positivism may be too close for a temperate presentation of the difference.[3]

Read, for instance, the first paragraph of section 18 in *Ideas I*. With a few minor changes, this could be read as a radical empiricist credo, reminiscent of J. S. Mill at his most positivistic. The basis of a science of principles, such as phenomenology seeks to be, Husserl tells us here, is the analysis of the role and relation of particulars and principles *in experience*. Not only that: he emphasizes that his own analysis proceeds independently of any theoretical presuppositions, not as a

§ 18a

speculation or as an interpretation but as a pure articulation of the evident givens of our awareness. The tone of the passage may be as important as its content. Let us listen in on his presentation, paraphrasing as we go along.[4] Here is Husserl speaking:

Wir haben unseren Aufbau der Idee einer reinen Phänomenologie, das sei scharf betont, nicht von einem vorgegebenen philosophischen Standpunkte aus doziert, wir haben nicht überkommene und sei es selbst allgemein anerkannte philosophische Lehren benutzt, sondern einige, im strengsten Sinne *prinzipielle Aufweisungen* vollzogen, d.h. wir haben nur Unterschiede zu getreuem Ausdruck gebracht, die uns in der *Anschauung* direkt gegeben sind. Wir haben sie genau so genommen, wie sie sich da geben, ohne jede hypothetische oder interpretierende Auslegung, ohne Hineindeutung von solchem, was uns durch überlieferte Theorien alter und neuer Zeit suggeriert sein mag.	Let me stress this sharply: when we built up our conception of pure phenomenology, we did not pontificate from some preconceived philosophical standpoint. Nor did we make use of any traditional philosophical doctrines, not even the altogether uncontroversial ones. Rather, we brought to fruition certain rigorously structural insights; that is, we have done no more than to articulate faithfully distinctions which are given directly in our awareness.[5] We took them just as they present themselves, without any hypothetical or interpretative elaboration, without injecting anything that might have been suggested to us not by pure awareness itself but by traditional theories, ancient or modern.

Das sei scharf betont can be rendered "to stress the point," but, reading the German, we can almost see Husserl, leaning over the table, voice upraised: "Now let me make one thing absolutely clear . . ." The emphasis is unmistakable, and Husserl wants no mistake about it. His phenomenology is not based on speculation, on a science as *strittig und verdächtig,* contentious and contemptible, as philosophy. Though phenomenology does take philosophy into account as one of our experiential data, it does not presuppose it. It is based solely on a faithful articulation of experiential givens, the data of our primary awareness. Husserl does not so much as pause for breath for a page and a half.

§ 18b   Such a vehement critique of speculation is familiar enough from empiricist and positivist writings, yet it is precisely this positivistic insistence on a direct experiental grounding of all knowledge which leads Husserl to criticize positivism and empiricism. The object of his attack is not empiricism as an appeal to experience but rather the traditional empiricist interpretation of experience—or the fact that empiricism interprets it at all. What Husserl questions is the assumption that a theory can arbitrate what should and should not count as experience, as well as the Humean conclusion that only sensory perception of particulars should do so. It is the predilection for particulars and the hostility to principles (*Ideenfeindschaft*) which, as Husserl sees it, render the empiricist interpretation of experience suspect.

Husserl's strident tone may well be unfortunate today, when the § 19a difference between phenomenology and traditional empiricism is familiar and the continuity between the two needs to be stressed. Two generations ago, however, it may have been necessary. Now the continuity still stands out from the text in spite of it. Husserl praises the basic thrust of empiricism toward an experiential grounding of knowledge but seeks to warn empiricism against what he considers its unwitting metaphysical bias—the restriction of "experience" to sensory perception and of sensory perception to passive recording of particular data.

The basic thrust of empiricism, Husserl maintains, is sound. It is the laudable effort to free knowledge of all the Baconian "idols," of dogmas, myths, and superstitions, and to find a firm foundation in the givens of experience, in *Sachen selbst*.[6] But it is easy to confuse experience with its noematic contents. Empiricism fell prey to that error, first restricting experience to sense perception and then taking only discrete sense data as genuine "experience" within it. Returning to experience and returning to "the facts" appeared, to the empiricists, as the same thing.

But the two conceptions are far from identical. Physical objects, § 19b the concrete particulars to which the empirical sciences turned, are no more identical with objects of experience than a set of movements is identical with an act. Primary experience includes, just as emphatically, the qualities an object has in subject experience as well as what in Husserl's time would have been called "ideal objects": structures and patterns of experience. To recall an earlier example, we do not, for instance, experience simply a smooth tall object and a fuzzy spherical one. We experience a wine bottle and a tennis ball, as well as a relation: "bigger than." The recognition that the tennis ball will not fit the mouth of the wine bottle is not a result of speculation, but just as much an experiential given as the two particulars, the ball and the bottle. So is the realization that not only will this tennis ball not fit into this wine bottle but that tennis balls do not fit into wine bottles and, for that matter, that large objects do not fit into small openings. Not only particulars, but patterns and principles are among the initial data of our experience. That, in fact, is what makes knowledge—as distinct from mere recording of data—possible in the first place. Husserl emphatically agrees with the turn to experience, but questions the conception of experience as the recording of "sense data."

The point is clear, though the English text is not. Husserl has been stressing the experiential foundation of knowledge, but in § 19b he suddenly seems to be criticizing empiricism for restricting knowledge to experience—and, in the first sentence of § 20, the English text actually has him substituting "intuition" for experience. With that sentence, his oft-repeated strictures against all "mystical connotations" go by the board as readers charge off on an orgy of "intuitions." After all, did not Husserl himself, in *I* § 20a, tell us that we have to substitute "intuition" for experience?

No, he did not, though that is how the Boyce Gibson translation does read: "Thus for experience (*Erfahrung*) we substitute the more general "intuition." But that hardly conveys the sense of Husserl's text, *Also der Erfahrung substituieren wir das allgemeinere "Anschauung."* The confusion, we would submit, is due in part to the differences between colloquial and technical usage, in part to the problems of translation between two cognate languages. Since experience does have a common structure, regardless of the languages in which we articulate it, the problem is not insurmountable. Since, however, the terms in which we articulate experience, unlike the deep structures of both experience and language, do not always coincide precisely in different languages, we need to turn to experience to surmount the problem.

Regardless of the language we speak, one sense of experience which we shall have to articulate, by some term or another, is simply the most general, neutral one of the sum total of all that a subject is aware of doing or suffering. That is "experience" as we use the term in English, with no qualifying adjectives added, neither stressing nor excluding either the subject or the object, simply noting that, in one sense or

§ 20a

another, certain events have in fact taken place within a subject's awareness. Nothing is excluded except any putative events inaccessible to the awareness of any subject.

However, again regardless of the language we speak, we shall need to articulate a narrower emphasis as well, seeing the sum total of all a subject is aware of doing or suffering in terms of its contents or in terms of the act of experiencing.

When, for instance, we say to someone, "Tell me what you *actually experienced,* not what you felt," we are normally asking for an account of the "objects" of experience, conceived as only accidentally related to the subject. To call it "objective" experience is, strictly speaking, a contradiction in terms, since experience presupposes an experiencer; but that is what we usually do call it and we know what we mean.

Finally, regardless of our language, we shall also have to articulate the opposite emphasis, as we do when we say, "Don't tell me what you experienced, tell me 'how it felt'." This time, we are excluding the objects of experience as only accidental and are stressing the *subject's response.* Again, to speak of this as "subjective" experience is, strictly speaking, redundant, since all experience is necessarily a subject's experience. But that is how we do speak of it and, again, we do know what we mean.

In some languages, there will be three different terms for the three distinct senses of experience. In Czech, experience considered in terms of its contents is *zkušenost* (I found out that *the dog really bites*); considered in terms of the subject's experiencing, it is *prožitek* (*I felt surprise, fright, and pain* when the dog bit me); while the middle, neutral sense (*I was bitten by a dog*) would be designated as *zážitek.*

German deals with the same three dimensions with two terms, *Erfahrung* and *Erlebnis.* Used in opposition or in a narrow sense, the term *Erfahrung* suggests the object content of an experience, the term *Erlebnis* (literally, "something lived through") the act of experiencing. To designate the neutral, general sense of the sum total of all a subject is aware of doing and suffering, either term will stretch. Ordinarily, the term *Erfahrung* would be the one most commonly used to speak of experience in general. However, if we wish to emphasize the intimate, personal nature of experience, we can also use the term *Erlebnis* in a general sense of something a subject is aware of doing or suffering rather than in a strictly internal, "subjective" sense.

In the course of his work, Husserl came to stabilize a technical usage which conforms, generally, to colloquial usage except that it restricts the term *Erlebnis* to its narrow sense. In the concluding sections of *Ideas I,* Husserl begins to use the term *Erfahrung* consistently both in the general sense (as when he asserts in *E & J* § 6 that evident givenness is *Erfahrung*) and in the technical sense of the noematic aspect of experience. When the term *Erlebnis* occurs, it is in the technical sense of a subjectively lived process of consciousness.[7]

If that were the sense of *Erlebnis* in *Ideas I,* Husserl would indeed be an out-and-out idealist. But in the first two-thirds of *Ideas I,* this usage has not yet been stabilized.[8] Here, as in colloquial usage, *Erlebnis* can still stretch to cover the general sense of experience, giving it a specific subject emphasis. However, unlike the case in colloquial usage, or in the rest of Husserl's works, in *Ideas I* the term *Erlebnis* strikingly predominates over *Erfahrung* as the general term for experience. While this is inconsistent with Husserl's later usage, it is entirely consistent with his purpose. In presenting his project of phenomenology, Husserl is seeking to break through our habitual ("natural") objectivism and make us aware of experience as *a subject's act*—not an event but an act intelligible in terms of intentional constitution. As we have noted throughout, Husserl is *not* seeking to substitute one specific sense of experience, the "subjective," for another. Rather, he wishes to stress that experience, as such, in principle, is *a subject's* experience. For this, the use of *Erlebnis* in a general sense, to cover the neutral middle ground, is the ideal tool, and that is how Husserl uses it here. The translation, "lived experience," inaccurate in later works, is an accurate rendering of the term *Erlebnis* in *Ideas I.*

The relevant point in our present context, however, is that in *Ideas I* the term *Erlebnis* effectively crowds out *Erfahrung* from the middle range, restricting it to the narrow sense of experience seen in a noematic perspective.[9] That is true generally through § 84, and especially so in § 20a. Here, after all, Husserl has been criticizing empiricism for restricting experience (*Erfahrung*) to the sense perception of individual data, the *Ideenfeindschaft* ("hostility to principles") of which he speaks. In that context, when he speaks of replacing "experience" (*Erfahrung*) as the ground of knowing, he is not proposing to replace experience in its generic sense, but rather a restricted conception of experience which disqualifies, as "not really experience," much of what is genuinely a primordial given of our awareness.

Note, however, that Husserl does not propose to replace *Erfahrung* (here the sense perception of particulars) simply with *Erlebnis* (here the generic term for experience, though with a subject-emphasis). In keeping with his "golden rule" (*I* § 24a), he objects to any narrowing of the concept of experience.

Instead, he offers us as a substitute the term *Anschauung,* which we have been paraphrasing as "seeing" in order to avoid the intuitive sterility of the more precise "apprehension." While not ordinarily so used, in this context *Anschauung* does function as the most general designation of experience. That experience, after all, in its most general sense does indicate the *awareness* of all that a subject does and suffers. In seeking to avoid the partial emphasis on the subject or the object, Husserl quite logically moves to the generic trait of experiencing, the *awareness,* or *Anschauung.*[10]

Returning to our problematic text, we can say that Husserl is proposing an empiricism—or, more accurately, an experientialism—based not on the sense perception of particulars but on experience in the broadest sense of all awareness, the totality of our "taking-in," our perceiving, grasping, seeing.

Now a hundred years ago it may have been the case that "intuition" had, in English, the literal sense of "in-tuition," the general taking-in, so that we might have said "I intuit a cup" or "I intuit that $2 + 2 = 4$" and meant no more than that I "see" it. Today, to say that we "intuit" a cup or a sum suggests something quite different, not clear seeing but its opposite—that we do not actually "see" it, but that we "sense" or "guess" at it, unclearly indefinitely, that in some unspecifiable manner we "have a feeling" that it is so.

In spite of Husserl's repeated warnings against "mystical connotations," the unfortunate translation, "substituting intuition for experience," suggested just that to many readers. But any such connotations are utterly inappropriate in *I* § 20a. Husserl wants a more, not a less, experiential basis; his aim is more, rather than less, clarity of sight. If we want to be faithful to his intent, we should translate the first sentence of *I* § 20a as "For 'objective' experience, let us substitute the more inclusive *awareness,*" or paraphrase it as "Not sense perceptions of particulars, but all our awareness, our taking-in" is the

primordial starting point of knowledge. The point of phenomenology
is not to substitute some extraexperiential "mystic intuition" for experience but rather to include *all* experience, the sum total of all of
which we are aware. Husserl's proposed substitution does not call for
replacing "experience" with "intuition" but rather for replacing a
restricted segment of experience with the whole range of our awareness
in its primordial givenness.

With that, the rest of § 20—and, for that matter, the entire point of
Husserl's critique of empiricism in §§ 18–20—becomes unproblematic.

§ 20b   Yes, of course, empiricism would inevitably lead to skepticism. If
we were to count as experience not what we in fact live and are aware
of living but only those disjointed fragments represented by discrete
sense data, then any order we might impose upon them would be
inevitably suspect, invented rather than given. That is emphatically
the case with the attempt to reconstruct a meaningful whole—a behavior—out of a compilation of observed movements, say, the meaning
of love out of buttons sewn on and bowls of goulash cooked. Sociology,
as Max Weber recognized, must *understand* in order to explain. It
cannot build on fragmented "data" passively recorded by a human or
a mechanical device. It must turn to experience in its primordial sense
of all we are aware of living, in the intelligible unity in which we are
aware of living it.[11]

Phenomenology, as Husserl presents it, is radically empirical in this
sense. It turns to experience in the sense of primordial awareness. It
may and must articulate experience critically, but it can claim no
other starting point than that evident givenness, and no goal other
than a clarified, transcendental awareness. Husserl, together with
many thoughtful empiricists, is criticizing the reduction of experience
to the recording of sense data. As a remedy, he proposes not some
extraexperiential "intuition" but a turn to experience in its full primordial sense. That is why he can say, with full justification, in § 20b:

§ 20b   Sagt *"Positivismus"* soviel wie   If "positivism" signifies basing
absolut vorurteilsfreie Gründung   all systematic knowledge on the
aller Wissenschaften auf das   "positive," that is, on what is
"Positive," d.i. originär zu   simply there to be grasped [rather
Erfassende, dann sind *wir* die   than "derived"], wholly free of
echten Positivisten.   all preconceptions, then it is *we*
                                        who are the genuine positivists.

But what is "simply there to be grasped," Husserl is pointing out, are not physical objects but objects in an experience which includes patterns and principles as well as particulars. A genuine empiricism, Husserl is claiming, would have to be phenomenological; it would have to start with the totality of human experience as humans are directly aware of living it. Any philosophy which a priori excludes our undeniable lived experience of principles—ideas—is equally a priori suspect.

Husserl's §§ 21–23: Phenomenology and Idealism

The recognition of the reality of ideas may be the reason why Husserl sets a markedly milder tone when he comes to speak of idealism.[12] It may also be that the idealists themselves set a milder tone in their disputations, treating phenomenology as erroneous rather than as a set of nonsense statements.

There is one other consideration. Precisely because of his radically experiential emphasis, Husserl has an instinctive predilection for idealism. As we noted earlier, humans in their ordinary experience are basically idealists. In spite of the naive reism of common sense, they do not orient their lives around beer and baseball but around far less tangible reference points—pride, hate, prejudice, esteem, love. Similarly, on a far more sophisticated level, humans in their reflection, even when proclaiming a positivist or behaviorist position, rely on the intelligibility of lived experience. "In Wahrheit sehen alle und sozusagen immerfort 'Ideen,' 'Wesen,' sie operieren mit ihnen im Denken, vollziehen auch Wesensurteile" ("In truth they see, all of them and, so to speak, constantly, 'ideas' and 'structures,' use them in their thought and formulate eidetic judgments"). Thus Husserl writes of his critics in *I* § 22a, though what he says applies to everyone. For Husserl, a philosophy which recognizes the reality of ideas is prima facie more credible than one which does not.

The trouble with idealism—and the reason why not only the man in the street but also the person in a philosophy classroom finds most overt statements of it farfetched—is, according to Husserl, that idealism denies the experiential grounding which makes it plausible, presenting its ideas not as experiential givens but as articles of faith or products of speculation. The man in the street "sees his duty" and,

§ 21

more often than not, does it; he "sees" the logic of a situation, say, that injustice creates resentment, and treats it as a "fact of life." But if he is told that these are eternal, a priori principles, innate or intuited rather than seen, he balks,

There is in fact no great problem about the necessity of, say, the assertion that the opposite angles of a parallelogram are equal. That is evident—I *see* it as much as I see the particular parallelogram illustrating it. Even the notorious assertion that "The Absolute is one" makes a great deal of sense as an observation report of a structure of experience which we encounter in direct awareness. The sense of unity of being in contrast with the multiplicity of its manifestations is not at all an uncommon experience, even though its curbside formulations may seem too crude to the philosopher or the poet.

Such perceptions, however, become highly problematic when they are presented not as experiential givens but as speculative dogmas. When the idealist, for fear of falling prey to the empiricist restrictions on experience, denies that he is seeing or that rational insight is really a presentative awareness strictly analogous to the awareness of seeing yellow, it becomes quite problematic just how we can be said to know *eidē* at all. Idealism can, of course, escape skepticism by claiming a "feeling" of certainty, but only at the cost of falling prey to a vicious subjectivism. Like facts, principles can be evident because they are *seen,* given in our direct awareness of lived experience, but their evidence becomes problematic when they are separated from their experiential matrix.

At this point, however, the man in the street is quite likely to feel uncomfortable for a different reason. To speak of "seeing" structures and principles will suggest to him that they are somehow "there" to be seen. As Husserl pointed out in § 1a, for the naive realism of common sense, to be real means to be there "in the world," as physical entities, occupying space. Our man in the street may be aware that the truth of $2 + 2 = 4$ is not simply "in the mind," but he is no less aware that "in the world" there is only 1,1,1,1, waiting to be counted. Ideas don't exist.

This is the objection to which Husserl turns in *I* § 22a. His tone throughout the section suggests that he considers this clearly a difficulty not worthy even of the man in the street, a sophism based on a willful confusion of reality and physical existence. To say that something is real means evidently that it is a datum of experience but not necessarily a physical entity. Even our man in the street knows that.

He knows, for instance, that guilt is not "there" as a can of beer is there, but that it can be far more real: "I feel so bad about it I don't feel like drinking." But when he is told that this means that the guilt he lives must exist, like the can of beer, though in some platonic realm, he retreats into subjectivism to preserve the reality of guilt while denying its existence. He will say that it is "real for him," though his expectations of understanding and respect from others amply testify that he does not think the guilt is real only "for him," but rather that it is really there, in the situation. To accuse him of attributing existence to his guilt is manifestly unfair. It is no less unfair to level a similar accusation against a philosopher who insists on the reality of ideas. Even when, like Plato, he speaks of ideas "existing" as prototypes in a heavenly realm, this is clearly a metaphor designed to stress their reality. To take it as a literal assertion shows a lack of experiential awareness.

But what if the man in the street chooses the other horn of the §23 dilemma and insists that, since ideas do not "exist," they really are just "in the mind," essentially subjective and private? The curbside phrase for that is "It all depends on how you look at it," while in the classroom it is "Everything is relative." To Husserl that is clearly a counsel of desperation to which the speaker is driven by the insistence that reality must mean either physical existence or existence as an a priori dictum, annunciated by professors rather than seen in experience. Yet once we lose sight of the fact that principles, like facts, are experiential givens, *seen* rather than arbitrarily posited and believed, such an argument does acquire a certain plausibility.

That plausibility, however, is based on the confusion of a principle with the reflective consciousness of a principle. The empiricist may claim to have derived his idea of hate by abstracting the common characteristics of numerous instances of hate. That is in fact how we frequently generate our definition of hate. But in order to carry out such abstraction we have first to select the experiences we shall consider. Only an initial awareness of the principle, hate, makes the subsequent abstraction possible. Once again, only because the principle, hate, can be *seen,* can it be studied—and our study will be no better than our initial grasp of direct awareness. Phenomenology, as Husserl notes in §25, does not propose to substitute awareness for scientific inquiry, but it does propose to see and grasp clearly the lived experience on which such inquiry is built.

But what about the products of pure imagination, such as Husserl's flute-playing centaur, or its English equivalent, the unicorn? Are they not also givens of experience? Certainly they are, though they are *given as imagined* rather than *as perceived,* as hoped for, or any other mode of givenness. They become problematic only when idealism (understood now as any philosophy which takes the data of awareness rather than putative physical entities as its starting point) forgets that ideas, like facts, are *seen,* and treats them as simply present in the mind. In that case, the distinction among the modes of givenness (given-as-perceived, given-as-imagined, or given-as-hoped-for) disappears as all data become equally and arbitrarily present. The cure for the ills of idealism, Husserl claims, is to recognize its experiential basis: ideas are real, but it is not the case that they are simply to be believed or denied. They are *seen,* given in primordial awareness of lived experience.[13]

That, however, raises one final difficulty. If ideas—hate, justice, the relationship of opposite angles of a parallelogram—are indeed *seen,* given in direct awareness, is a meaningful disagreement ever possible? Or, in traditional terminology, is error ever possible? After all, one man in the street may "see" a duty where another sees a prohibition. Would not a disagreement between two observers, both of whom truthfully and accurately report their awareness of the structures of experience, prove either that the "reality" they describe is in fact private and subjective or that the sole pure datum we have, our awareness of experience, is itself unreliable?

Not really, any more than in the case of sense awareness. On that level, we accept it as nonproblematic that two observers can perceive the same aquamarine surface and truthfully report seeing two different colors, blue and green. We accept it as a fact that some (sense) perceptions are clear while others are not, that some are confused and we have to look again. We find the possibility of confused sense perception entirely compatible both with the recognition of its primordiality and its veridicity in principle. Why should the same conditions be problematic in the case of our awareness of structures and principles?[14]

The fact of confused, unclear perception of principles becomes problematic only if we separate the principles from their experiential grounding and hypostatize them as "platonic" essences, at least in the sense in which some scholars interpret Plato in spite of his insistence that "rational intuition" is a seeing, analogous to sense perception. In the act of seeing, on the level of fact as well as principle, unclear perception may be a problem but it is not in principle problematic. As Husserl pointed out in his chapter on method (*I* §§ 66–70), we need to look again until we see clearly. The letter on the chart may appear as a blurred shape—I have to look again, focus, come closer, until I see it clearly. Analogously, I may sense vaguely that there is something wrong about taking advantage of a human's ignorance to defraud him, but I have to look again, focus, before I see the principle of injustice clearly. In either case, however, a clear grasp of the given is the rock-bottom basis of all knowledge claims. The idealist grasp of principles becomes problematic only when we forget that it is ultimately a *seeing,* not some mysterious intuition.

Ultimately, as Husserl sees it, the trouble with idealism, just like the trouble with empiricism, is not its basic contention. Of course ideas are real, just as facts are real. From a transcendental viewpoint, we can even say that yes, of course, reality is intelligible as idea, as perceived, just as its intelligibility is significant as acted out *in carne.* But, in both cases, life is prior to reflection and the experiential grounding is prior to both idealist and empiricist analysis. The problems of idealism, like those of empiricism, can be resolved once we recognize that, as Husserl concludes at the end of *I* § 23b,

Wesenserschauung ist ein originär gebender Akt und als solcher das Analogon des sinnlichen Wahrnehmens und nicht des Einbildens.	Awareness of principles is a primordially presentive act and, as such, is analogous to sense perception, not to imagination.

Phenomenology can be a radical empiricism as well as a transcendental idealism, because it does not start with either naive realism or subjectivism but with a faithful articulation of lived experience.

Husserl's § 24: Phenomenological Experientialism

§ 24

By the end of § 24, something seems amiss. All the conceptual clarification of the preceding sections may be well and good, but phenomenology is supposed to be about *seeing,* not about speculation. Husserl agrees: "Doch genug der verkehrten Theorien," he exclaims in § 24a —"Enough of such inverted theories!"—and, in experiential terms,

§ 24a

they are quite literally inverted, arguing from concepts to experience. That, from Husserl's viewpoint, is the one real trouble with all theories. To be legitimate, they must rest on experience, as it is given in direct awareness, prior to any theoretical processing, and so on phenomenology, with or without its Husserlian paraphernalia. The purpose of phenomenology is not to refute theories but rather to ground them in experience, though it may have to refute their claim to represent a reality more fundamental than experience.

Thus, in a very real sense, phenomenology has no quarrel with any theory whatever. Quite the contrary; its relationship with all sciences should be basically symbiotic. There is, for instance, a very real kinship between phenomenology and behaviorism. Both approaches seek to eschew obfuscation and to grasp human experience in terms of praxis rather than of theorizing. To be sure, from a phenomenological perspective the behaviorist conception of praxis—"behavior"—seems experientially inadequate. Behavior, after all, is intelligible only as it is lived, as an intentional unity, not as a set of discrete movements susceptible to being recorded by a camera. Behaviorism needs a phenomenological foundation to provide it with a basic grasp of its central category. But, in turn, behavioral data are crucial to the application of phenomenological insight. Without behavioral instantiation, phenomenological insight into the structure of praxis remains barren.[15]

At the other extreme, there is considerable kinship between phenomenology and idealism, based on far more than Husserl's later use of that term. Several idealist philosophers (Royce, James, Otto) worked along distinctly phenomenological lines. In particular, the American Personalist thinkers, who use the term "Person" as a primordial category, have much to contribute. In turn, a thorough phenomenological critique of their categories can make the Personalists' valuable contribution far more readily available than a conventional presentation that treats it as a speculative thesis.

A promising symbiotic relationship is in principle possible with Marxism, at least to the extent that Marxism can be an experientially grounded study of the dynamics of historical wholes rather than a dogmatic attempt to make reality conform to the Marxian corpus. Sartre's *Critique de la raison dialectique* represents an interesting attempt to explore this direction. If that attempt fails, it is because

Marxism, in becoming the mystified ideology of an economically obsolete ruling class, the armed ideologues, has lost its experiential grounding more than any other version of Hegelian idealism. It may well be that East European Marxists, who in revolting against their political masters must also reject ideology's claim to power, will make that symbiosis possible, as Karel Kosík showed in his *Dialectics of the Concrete*.[16]

Altogether, phenomenology in principle does not stand in conflict with any particular regional theories but is necessarily prior to them as the articulation of experience—of awareness—on which all theories build. The phenomenologist, far from being a sectarian, should be the most compatible member of any professional collective. He can make a contribution to the work of all his colleagues because his starting point is one to which they all appeal: experience, about which they make judgments but which it is his task to describe, faithfully, in its full structured richness, as it is initially given in the awareness which accompanies all lived experience. Phenomenology becomes precarious when it poses as an esoteric gnosis. It is on safe and nonproblematic grounds as long as it holds to what Husserl presents as his "principle of principles":

. . . dass alles, was sich uns *in der "Intuition" originär . . . darbietet, einfach hinzunehmen sei, als was es sich gibt,* aber auch *nur in den Schranken, in denen es sich da gibt.*	. . . simply to accept as given everything we encounter in perceiving awareness, as it confronts us, but also only within the limits within which it confronts us.	§ 24a

What Husserl really proposes is an experientialism so radical that it does not pretend to bestow patterns of meaning upon a meaningless universe by a miracle of induction but discovers—literally, *sees*—them in experience and applies them to understanding particular instances. Just as science, insofar as it deals with facts, must let itself be guided by those facts, so in dealing with principles it must let itself be guided by the principles and structures given in experience.

As a matter of fact, as Husserl noted in § 22, scientists who may deny all knowledge of structures and principles of experience in theorizing about their work do make constant use of them in practice. Even the behaviorist assumes a sufficient grasp of the intentional unity   § 25 of a subject's acts to be able to isolate a particular set of movements as constituting "behavior." To "explain" this genetically is legitimate as a special regional endeavor, presupposing a prior eidetic grasp. It may be the case, for instance, that our conception of marriage developed under particular historical or contextual circumstances. But the point of science is not just to "explain," in the sense of accounting adequately for what is the case, but to *understand,* to grasp its present and future significance, to be able to respond adequately, and to guide future development in desirable rather than simply understandable directions. For that, a "causal" explanation is less important than an experiential grasp of the essential structure of marriage as a human way of being-in-the-world, of its intentionality far more than of its origins. Though Husserl would never put it in those terms, Bowne's insight applies: efficient causal explanation is relevant—and possible —only as a retrospective reading of a teleologically structured experience.[17] Only because the subject—an I—wishes to achieve something, whether to make a marriage work or send a rocket to Mars, does the multitude of experiential data become intelligibly ordered enough to permit him to see it as a causal chain. Only for that reason does such an explanation become relevant. The dependence of efficient explanation on teleological understanding does not call for the speculative construction of a teleological explanation but for a faithful articulation of the teleology of lived experience.

§ 26   In this sense, the "dogmatism" of the natural sciences—the impatience with epistemological doubts about their work, the insistence on presenting their findings—is quite legitimate. Husserl posits what is in fact a division of labor. The task of the "dogmatic" ("without prejudice") sciences is to present the givens of experience.[18] Critical analysis of their assumptions is a task of the reflective sciences, those of a philosophical standpoint. Problems arise, as Husserl has stressed throughout, when the special sciences interpret such legitimate "dogmatism" of the given far too narrowly, as a dogmatism of "facts" rather than of experiential data.

The entire schema of dogmatic and philosophic sciences cuts across our conventional classifications. Even phenomenology comprises both kinds of science. Much of Husserl's work belongs to the "philosophical," critical concern. But, insofar as a phenomenologist is not reflecting upon phenomenology but actually *doing* it, providing a clearly articulated grasp of directly lived and perceived structures of experience, he is engaged in a "dogmatic" science. Or perhaps, more accurately, he is engaged in a prescience, in the articulate seeing of the essential structure of experience which alone can provide a secure foundation for all scientific speculation.

Phenomenology As a Metatheory

What is phenomenology, not in its role of rigorous description of lived experiences but as a philosophy, a "science of the philosophic standpoint"? As Merleau-Ponty notes, it seems riddled with contradictions.[19] It is an empiricism which considers necessary principles its data, as well as an idealism which insists on a positive experiential grounding. It could be read as a particularly obscure realistic theory or, equally well, as a particularly abstruse idealistic one; and in fact it has been interpreted along both lines.

Yet neither interpretation seems quite to fit. Thus it might not be amiss to consider a different approach. Perhaps phenomenology as a philosophy is not at all a theory, proposing a particularly obscure solution to problems conventionally defined within a naturalistic or idealistic matrix. Perhaps it is a metatheory, like naturalism or idealism, proposing a matrix within which problems can be defined.[20]

Here some attention to the terms "theory" and "metatheory" might be worthwhile. The distinction we wish to make is basically analogous to that between what we are accustomed to calling a "scientific theory" and a "metaphysical theory." Oversimplifying greatly, a "scientific theory" is any set of propositions which proposes a specific solution to a conventionally defined problem, within a commonly accepted intelligibility matrix. A metatheory ("metaphysical theory") is a set of propositions proposing such a matrix: what we shall treat as real and what as derivative, what as desirable and what as to be avoided, what as the *explanans* and what as the *explanandum*.[21]

A scientific theory presupposes an intelligibility matrix, but within that matrix it is capable of being true or false. The universe is not irrelevant to it; some conditions render it more probable, verify it, or, according to Karl Popper's ingenious suggestion, falsify it. By contrast, a metatheory must be compatible with all possible states of the universe, but it does not presuppose an intelligibility matrix; rather, it proposes one, more or less adequately.

Thus the proposition "Stones fall" is a rudimentary scientific theory.

It presupposes an intelligibility matrix—conceptions of evidence, a definition of up and down—within which it can be true or false. Should stones habitually waft gently skyward, the theory would be rendered less probable. By contrast, the proposition "Stones are the ultimate reality" (or, more familiarly, "reality is material") cannot be rendered more or less true, regardless of what we may learn about stones. It defines a perspective in which "explanation" shall ultimately mean the reduction of any phenomenon to its petrological "real basis."

The crisis of Western thought may well be basically a metatheoretical one. Modern science, with its positivistic bias, largely dismissed metatheoretical considerations as meaningless, or at best as irrelevant, while tacitly accepting a materialistic metatheory. The decision freed it from the interminable debates over the ultimate nature of reality, and, for the purposes of describing the physical universe, it did seem irrelevant whether we regarded the ultimate nature of that universe as material or mental, the world as a cosmic accident or as God's creation. The incredible technological advances of the last century seemed to justify the decision.[22]

That decision becomes problematic when we begin to deal with human beings—metaphorically, when we raise not only the question of how to build a hydrogen bomb but whether to build one and on whom to drop it. For the purposes of description, any metatheoretical matrix may do equally well, but the prescriptive consequences will differ. We may, for instance, be able to describe human behavior equally well as the self-realization of human freedom or as a deterministic stimulus-response system, but the prescriptive conclusions with respect to the relative value of human freedom and material welfare will be drastically different. When we have to make decisions on what to safeguard and what to sacrifice, our metatheoretical matrix becomes crucially important.

Modern Western thought has operated with two basic metaphysical models. Husserl speaks of them as "naturalism" and "platonism"; ordinary philosophical usage relies more frequently on the terms "empiricism" and "idealism." But the labels are trivial. What is fundamental are the two basic metaphysical proposals—either to treat matter as real and idea as derivative or, conversely, to treat idea as real and matter as derivative, with all the prescriptive consequences each proposal implies.

In principle, either approach is possible. Our lived experience does include, as an irreducible datum, the experience of the dependence of idea on matter. The effect of hunger on my thought makes the point. But that experience includes, no less irreducibly, the opposite awareness: the utter irrelevance and meaninglessness of the world until a subject gives it meaning, even if only by recognizing it as a means of satisfying hunger. Herman Melville's Queequeg, carrying a wheelbarrow on his shoulder, shows that lacking the idea of a wheelbarrow is no less restrictive than lacking a wheelbarrow. It is equally true that, given the idea, I can always rig a wheelbarrow, and that, given the object, I can always figure out a use for it. Though the prescriptive consequences of choosing either as basic will differ, both experiences are real. Neither is given as illusory; to claim that, contrary to actual experience, one is illusory and the other "real" makes reality arbitrary. Similarly, while a metatheory can be based on either, there is something intrinsically suspect about a metatheory which must dismiss fully half of our experiential givens as "apparent" only.[23]

Phenomenology may well be presenting an alternative, not as a particularly intricate form of naturalism or of idealism but as an alternative to both, taking experience in its lived unity—rather than either of the poles in which reflection splits it—as its basic metatheoretical referent.

The radical novelty of Husserl's work tends to be obscured by his use of the traditional term "transcendental *idealism.*" That is why I have preferred the term "transcendental experientialism," since, I would submit, Husserl's great contribution to philosophy is his conception of experience as *Evidenz* and of subjectivity as transcendental. Both naturalism and idealism, we can argue, begin not with lived experience but with experience interpreted from the standpoint of its material or mental contents. Husserl is taking the lived experience as basic for interpreting both poles.[24]

If our predilections are naturalistic, we can present what Husserl is doing as a radical empiricism, as he does in § 24 of *Ideas.* If they are idealistic, we can, with equal justification, present it as a transcendentalism, as Husserl (speaking to a French audience) did in his Paris lectures.[25] Stripped of their speculative connotations, those two terms become functionally equivalent. "Experience," in its radical, primordial sense, does not indicate the "fact-content" of experience but the experiencing itself, and so "radical empiricism" can be a faithful description of what phenomenology is all about. But neither is experience, as lived, equivalent to a set of subjective ideas or feelings about it. Since phenomenology does not identify with such subjective perspective but stands beyond the "subjective" and the "objective" alike, seeking to grasp the experience in its primordial unity, it is genuinely transcendental.

But while either label is justified, both are rather misleading if what Husserl proposes to do is not a particularly cunning version of either "naturalism" or "platonism" but an alternative capable of subsuming both while more fundamental than either. If that is the case, phenomenologists will not construct or attack particular naturalistic or idealistic theories, but rather will seek to show that either approach is inadequate as a metatheoretical matrix and that the virtues of either can be subsumed more adequately within a phenomenological metatheoretical perspective.

As a matter of fact, that is how phenomenologists do habitually approach other philosophies. Frequently they frustrate their colleagues by failing to address themselves to a specific contention, the latest article, or a particular book. At times they seem to argue with straw men. But the reason is not faulty scholarship. Rather, because they are presenting a metatheory, they address themselves to the metatheoretical assumptions beyond the particular contentions of this or that volume. They do not seek to show that this or that particular theoretical contention is faulty, tacitly assuming the adequacy of its metatheoretical matrix. Rather, they seek to elaborate an alternative metatheory, to show that such alternative metatheories are not capable of providing a consistent metatheoretical basis and that the phenomenological metatheoretical basis is capable of generating a more adequate theoretical analysis of experience.

Phenomenology, finally, is not simply another philosophy within a traditional framework. It is a *way of doing* philosophy, a "method" in the profound sense of a metatheoretical framework within which we can raise the whole range of problems presented by being-human and re-presented in traditional philosophy. It will stand or fall with its ability to provide a more adequate treatment of those problems. Husserl concludes his *CM* with a quotation from St. Augustine: "Seek not to go forth: turn within. Truth dwells within the human." He might have chosen another quotation from the same author: "Where will the heart find rest except in the truth?"

The Horizon of Phenomenology

More than three score years after the publication of *Ideas I,* though some problems of
comprehension still linger, phenomenology
itself has largely ceased being problematic.
Not that philosophy has become phenomenological in the sense that Husserl en-
visioned; it has not. But phenomenology
did become an intrinsic part of the Western
philosophical milieu, profoundly affecting
the tenor of Western thought even in the
case of overtly antiphenomenological directions. To gauge its impact we need but
compare the classical Marxism of, say,
Engels's *Anti-Dühring* with its contemporary namesake in, say, Karel Kosík's *Dialectics of the Concrete.* The difference is
striking. While nineteenth-century thought
was still predominantly metaphysical in
temper, acknowledging the individual subject at best as one of the components in a
global system, in the twentieth century the
mainstream of Western thought has come
to treat subject experience as a primordial
datum.

It would be foolhardy to claim that Husserl or phenomenology single-handedly
brought about that basic reorientation.
Phenomenology did, however, provide
some of its crucial components, notably a
conception of lived experience as primordially intelligible, or, in Husserl's terms, of
experience as *Evidenz.* As long as the West
assumed that experience is opaque as lived
and becomes transparent only as observed,
it inevitably remained locked in the Car-

tesian categorial schema of "mind" and "matter." Experience is one
in the unity of the *act of experiencing;* in the act of throwing, for instance, the intent is acted out in the movement, while the movement
is meaningful as acting out an intent. As observed, even in self-
observation, it automatically becomes polarized between a disem-
bodied observing mind and a meaningless observed movement, giving
rise to the problem of their relation and of the primacy of one or the
other. In recognizing the primordial intelligibility of the act *as lived,*
as primordially given in subject awareness, phenomenology prevented
(in the strict etymological sense) that problem and made possible a
radically different starting point, a philosophy grounded directly in
lived experience itself. The concept of experience as *Evidenz,* a primordial intelligible given, may well constitute Husserl's greatest
contribution to contemporary thought.

That contribution, however, raises another problem, that of the
intersubjective validity of statements based on lived subject experience. Here Husserl's contribution is no less crucial. This time it is
the recognition that subjectivity does not consist solely of contingent
particularity but has a transcendental dimension as well, one valid for
any subject qua subject. The recognition that $2 + 2 = 4$ or that unprovoked injury creates an obligation to repay is a subject act, but it is
not subject specific. It is transcendental. While Husserl's recognition of
experience as *Evidenz* gave Western thought the tool for overcoming
uncritical objectivism, his recognition of the transcendental dimension
of subjectivity offers a tool for overcoming relativistic subjectivism.

Philosophy has been far slower to make as full use of Husserl's
conception of subjectivity as transcendental as it did of his recognition
of subject experience as intelligible. In part, the problem may be one
of comprehension; much of the criticism directed against Husserl's
conception of the transcendental dimension of subjectivity is clearly
based on a misreading of his text.[1] But only in part. There is also the
problem that, in Husserl's original conception, the transcendental
dimension of subjectivity, the *reines Ich,* can appear as a sterile vanishing point of perspective rather than as a full Person-al presence.[2]
Much of the energy of Husserl's successors has in fact gone into
recognizing the full Person-presence of the subject.

That recognition of the subject as a transcendental Person-presence
rather than a vanishing point has emerged gradually in the work of
thinkers like Heidegger, Merleau-Ponty, Landgrebe, and Ricoeur.

Step by step, they overcame the anthropologism which plagued Heidegger's and Merleau-Ponty's pioneering efforts yet have retained the conception of the subject as a Person-presence in all its density.[3]

That conception, however, is raising new problems which today constitute the leading edge of philosophy. The (transcendental) subject as Person includes dimensions of subjectivity which cannot be brought to the pure *Evidenz* of subject consciousness. They include both Husserl's "twighlight zone" of *I* § 69c and the irreducible "X" of *I* § 131, *die Härte des Realen,* which includes not only the transcendence of the object but also that of nature and history. That dimension of subject being requires a methodological extension of phenomenology in hermeneutics and so raises the problem of incorporating hermeneutically gained insight into the fundamental awareness of the self-constituting subject.

Such problems, while no longer strictly a part of the presentation of the project of phenomenology, do constitute its horizon. Before we conclude our examination, we shall do well to cast a summary glance about that horizon. We shall focus first on Husserl's twin contributions, the recognition of experience as *Evidenz* and the transcendental dimension of subjectivity. We shall then examine the labor of transforming that transcendental dimension from an epistemological vanishing point to a conception of the Person as a transcendental presence. Finally, we shall point to the problems of the hermeneutic extension necessitated by the conception of the transcendental subject as Person.

Experience As
Evidenz

Husserl's affirmation of experience as intelligible and intrinsically susceptible to faithful articulation represents both a basic contribution to contemporary philosophy and an affirmation of the most audacious link in the Western philosophic faith—that the human, simply qua human, is *capax veritatis.*

It is a daring affirmation. At most times, and for the most part, humankind has lived in the shadow of a profound suspicion that appearance is the mask rather than the face of reality, a veil of *maya* behind which there may be no truth, that if there were, it might not be knowable by mortals, and that, even if knowable, it would be so concealed in articulation as to be incommunicable.

Against that lingering skepsis, Husserl presents his conviction that appearance is not a mask but the presence of reality, overt rather than latent, to be *seen* rather than conjectured, the birthright of all humans rather than the privilege of poets, seers, or ideologues.

Far more is at stake here than an obscure point of epistemological theory. If individual consciousness were indeed false or unintelligible as lived, covertly ordered by the hidden dynamics of the psyche or the economic determinism of History, then the Western commitment to the value, verity, and freedom of the human individual would be an elaborate self-deception. Yet the issue does hinge on a point of epistemology. If experience in its primordial givenness were indeed a buzzing, booming confusion until ordered by a reflective judgment, then all knowledge would be conjecture, distorting and concealing as it revealed. If, on the other hand, experience is *Evidenz,* primordially intelligible as lived, then knowledge can be a faithful articulation grounded in immediate awareness. Or, in the most primitive terms, the question is that of the grounds of knowledge, whether knowledge is grounded in the *living of* experience or only in thinking and speaking *about* it.

Husserl is utterly committed to the primordial intelligibility of experience. He is not denying the reality of those aspects of experience which in principle can be grasped only indirectly, as the "twilight zone" of *I* § 69c. Nor is he denying the difference between act and awareness, except in purely immanent *Erlebnisse,* such as feeling pain. Phenomenology, after all, is a process of *bringing to awareness.* But he insists that the intelligibility of experience really needs *only* to be brought to thematic awareness; it does not have to be created or imposed by reflection. Experience, Husserl insists, is intrinsically intelligible.[4]

Given Husserl's entire approach, that assertion cannot be presented as the conclusion of a speculative argument. Rather, it itself must be capable of being simply brought to thematic awareness as something that, marginally, is already there in lived experience. So, prima facie, it is. Stumbling about in total bewilderment is an exception occasioned by a specific cause, not our usual modus operandi. For the purposes of bringing it to thematic awareness, however, we might do well to examine it in three parts: the recognition that experience is intrinsically conscious, that it includes a dimension of self-reference, and that its data include not only a factual content but also an intentional order.

First of all, the claim that experience is intrinsically intelligible reflects the recognition that it is not an unconscious happening to which reflection must be added but that it includes awareness intrinsically and *ab initio*. Even when he is not reflecting upon them, the ordinary subject is *aware*—or at least is not unaware—of his actions. He registers changes in his mental states as well as in his physical context, sees his acts as serving a purpose, makes choices, and altogether gives direction and meaning to his movements. He is aware of *acting,* not merely of performing random movements, and can, if challenged, bring that awareness to thematic focus.

The subject may, of course, be in error about the ultimate effect of his acts, and no less so about their motives. He may also interrupt his act and stop to reflect upon it. Common usage would describe this by saying that "I became aware of what I was doing." But that is not strictly accurate. Even though the subject may not have been reflecting upon it, he was aware of his acting. In fact, he can begin to reflect only because he is already aware; as we have noted already, even behavior*ism* is possible only because we experience human acts as constituting the meaningful unity of *behavior* rather than as discrete movements. While awareness is not yet reflection, it is awareness. To speak of ordinary experience as intelligible means first of all to recognize that a subject is in fact aware of acting.

Second, to speak of experience as intelligible means to recognize that the subject is not only aware of acting but is also aware of himself as the subject of his act. Again, this does not mean that the subject *reflects* on his role, but simply that he is aware—or not unaware—of himself as the focus of the action. *The subject is always an I.* It may be stylistically awkward, but it is quite accurate to speak of the subject in the first person singular: "An I does" or "I do."

As a matter of ordinary experience, that awareness often occupies a very small part of our attention. Especially when preoccupied with a demanding or difficult task, we often have a sense of losing all awareness of ourselves. But the point is that bringing such awareness to thematic focus is a matter of shifting attention within my present phenomenal field rather than of "turning" from one field to another. What common sense terms "becoming aware of myself" does not call for a mental about-face, turning my back upon the world and becoming preoccupied with my subjectivity, but simply for a shift of focus and emphasis in the awareness which already accompanies my experience. Ordinary awareness, finally, is not polarized; rather, it forms a continuing horizon which includes both the object and the subject of the act.

Thus when a subject is—or, when I am—totally preoccupied with the task of sailing a small craft in heavy weather, my attention focuses almost exclusively on the luff of my sail. Yet I remain aware—out of the corner of my eye (phenomenologists speak of it as "circumspective" awareness)—of the sail as secured to a gaff, a boom, and a mast, of the mast as stepped through the foredeck in the hull, of the hull boiling through the water, which forms a horizon around me and presses through the rudder on the tiller in my hand, and so of myself as controlling the helm. My consciousness is not simply of "a boat to be steered" but rather of the act of steering, which, circumspectively, entails both an I and an object: (I) *steering* (a boat). When I steer badly, I need not put all this out of my mind to concentrate on myself; all I need do is shift attention to a different segment of the circle. Awareness of myself as the subject of my experience, as Kant notes in the famous passage which Husserl quotes,[5] accompanies all my perceptions; it is not simply a retrospective hypostatization of remembered acts.

Finally, to recognize ordinary experience as intelligible means to recognize not only that ordinary experience includes, *ab initio,* both awareness of an act and of a subject but also awareness of experience *as meaningful.* At its most ordinary, quite prior to reflection, it includes an awareness of what common sense misnames "logical" connections such as appropriateness, sequence, meaning, consistency. Awareness of doing and of being-subject is inseparable from the *intentional structure* of experience. Experience is not a random set of happenings but a subject's way of being in his world, of coping, adjusting, interacting, which constitutes the world as a meaningful context of action. Even if my acts were "arbitrary" in some grand cosmic sense, within my experience they exhibit an internal structure within a structured context. I am present in my world, not aimlessly but as an *intentio*. The contents of my world, in turn, confront me not as atomic bits but as near and far with reference to my location and locomotion, as large and small in relation to my size, as crucial and trivial in relation to my concerns, as propitious or noxious in relation to my well-being— in short, as making sense. By my very presence as subject, I constitute the world as a meaningful context and so, in turn, experience it, not as a matter of reflection but already in direct awareness.

Altogether, the three assertions add up to the recognition with which we began, that experience is intelligible in its initial givenness, as subjects live it. That is why reflection need not be an arbitrary construction of meaning but can be a process of *becoming aware* of lived meaning. The meaninglessness which figured prominently in postwar existentialism is not a datum of ordinary experience but something a subject imposes upon it. Of itself, as a given, ordinary experience does make ordinary sense: it is intelligible.

The affirmation that the truth is overt rather than latent does not, as Husserl notes repeatedly, mean that it is effortless or obvious. It is not; to see clearly calls for a strenuous effort. Nor does that affirmation mean that there are no zones of twilight or even of utter darkness. Clearly there are, as God reminds Job and as the vicissitudes of fortune constantly remind us. But it does mean that the obstacles which call for an effort, as well as the zones of darkness which call for an oblique approach, confront us *within* the being of a subject who can aspire to and achieve a clear grasp of the truth, not as a function of some putative whole but directly as a subject in lived experience. Again, it does not mean that wholes may be unreal. Clearly they are real, but in the context of the lived experience of individual subjects whose experience as subjects rather than as objects of history is intrinsically intelligible.

Whatever our ultimate assessment of phenomenology—and some of Husserl's claims in its behalf might prove hard to sustain—its conception of experience as primordially intelligible represents a crucial contribution to the work of philosophy. If lived experience were intrinsically opaque and unintelligible, we could offer only speculative or symbolic statements about it. Because experience is intrinsically intelligible, the human, through groping and stumbling, remains *capax veritatis* as the subject of his life, not merely as the object of Nature or History.

The Transcendental
Dimension of Subjectivity

Husserl's affirmation of the primordial intelligibility of lived experience provides an answer to objectivistic skepsis, but in its turn invites a different, subjectivistic skepsis. Experience becomes intelligible as a subject's experience, but by the same token its intersubjective validity becomes problematic. Only if subject experience is not merely contingent and particular but has, intrinsically, a transcendental dimension can it be the source of intersubjectively valid insight.

Here phenomenology represents one of the three basic possibilities which Western thought has explored in our time. Three creative thinkers who helped shape that thought, Carnap, Wittgenstein, and Husserl, all started with a conception of lived experience and all encountered a critical challenge in the problem of the intersubjective validity of such experience. Each offered a solution which defined a major possibility. Carnap's forceful reconstruction of physicalism was no uncritical codification of our *sensus naturalis*. It was a brilliant attempt to escape privacy of lived experience by translating it into its public physical counterparts. The accomplishments of the positivists and the behaviorists demonstrate the vast possibilities—and limitations —of that alternative.

Analogously, Wittgenstein's ordinary language philosophy was not simply glorified linguistics. Rather, it outlined a second major possibility for overcoming the relativity of lived experience, this time by substituting for it experience made public by an embodiment in language. Here the achievements of scholars like Chomsky, especially his recognition of the deep structure of language, show the scope of Wittgenstein's alternative.

Husserl's transcendental philosophy, too, is no fortuitous revival of idealism but an attempt to overcome the relativity of subject experience. Unlike Carnap and Wittgenstein, Husserl seeks the basis of intersubjectivity not in the translation of lived experience to a public counterpart, physical or verbal, but in its own necessary and universal structure. Husserl's cue may have been the experience of growing up in the multilingual Moravian village of Prosnice among playmates whose languages differed but who still lived the same experiences of joy and pain and understood one another. It may have been his exposure to the eminent mathematician, Karl Weierstrass, whose intuitionism would lead to the realization that when two subjects, individually and privately, add two and two to arrive at four, their *Erlebnisse,* while individual, are in no sense relative or private but necessary and universal. The subject as a mathematician is individual in his act of counting yet transcends the relativity of his natural subjectivity in its necessary structure. Husserl's exposure to Franz von

Brentano would lead him to similar conclusions. Brentano, speaking of the experience of love and hate, also recognized the universal and necessary structure of subject experience even though in each instance we live that experience individually.

Whatever the stimulus, Husserl's critical recognition is that the subject is capable of transcending the primacy and relativity of his natural subjectivity not only through objectification, by referring to a putative objective third, be it a thing or a word, but also as subject, by virtue of the universal, necessary dimension of (any) subject's experience. The claim is analogous to Kant's, but with a significant difference. Husserl does not claim that the human mind imposes necessary categories upon reality, but rather that subject experience as such is necessarily structured in a particular way. Subjectivity, though always individual in act, has a transcendental dimension.

That, incidentally, is what distinguishes Husserl's conception of transcendental subjectivity from that of nineteenth-century idealists like F. H. Bradley or T. H. Green. For both, transcendental subjectivity, stripped of all natural or psychological particularity, became not only nonparticular but nonindividual as well. Its relation to individual subjects then became an unsolved and insoluble problem. By contrast, Husserl's starting point is individual lived experience in its primordial *Evidenz*. Its transcendental dimension is not a duplicate ego but a dimension of a subject's being individual in his act of being, quite independently of any particularity or lack thereof. Metaphorically, the sum $2 + 2 = 4$, taken in principle, is neither individual nor particular. The subject act of adding two and two to get four, however, is individual (it is *I* counting) even though it is universal (any subject will reach the same sum) and not particular (I distinguish the act as mine by counting myself, personally, not by arriving at an idiosyncratic result, say, $2 + 2 = 3.9$). *I* function in a transcendental (and so universal) dimension; I do not "have a transcendental ego." At best, we could say that *I am* (also) that, though the term "transcendental dimension of subjectivity" remains more accurate.[6]

Husserl does occasionally refer to his position as one of transcendental idealism, though more frequently he speaks of transcendental phenomenology or simply transcendentalism. The first term is misleading, not only because of Husserl's basic experientialism (pp. 165–69, above) but also because we could describe the recognition of transcendental subjectivity as well (and as inaccurately) as a recognition of transcendental objectivity. Husserl is pointing to the possibility of a necessary, universal viewpoint in place of all particular ones, whether of natural objectivity or natural subjectivity. Instead of speaking of the world as it might appear apart from all subjectivity or as it appears to a particular subject, he proposes to view the subject and his world as they necessarily appear to any subject simply qua subject.

That distinction, again, is crucial. A world apart from subjectivity would be a world devoid of meaning. Meaning, whether as elementary as "to the right/left of" or as fundamental as right and wrong, good and evil, becomes arbitrary when it is taken out of the context of subject experience. But a world meaningful only in relation to this or that particular subject experience, in the stifling parochialism of individual or cultural particularity, would be a world condemned to relativism. In such a world, normative judgments would become a function of preference or consensus, or, in the absence of a consensus, of superior force. For a humankind endowed with the capability for global self-incineration, it is cold comfort to dignify that predicament with the title of "conflict theory." We need, urgently, to rediscover the common reference point of the transcendental dimension of our subjectivity.

Husserl points the way. While the recognition of the primordial intelligibility of subject experience may be his greatest contribution, the recognition of the transcendental dimension of subjectivity may be his greatest challenge to his successors.

Transcendental Subjects and Transcendental Persons

Relatively few of Husserl's successors took up the challenge of exploring the transcendental dimension of subjectivity. Those who did —such as Eugen Fink, Ludwig Landgrebe, and Maurice Natanson— have shown how fruitful such investigations can be. A great many others, however, including scholars as profoundly Husserlian as Aron Gurwitsch and Jan Patočka, found the conception of the transcendental ego profoundly problematic.

Jean-Paul Sartre's critique in *The Transcendence of the Ego*, though admittedly flawed as Husserlian scholarship, is helpful in pinpointing the reason. If we conceive of the transcendental dimension of the ego in sufficiently rigorous terms to escape psychologism or anthropologism, it seems to become sterile, a mere vanishing point of subjectivity. If we do not so conceive of it, Sartre claims, it becomes transcendent.

The point, while characteristically dramatic in Sartre's presentation, is not original with Sartre. Husserl, ever his own most perceptive critic, notes it quite explicitly in *C* § 43:

. . . der viel kürzerer Weg zur transzendentalen Epoché in meinen *Ideen* . . . , den ich den "cartesianischen" nenne (nämlich als gewonnen gedacht durch blosse besinnliche Vertiefung in die Cartesianische Epoché der *Meditationes* und durch kritische Reinigung derselben von den Vorurteilen und Verirrungen Descartes') den grossen Nachteil hat, dass er zwar wie in einem Springe schon zum transzendentalen ego[7] führt, dieses aber, da jede vorgängige Explikation fehlen muss, in einer scheinbaren Inhaltsleere zur Sicht bringt, in der man zunächst ratlos ist, was damit gewonnen sein soll . . . Daher erliegt man auch, wie die Aufnahme meiner *Ideen* gezeigt hat, allzuleicht, und gleich bei den ersten Anfängen, den ohnehin sehr versucherischen Rückfällen in die naiv-natürliche Einstellung.

. . . the far shorter way to the transcendental *epoché* in my *Ideas* . . . , which I labeled "cartesian" (since it is conceived as being attained through sheer meditative immersion in the Cartesian *epoché* of the *Meditations* coupled with their critical purification from all of Descartes's preconceptions and confusions), has the great drawback that it leads, as in a single leap, straight to the transcendental I, but, in the inevitable absence of all preliminary explanations, brings that *I* before us apparently empty of content, leaving us at a loss as to just what it is supposed to have achieved. . . . Consequently, as the reception of my *Ideas* had demonstrated, it becomes all too easy, right at the very start, to yield to the tempting lapse into a naive natural orientation.

This passage deserves examination. It poses the challenge of recognizing the full Person-al density of ego, even in my function as transcendental subject, without lapsing into anthropologism. That anthropologism is a broader version of what Husserl, referring more narrowly to pure consciousness, had called psychologism. In principle, it is the temptation to provide a density to ego as transcendental by coupling to it my transcendent being—whether body, psyche, social function, etc.—rather than by recognizing the full breadth of my presence as transcendental. Heidegger, while starting out on the solid Husserlian grounds of ego as a transcendental *presence* (*Dasein*), lapsed into anthropologism when he utilized the contemporary National Socialist critique of the Weimar bourgeoisie as a datum for his description of the subject's way of being present (*Dasein's sein*) in average everydayness. Similarly, Merleau-Ponty, in his elaboration of Husserl's "somatology" of *Ideen III* § 2, lost sight of the subject's primordial transcendental presence, substituting for it a generalization of his transcendent reality as a body-subject. Merleau-Ponty's works, along with Heidegger's investigations in *Being and Time,* unquestionably provide a vast body of material which can become invaluable once subsumed within a transcendental perspective; but, of themselves, they do not meet Husserl's basic challenge— to recognize the full density of ego *as transcendental.*

Husserl addressed himself to that challenge quite explicitly. In the subsequent volumes of *Ideen,* he set about examining the social and physical density of ego strictly as transcendental. In *Crisis,* he added an examination of historical and psychological density as well. Ludwig Landgrebe continued his work. For instance, in dealing with the vexing problem of the irreducible givenness of the transcendent, the "X" of *Ideas I* § 131, he recognizes that, contrary to Husserl's claim in that passage, far more can be said about that "X" once we recognize the transcendental ego not simply as a cognitive vanishing point but in the full density of his presence—in Landgrebe's term, as a Person.[8] That, finally, is the significance of Ricoeur's investigations as well. Ricoeur works in rigorous brackets; his starting point is not the anthropologistic human as an empirical fact but the essential possibility of being-human as the perennial transcendental subject. Ricoeur recognizes that precisely in that sense ego is—or *am* —more than a clear reflective consciousness. His being includes what, in *The Philosophy of the Will,* Ricoeur calls "the involuntary," that dimension of subject presence which confronts the subject as intrinsically a part of him, not alien yet intractable: again, the density of the ego even as transcendental.

The recognition of the full density of the subject as transcendental is a problem that Husserl's successors approach in varied ways but which remains constant. Since these successors are inevitably heirs to the temptation of premature transcendentalism, of which Husserl accuses himself in *C* § 43, it is helpful to note also the work of philosophers who grappled with the problem independently of Husserl, European "humanists" such as Masaryk or American Personalists such as Bowne. To a reader steeped in phenomenology, their work is not easily accessible. Rather like the writings of William James, they are precritical, subject to all the dangers of which Husserl warns in *I* § 51.[9] Their conception of Person as a fundamental metaphysical category or the Human as a moral ideal can appear grossly anthropologistic. In the wake of the defeat of national socialism, Heidegger in fact attacked humanism precisely as anthropologistic, or, in his terms, as being culture-bound by a *specific metaphysical conception* of the human.[10] As a critique of the lingering anthropologism of the European "humanists" and the American Personalists, his observations are surely valid. But that is not how Masaryk conceived of the human as a moral ideal or how Bowne conceived of the Person as the ultimate metaphysical category.[11] For both, the Person is precisely the transcendental I in its full density but prior to the peculiarities of a culture or a personality. Here, again, there is valuable material for meeting Husserl's challenge.

But can that challenge be met, or is the very idea of a transcendental *presence,* of Person in a nonanthropologistic sense, a *contradictio in adiecto?* The answer, as always, must come from the data of lived experience in clear primordial awareness, but Husserl does suggest the ways to look in the second volume of *Ideen: Phänomenologische Untersuchungen zur Konstitution.* The "constitution" of the title is the meaningful coherence of experience from the standpoint of transcendental subjectivity. In the course of his investigations, Husserl takes up, one by one, all that his less perceptive critics have urged against him as "problems"—the conception of nature, the transition from solipsistic to intersubjective experience, the pure I and its being as soul and body, the will as free and located, as well as a range of other philosophical problems.[12] In many ways, *Ideen II* is the payoff of the methodological inquiries of *Ideas I:* a phenomenological philosophy.

For our purposes, the most interesting discussion is in section III, amplified in appendix XII. Here Husserl elaborates what we would (and he might) call his "personalism." The framework of his inquiry remains constant: the transcendental subject as a pure given, the Person-al I as constituted. The crucial point, however, is that the

I as Person is not an anthropologistic transcendent entity but, as Husserl presents it, precisely what we have been calling the *density* of the transcendental presence.

The heirs of European "humanism" and of American personalism find themselves on familiar grounds. The phenomenological perspective of *Ideas I,* when applied to an examination of being-human, yields a philosophy of the Person which Masaryk or Bowne (and their successors) would readily recognize. There is, however, a crucial difference: Husserl's personalism (or "humanism") is a self-consciously critical one, free of anthropologism and so immune to Heidegger's critique of humanism.[13]

An examination of Husserl's "personalism"—his phenomenological investigation of the transcendental dimension of human subjectivity—is the topic for another book, which, *Deo volente,* will follow in due time. In examining the experiential horizon of Husserl's project of phenomenology we can, however, legitimately note the experiential basis of such an extension of the conception of the transcendental dimension of subjectivity.

That experiential basis is far less problematic than philosophical reflection would make it appear. The I which I am and am aware of being is emphatically not an epistemological vanishing point. In all that each of us does and suffers, we are aware of our presence as anything but ephemeral. We sense our selves as "really here," tangible, in solid flesh. This is not a matter of a reflective self-constitution or of our putative image in the eyes of another. Rather, it is the primordial sense of ourselves as present as we bring down the hammer on the glowing stock firmly gripped in the tongs on the anvil, sparks bursting against our apron; as we share a friend's grief; or, like Sartre, as we race after streetcars, lungs bursting and boots pounding on the cobbles. Here Sartre's description of the act as anonymous is surely hopelessly artificial. Even in moments of greatest preoccupation, the act is not simply being done; it is *we* who are acting, even prior to all reflection. Similarly, quite prior to all reflection, that "we" has a density, in the sense not of "having a body" but of being present as "real," effective, in power. The fact that so many philosophers have been led to (and misled by) the metaphor of "power" is not fortuitous.[14] That is how the sense of subject presence presents itself in its primordial givenness, entirely prior to any attribution of a "body."

Within purely epistemological limits, Kant recognized this focal presence as the transcendental unity of apperception, but, even within those limits, that presence has a density. Kant's term, "unity," is not altogether accurate. As lived, the unity of cognition is not so much a point of self-identity as a process of self-identification. In noticing, for instance, the third elephant today, I am concurrently affirming my unity with the I who saw the first and second elephants. In ordinary experience, that affirmation may be entirely unspectacular, but it is there as a self-imputing sense of continued presence. The transcendental unity is a transcendental unification, a relation, as Kierkegaard noted, relating itself to itself.[15] Even within epistemological limits, the subject presence already has a density.

However, that density is not only epistemological. Quite apart from any anthropologistic reference, strictly in terms of the experienced subject presence, it is spatio-temporal as well. The temporal density is obvious in terms of conscious anticipation and recollection, without which the present consciousness would be unintelligible. That, however, can still be criticized (even if the criticism is rather farfetched) as the product of reflection. But even apart from the act of reflection, simply in what Husserl calls the primordial "passivity," the present I-awareness is not a razor-edged moment. As we noted earlier, it includes the sense of "having just been . . ." and of "being about to . . ." which Husserl labels "retention" and "protention."[16] Not as observed from an anthropologistic perspective but as lived, the subject presence has a temporal density.

That density is spatial as well, which again is obvious, this time in Merleau-Ponty's sense of being a bodily presence. Once again, we could make a farfetched criticism, that this is anthropologistic since it does not hold of, say, angelic or dream consciousness. But even an angelic or dream consciousness *locates itself* with reference to what is not itself. That not-itself may be dreamed or anticipated as well as perceived, but regardless of its mode of presentation it is removed from the I, not identical with it, and so gives it a spatial density as the I goes out toward it in locating itself. The temptation of anthropologism is great because, ordinarily and for the most part, the primordial temporal and spatial density are so acted out. Anthropologism is not inescapable, because that density is more basic than its acting out in flesh; it is intrinsic to being-a-subject.

The recognition of the intrinsic density of being-a-subject has far-reaching consequences which, without elaborating upon them, we do need to note. The fact that the transcendental unity of the subject is a self-relation explains why everything that traditionally was lumped under terms like "laws of thought" or "laws of reason" is neither an arbitrary imposition nor a peculiarity of the human mind but a necessary condition of subject being. Self-contradiction, as the Personalists have always recognized, is a logical flaw because it is first an ontological one.[17] It is a negation of the unity of a subject's being, a self-destruction. The demand for self-consistency is, primordially, the need for self-respect. Logic, far from being a generalization of transcendent experience, now appears as an elaboration of the condition of transcendental experiencing.

Moreover, the fundamental self-relation which constitutes the unity of the subject is not only solipsistic. Self-identity is not primordially given in the mode of the Cartesian 'I think" but rather in the mode "we speak." Just as vision does not begin with staring into space but with seeing an object, so self-awareness begins with the encounter with an Other. We may dismiss as anthropologistic the recognition that language is a social product, but we cannot expunge the recognition that, precisely in primordial awareness, the ego is always ego-et-alter. We may be able to "think away" the Other, all Others, as dead, absent, unreal, but we cannot be aware of ego without being aware of alter in some mode, if only that of negation.

To conclude from the social density of subject presence that "man is a social animal," in the sense of being produced or constituted by a society, a class, or a *Volk,* is clearly unwarranted. The subject remains a subject, constituting such social objectivities. But what does follow is that such constitution is not arbitrary. Rather like the "laws of thought," "moral laws" represent neither an arbitrary conventional imposition nor some peculiarity of "human nature"; rather, they are a necessary condition of subject being, since being-subject means intrinsically being-with-Other.[18]

For a mind impoverished by a hundred years or more of uncritical natural science, it is not the social but rather what we might call the *metaphysical* density of subject being that is most problematic. That density is real because the Other of our intrinsic being-with-Other is the other not only as a Person but also as artifact and as natural object.[19] That world appears as alien and incomprehensible until we overcome our deeply rooted objectivism and learn to recognize it in its primordial givenness as a sphere of "mine-ness," a context into which we are not contingently thrown, but which we constitute as a meaningful whole by our presence, as our *Umwelt* and *Lebenswelt,* the world constituted by our living presence.

That sense of mine-ness we recognize readily enough in the coherence of our social world ("my friends and relations") and our immediate environment ("my home," with its familiar objects and accustomed places). We can, analogously, recognize the cohesion of the Other's *Umwelt* ("Rabbit's friends and relations," "somebody's home") as meaningful in terms of another subject's being. On entering someone's home, we can sense that there is an order, that things have their place and a meaning which is real yet is not ours. The humble experience of trying to cook in someone else's kitchen brings home the point.

That sense of a mine-ness not mine own, however, pervades the world of nature as well. We can obscure it by entering that world in a special role, as *homo faber* or *homo sapiens,* reducing the world to tools or problems. But when we enter it simply as Persons, we encounter the woods, the hills, and the skies, with the many creatures who inhabit them, as fitting together in an intimately coherent sphere of mine-ness that is neither ours nor any human's—yet is real and demands our respect. The classical Personalists did not hesitate to draw the evident conclusion: the world is transcendent yet intelligible as *created,* a *Lebenswelt Gottes.* Today, we tend to be far more circumspect; perhaps the awareness of our record makes us wary of acknowledging the reality of God's presence. But, though we stop short of the admission, there still remains the recognition of that aspect of the density of being-a-subject which challenges the naive egocentrism of our subjectivity. Being-a-subject entails both the recognition of being the center of a private and intersubjective unity of meaning and being at home in a context which transcends us. Being a Person entails all that, and if we are to recognize the full existential density of the subject, even strictly in his transcendental role as sheer subject, we need to recognize his reality as Person.

Hermeneutics and the
Return to Phenomenology

Phenomenology's "personalist turn," foreshadowed by Husserl in *Ideen II* and elaborated over the years by his successors, helped overcome the dilemma of a sterile transcendentalism or a relativistic anthropologism by its recognition of the full Person-al density of the subject as transcendental. With that, Husserl's project of phenomenology could become fully productive, though, as Husserl anticipated in *C* § 43c, no longer as a monadic egology but as what we have called a *transcendental personalism*.

The personalist turn, however, inevitably focuses attention on the recalcitrance of reality, masked but neither removed nor resolved by the transcendental bracketing.[20] That recalcitrance poses a problem. The bedrock of the entire project of phenomenology, as we have noted, is Husserl's conviction that reality is accessible to consciousness. That is his answer to the gnawing suspicion of Western philosophy that truth may be illusion. Reality, Husserl insists, is intelligible as lived experience; it is susceptible to being brought to clear awareness (*Anschauung* and *getreuer Ausdruck*) and, as such, is univocal and interpersonally valid (the transcendental dimension of subjectivity). The recognition of the full density of subject presence, however, leads to a recognition of dimensions of reality which are opaque to awareness and inconsistent with its eidetic coherence. Noetically, this calls into question Husserl's confidence that conceptual articulation of experience can be genuinely a true expression. If reality were intrinsically opaque, then language would not only reveal but also distort and so conceal it. The noematic aspect of the problem is what philosophers have traditionally designated as the problem of radical evil—the reality of aspects of experience which are radically inconsistent with its basic human coherence, aspects which are neither will nor capable of being consistently willed but which nonetheless are irreducibly real. If the full density of subject presence included dimensions which the subject can neither know nor consistently will, then the project of phenomenology would become problematic except as a regional study.

The problem of the alleged opacity and inconsistency of experience barely emerges in Husserl (or, for that matter, in the humanists [Masaryk] or Personalists [Bowne] of his time). As we have noted, Husserl does acknowledge a "twilight zone," but he does little more than that. To the end of his days, Husserl, again like Masaryk or Bowne, clung to the conviction that the opacity of language is a problem of practice rather than of principle and so can be resolved by the kind of rigorous analysis which he presents in *FTL* or *E&J*. Similarly, as *Crisis* and the "Vienna Lecture" testified, he remained convinced that the radical evil whose reality was being brought home to the Europe of the thirties by Stalin and Hitler is a corrigible deviation from a consistent norm rather than an ineradicable contradiction in the very nature of being.

Amid the ideological turmoil of the thirties, with its facile relativization of both good and evil and truth and falsehood in the name of class or *Volk,* Husserl stood out as a witness to the conviction of the consistency, moral coherence, and clarity of being as *unum, bonum, verum.* That conviction is the philosophical basis of the European and now Western ideal of humanity, that unique fusion of Greece, Rome, and Jerusalem with its affirmation that the individual human, for all his cosmic insignificance, is infinitely valuable as *capax boni et veritatis.*

We are utterly convinced that, ultimately and in a profound sense, Husserl is right in his affirmation. The way to that affirmation, however, is proving far more circuitous than Bowne, Masaryk, or even Husserl, in spite of *C* § 43c, ever anticipated. Before we can affirm the transcendental clarity and consistency of being-human, which is the project of phenomenology, we need to come to terms with the phenomenal ambiguity and inconsistency of its horizon.

The problem emerges more clearly in the work of Husserl's successors than in that of his followers. Martin Heidegger recognized the density of subject presence from the start with his conception of the subject as *Da-sein.* Quite early in his investigations, however, he had to confront the question whether Dasein's being, as accessible in direct awareness, represents what being genuinely is or whether that is an appearance, distorting the primordial reality of being as it reveals it. Heidegger was led increasingly to the latter view. The contradiction of being genuinely and not genuinely, that of life and its innermost possibility, death, that of being and nothing—all appear to him not as accidental but as intrinsic to finite being.

Ricoeur's investigations, while far less encumbered by obscure romantic mysticism than those of Heidegger, still encounter analogous problems. Being-as-subject in all its density, represented for Ricoeur by the will, is a fusion of the voluntary with an involuntary which is intrinsically a dimension of being subject and so cannot be dismissed as alien (as it is by Sartre) but which still is partially or fully opaque to clear awareness. The subject wins the unity of his being in an act of appropriation. In that act, however, he also confronts the absolutely unacceptable, the inconsistent reality of radical evil. There is, to be sure, an important difference between Ricoeur's and Heidegger's readings of that contradiction. Ricoeur shares the Christian conviction that the radical contradiction is not a function of finitude as such, but rather of a *fall,* and so is characteristic of our present state, inevitable but not intrinsic. Yet, *pro statu isto,* his diagnosis parallels Heidegger's: there is a deep opacity and contradiction in the very being of the finite subject.

Confronted with opacity and inconsistency of the subject's horizon, both Ricoeur and Heidegger turn, as humankind has at least since the time of Job, to a poetic reconciliation. Unable to resolve that contradiction in positive terms, humans have ever turned to myth, seeking to transcend it in symbols which point beyond the articulate conflict to a prearticulate unity, beyond true and false, beyond good and evil. Heidegger, in his later work, seeks to transcend the opacity and inconsistency of finitude in the poetic evocation of a unity so primordial that it cannot be named. As the Hebrews used the tetragrammaton יהוה , Heidegger uses an archaic spelling of the word for being, canceled by lines drawn through it: S̶e̶y̶n̶. For Heidegger at least, positive descriptive phenomenology, with its hope of rigorously bringing the reality of lived experience to clear awareness, becomes eclipsed by a hermeneutic uncovering of the alleged primordial reality of being.

Heidegger's turn to the mystery of being, leaving behind Husserl's positivistic emphasis and reclaiming the great romantic tradition of Goethe, Schelling, and Hegel, can appear most impressive. The positivism of Hume—whom Husserl studied persistently—and even the critique of Kant can appear mundane and superficial alongside the profound grounding of the deep calling to the deep in German romanticism. The romantic vision, capable of embracing in a sweep of symbol the problems and contradictions of the particular, offers a depth and a scope that make the epistemological positivism of Hume and the moral positivism of Kant appear trivial.

But that turn raises a rather vexing question. For all its mundane superficiality, British positivism has consistently led to benign social and human results. It has given us Mill's conception of liberty, Locke's conception of democracy, and it has articulated our ideas of human rights and common weal, ever tempering the aspirations of autocrats and ideologues with the mundane reality of everyday human being.

The record of profound romanticism has been rather more am-
biguous. Both left and right Hegelianism, perhaps against the wishes
of their philosophic spokesmen, became the ideologies of stifling, soul-
and body-destroying political orthodoxies. Why didn't Heidegger's
profound insight warn him against national socialism? The perennial
appeal of revoluntionary movements for academic enthusiasts is understandable and is making itself felt today no less than in Heidegger's time, when German national socialism and Russian Marxian
socialism were revolutionary movements. But a philosopher's insight
ought to warn him against the excesses of political passion. Why did
the profound romantic tradition fail in the case of Heidegger, as it had
before and after?

In principle, the answer is no mystery. In relativizing the finite,
Hegelianism may be able to transcend the opacity and inconsistency
of the particular or even see it as "dialectically" consistent, but it
does so at the cost of giving up the clarity of moral insight, good and
evil, truth and falsehood. In human terms, that is a desperately high
price. Perhaps it is the case that, ultimately, good and evil, truth and
falsehood fuse in an ineffable unity in the all-redeeming sight of God,
but in the lives of humans in which moral choices must be made they
function as contradictions, not as dialectical complements. Nazism
and Stalinism do not complement the ideal of humanity; they kill
and destroy and must be confronted with a clear vision of truth and
justice. Philosophy needs the wisdom of Job because humans must
live with the failure of effort, but it also needs the moral perspective of the Psalmist: "So teach me to number my days that I may
discern between good and evil." The hermeneutic poetics of being is
legitimate as a tool for grasping the full cosmic and historical density
of the moral subject. It becomes vicious when it obscures the clarity
of the moral subject with a putative higher whole, be it class, *Volk,*
or ~~Seyn~~.

Paul Ricoeur, in his use of hermeneutics, is keenly aware of the
difference. For him, hermeneutics extends rather than replaces the
clear phenomenological vision. The "long route" which he proposes
leads to an affirmation of the subject in his full density, his full cosmic
and historic context, not to an abandonment of the subject.[21] It includes an analysis of the opacity of the subject's mirror image, which
is objectified in depth psychology and linguistics, but appropriates
that mirror image in the name of the subject. It includes a confronta-

tion with the reality of evil and the cosmic horizon of the subject which denies him the pride of place as the creator of all he surveys, but which is nonetheless the cosmos of his being. Hermeneutics, in Ricoeur's use, becomes an extension of the fundamental phenomenological affirmation: the oblique survey of the subject's horizon.

With that, however, Ricoeur's own claim that his "long route" leads to the same point as Heidegger's short turn becomes slightly problematic. Whether Ricoeur so intends it or not, his long route does not displace the merely finite being as relative or transient by an ineffable ~~Seyn~~. The congruence holds only if we accept Ricoeur's generous interpretation, according to which Heidegger, in attributing to the subject the role of fusing and articulating being, also returns to an affirmation of subject reality. For, whatever may be the true reading of Heidegger, Ricoeur's ultimate affirmation is not Hegelian or holistic but profoundly humanistic, personalistic, and Husserlian.

And that, we would submit, is the full significance of Husserl's phenomenology: the affirmation of the primacy of the subject, though in his full density and context. Husserl, a continental European, was also a student of Hume, keenly aware of the crucial role of the positivist insistence on rigorous grounding of knowledge in lived experience. As a European, he recognized the need to broaden that conception of experience from the British positivist restriction of sense experience of particular data to the primordial awareness of experience in all its immediacy and fullness. But he recognized no less keenly the need for grounding such full eidetic awareness in primordial givenness, in *Evidenz*. Metaphorically, we could say that Husserl fuses Hume and Kant, and the fusion yields a powerful insight into the being of the subject.

We began with the analysis of subject consciousness as phenomenology's central contribution. We have returned to that subject, though now in the full density of his presence as Person and with a hermeneutic vision of the horizon of his presence, as Person in God's world. The insight we have won is not new—it is at least as old as St. Augustine, as perennial as the Western affirmation of the reality, univocity, and value of the moral subject. But we have won that perennial insight in a new way. What Husserl has added is a keen-edged philosophical tool capable of making humanism (or, in the term we have used, personalism) a rigorous *scientia*.

Notes

Preface

1. Since pages differ in various editions, we shall use Husserl's section numbers as reference points. Where more precise reference is needed, we shall use lowercase letters to indicate paragraphs within each section. Thus § 19c refers to the third paragraph of section 19. See the List of Abbreviations following the Preface, and also the Bibliography. Unless otherwise noted, all translations are mine.

2. Aron Gurwitsch, *Studies in Phenomenology and Psychology,* p. xviii.

3. We are citing examples, not offering a list; otherwise the omission of names like Maurice Natanson, Richard Zaner, David Carr, and many others would be inexcusable.

4. Dorion Cairns, "An Approach to Phenomenology," p. 3.

5. See the Bibliography at the end of this volume for a survey of the three "introductions" and a more detailed justification for choosing *Ideas I.*

6. Gurwitsch, *Studies in Phenomenology and Psychology,* pp. xiv–xv; similarly, Cairns, "An Approach to Phenomenology," follows *Ideas I* in what was then (1940) a pioneering presentation of phenomenology in America, even though, in his *Conversations with Husserl and Fink,* Cairns reports that, in 1932, Husserl, having just completed his *FTL,* considered that his best introduction.

7. Since we shall be *pointing out* what is there to be seen in the text, the reader will find it helpful to follow Husserl's text side by side with ours. For texts and translations, see the Bibliography.

1   **Ordinary Experience and Common Sense**

1. *Ideas I* § 20b.

2. Husserl identified himself as an idealist most explicitly in *CM* (note especially § 41), although the title of *I* § 49, "Absolute Consciousness as the Residuum after Nullifying the World," can already be read as explicitly idealistic.

3. In practice, phenomenology obviously does not operate in a philosophical vacuum. For its relation to the history of philosophy, see Husserl's *C,* pt. II; the schematic presentation in *I,* chap. 2; or above, pp. 153–65.

4. This, in effect, is how common sense poses the problem of solipsism.

Husserl notes it in *CM* § 8. *CM V* and *C* §§ 53–55 sum up his conviction that the necessary structure of any subject experience is the basis of the answer to the problem, which is posed not by experience itself but by our common-sense interpretation of it.

5. The pregivenness of such meaning structures, we need to note, is *not* a matter of cultural conditioning. Such conditioning affects the content of the structures we habitually employ (say, comparing in terms of beauty rather than wealth) or of particular judgments. The point here, however, is not what structures we "in fact" note but that, in principle, our experience presents itself to us as including patterns, whatever their source, as well as particulars. Cultural conditioning is irrelevant to Husserl's concern in *I* § 1. Ricoeur's investigation of the relationship between "preformed skills" and their cultural extension (Ricoeur, *Freedom and Nature,* pp. 231–49) is more to the point.

6. That is the "principle of principles" which Husserl states in *I*-§ 24a, restates in *CM* § 5, and repeats in all of his work. The idea of providing an "absolute"—primordial, underived—grounding for knowledge in originary *Evidenz* (see *FTL* §§ 105–7 or *CM* § 24), that is, in a direct grasp of experience in full clarity, is the driving force of Husserl's investigations, presented repeatedly as a credo (see *CM* §§ 1–2 or *C* § 17). It is such grounding that would make philosophy (or, for that matter, any of the special sciences) truly a *strenge Wissenschaft,* a genuinely *rigorous* science.

7. Alfred Schutz introduces the concept of "ideal type" as a *terminus technicus.* While the term is not an exact equivalent of Husserl's *Wesen* or even *eidos,* it is clearly continuous with both (see *CM* §§ 20, 46; *C* § 48) and indicative of their thrust. (See Schutz *The Phenomenology of the Social World,* §§ 1, 37–38 and passim.)

8. Please note well that we are *paraphrasing* in order to render the passage "intuitable" rather than translating it to re-produce it in English. As of this writing, the only translation available is W. R. Boyce Gibson's *Ideas* (see the Bibliography), which suffers the failings of all pioneering works and, for all the credit due a pioneer, should be used with extreme caution. A new translation by Fred Kersten is in preparation by Martinus Nijhoff of The Hague. In this volume, all paraphrases and translations are mine, unless explicitly noted otherwise.

9. The recognition of experience as constitutive and of the surrounding world as constituted anticipates the argument. Husserl himself does not develop it fully until *CM* III–IV and *C* § 17, and with reason. Unless we first grasp and fix the reality of lived experience in phenomenological brackets (the task of *I*), constitutional analysis will be no more than a subjectivistic version of objectivism. We shall return to the point below, p. 230.

10. The conventional English translation, "primordial dator intuition" (Boyce-Gibson) or "primordial presentive intuition" (Dorion Cairns) is inappropriate here, since Husserl speaks of *Erfahrung,* that is, *experience.* But it is misleading even when Husserl speaks of *Anschauung,* or, rarely, *Intuition.* First of all, "intuition" in English has pronounced mystical, extra-experiential connotations which Husserl explicitly rejects (*I* § 3g; *C* § 39). As he uses the German *Intuition,* it is simply a neutral term for taking in information and can cover even instances like the "sense intuition" seeing green. Second, the term "dator" has no connotations at all, while the *gebende* it translates does: it refers to awareness that provides new information, which in English is normally designated by the Kantian term "synthetic." Finally, "primordial" has connotations which Husserl rejects explicitly in *I* § 1n.1: *originär* means "underived; experientially rather than historically primary." Thus, while *originär gebende Anschauung* might be translated "primordial dator intuition," the paraphrase "primary synthetic awareness" might be less misleading.

11. Should Husserl's assertion seem exaggerated, we need but recall Lundberg's classic essay "The Natural Science Trend in Sociology" (*American Journal of Sociology* 61, no. 3 [November 1955]: 191 ff.). Or compare Husserl's statement in *I* § 1c with what might be a paraphrase of it: "Modern science is a unified body of knowledge. Each individual science has a fixed objective, a well defined terrain and a specific methodology within the greater body." The speaker is Henri Ellenberger, author of the monumental *The Discovery of the Unconscious,* in an interview with Jacques Mousseau ("Freud in Perspective," translated by Paule Caillat, *Psychology Today* 6, no. 10 [March 1973]: 56). While contemporary thinkers like Hempel, Nagel, or Skinner are far more sophisticated than their predecessors (say, Watson or Lundberg), the principle that even social science describes regularities in the behavior of objects remains unchallenged.

12. For what it is worth, the term *Wesen* troubled Husserl as well, with its *ärgerliche Aequivokationen* ("annoying equivocations"), though he found it, together with the "still unused" term *eidos,* less misleading than the *Idee* he had used in his *Logische Untersuchungen* (*I* "Introduction," penultimate paragraph). In the Introduction to *Ideas,* Husserl speaks of *Wesen* and *eidos* as functionally equivalent. In the course of the work, a not altogether consistent pattern emerges: he tends to use *Wesen* when he is speaking of a principle or a typical way of being as exemplified and seen in an instance, and to use the term *eidos* when speaking of it in isolation. This pattern persists in *CM* and *C.* (The plural, *eidē,* does not, to my knowledge, occur in Husserl's writings.)

13. The direct givenness of *eidos,* which is not abstracted or constructed

but "seen," given in primary synthetic awareness, is crucial, not only to *I* but to all of Husserl's work. Husserl elaborates it in all his works, e.g., *CM* §§ 4, 17; *C* § 48). Yet we need no phenomenological theory to recognize that even in ordinary experience we see not only two circles but also the relationship "bigger than" between them. See also n. 16, below.

14. This familiar process is what Husserl describes in detail later, when speaking of the "method of perceiving clearly" (*I* §§ 67–69). The evident, while self-given (*CM* § 24), is not necessarily obvious (*CM* § 6).

15. Husserl, in the context of the example of tone and color, uses an artistic metaphor, *Abschattungen,* which can mean "shading-off" or "sketches, adumbrations." We shall employ a cinematographic one, "exposures," which can describe discrete perspectival views as well. See also Husserl's detailed analysis in *I* § 41, and cf. pp. 66–68, above.

16. This is the crucial difference between a phenomenological and an empirical perspective. For instance, psychoanalytic explanation deals with a phenomenon as the effect of hypothetical causes which are not given in experience but are postulated speculatively to account for it. By contrast, phenomenology seeks not to explain but to understand: to grasp the phenomenon in its lived intelligibility. In principle, this is the difference between grasping, say, paranoia as a subject's way of being-in-the-world and explaining it as the effect of an infantile trauma. As we shall stress later (pp. 167–69), the two are not incompatible. Husserl's point is that we have to *understand* a phenomenon before we can start explaining it, since reality is always lived experience, given in awareness—not the explanation we construct subsequently to account for it.

17. See *I* § 39, where the difference between immanent and transcendent perception leads Husserl to speak of immanent and transcendent typical structures, that is, those of lived experience in its immediacy and those of experience as observed.

18. This is not just a matter of proof texts like *I* § 3g or *C* § 34. The entire spirit of Husserl's enterprise is thoroughly antimystical and anti-"intuitive", in the usual sense of that word. Its aim is to provide a rigorous experiential foundation for knowledge. See Husserl's affirmation of positivism in *I* § 20.

19. So-called *verstehende Soziologie* demonstrates this. Its practitioners avoid factual conclusions on eidetic grounds but use eidetic grasp to prepare explanatory models. Thus Max Weber in his classic *The Protestant Ethic and the Spirit of Capitalism* does not base his factual assertions on his eidetic grasp of the Puritan ethic, but uses that grasp to render factual materials intelligible. T. G. Masaryk makes a similar use of Russian novels in *The Spirit of Russia.*

20. See constitutive synthesis (*CM* § 17) as projecting a horizon of

possibility (in *CM* §§ 19, 38). The foundations of that analysis lie in ordinary experience and in its description in *I* § 4.

21. *Being and Time,* pp. H.135 ff. This concept became a great favorite with postwar existentialists, but, in terms of Husserl's perspective, it requires the kind of critical examination which Paul Ricoeur provides in his *Freedom and Nature.*

2   **In Search of Pure Experience**

1. See *I* §§ 67–70; also above, pp. 143–47.

2. When we isolate lived experience in its purity, we raise the problems of objectivity (how can lived experience apply to an objective world) and intersubjectivity (how can individual experience apply to anyone but the speaker). Husserl deals with these in §§ 33–35, which we shall examine in chapters 3 and 4.

3. We do not mean to suggest that the picture of reality drawn by theology or physics is arbitrary. Clearly it is not, just as the order of a set of numbered balls of different sizes and colors arranged by their numbers rather than by their sizes or colors is not arbitrary—no. 3 must come after no. 2 and before no. 4. Such ordering is relative to a subject. Specifically, it is made possible by our decision to arrange by numbers. Similarly, the ordering of a special science, whether physics or theology, depends on the special questions it asks (hence the term "special" sciences). Most generally, "causal" explanation is contingent on a teleological decision. Or, in Bowne's aphorism, mechanism is teleology read backwards (*Philosophy of Theism,* p. 94). Husserl does not examine the implications of this recognition except in speaking of the "we" as functioning as a subject in *C* § 54a (see also Schutz, *The Phenomenology of the Social World,* §§ 33–40). Those implications are barely acceptable today. A reader reckless of respectability will find them traced out in, for instance, Bowne, *Metaphysics,* pp. 94–120.

4. See above, pp. 175–79; *I* §§ 57, 80; *CM* § 11; and *C* § 19.

5. The "existentialists" in fact frequently used fiction and theater as philosophical vehicles and drew their examples from crisis situations (cf. Dorothy McCall, *The Theatre of Jean-Paul Sartre*). But, as philosophy, that is problematic. Drama may be the ideal vehicle for presenting experience to our seeing, but that is all it does. Crisis situations do bring out an experience in lived purity; however, that experience is no longer an ordinary or typical one, but rather one distorted by the same elements which exhibit it. Colloquially, crisis situations do not show us what a human "really" is but only to what he can be driven under extreme duress. Thus Ricoeur's

insistence on suspending both "the bondage of passion and the vision of innocence" (*Freedom and Nature*, pp. 20–34) and on the need to develop phenomenological bracketing as an *ordinary* philosophical procedure.

6. In the *Husserliana* edition of the German text, chapters are numbered consecutively within parts; in the English translation, they are numbered consecutively throughout the book. To avoid confusion, we shall use the section (§) numbers. The chapter under discussion here—chapter II.1 in the German and chapter 3 in the English—is §§ 27–32.

7. *I* §§ 31–32; *CM* §§ 1–3; and *C* §§ 17–19. Husserl is never strictly Cartesian; even in *CM* he likens the phenomenological *epochē* to Cartesian doubt *only* in the sense that both—more precisely, each in its own way—represent a radical alteration of the natural standpoint. He makes his critique of the "Cartesian way," including whatever Cartesian leanings there might be in *CM*, in *C* §§ 43 and 55d.

8. "Subject-function" might be a more accurate term, since in relation to, for instance, my world of mathematics I do not function as a natural being. My body is irrelevant, and so, for that matter, is my mind in any empirical sense. I am relevant to the world of mathematics solely as positing it, thus, as a subject-function rather than as a natural subject. This is what Husserl will describe below (*I* § 57) by the much misunderstood term *reines Ich* ("sheer I") and in far greater detail in *CM* §§ 30–33 as the even more misleading *transzendentales ego*, clarifying it later, in *C* § 55, by speaking of the *Ich als Ur-Ich*—"the primordial I-function." See also Gurwitsch, *Studies in Phenomenology and Psychology*, pp. 287–300.

9. Not only common sense but also much empirical psychology yields to this temptation. Behaviorist and existentialist psychology rightly reject this conception of a substantive pure ego but, lacking Husserl's conception of the sheer I-function, reach the paradoxical conclusion that acts have no subject, as did Watson in his classic *Behavior: An Introduction to Comparative Psychology* (New York: Henry Holt, 1914) or Sartre in *The Transcendence of the Ego*. Bertocci, using the term "Person" as distinct from personality, presents an interesting alternative in "A Temporalistic View of Personal Mind" (*The Person God Is*, pp. 41–93).

10. Husserl actually uses the words "common sense," in English, in the text of *Crisis* (§ 53c). Concerning the "natural" world as habitual, see Jan Patočka, *Přirozený svět jako filosofický problém*. Patočka uses the word "přirozený," suggesting that which comes "naturally," effortlessly, rather than the word "přírodní," referring to a physical "nature." See also Ludwig Landgrebe, "The World as a Phenomenological Problem," trans. Dorion Cairns, in *Philosophy and Phenomenological Research* 1, no. 1 (September 1940): 38–58.

11. Husserl states this most clearly in *C* § 55d, when he calls the

attempt to attack transcendental phenomenology as a "Cartesianism" a "ludicrous if common misunderstanding" and adds, *Es gilt nicht, Objektivität zu sichern, sondern sie zu verstehen* ("The point is not to secure objectivity, but to understand it").

12. The term "phenomenon" as Husserl uses it has none of the ordinary connotations of unreality, of a "mere" appearance hiding a "true reality." If reality were transcendent, whether as "noumenal" or "material," and merely recorded in the mind, a phenomenon would be "mere" appearance. But Husserl's point is precisely that it is not. Reality is experiential. The ashtray of the earlier example, which appears in our experience, is not a "mere" re-presentation of some transexperiential "real" ashtray. The phenomenon, ashtray, as it functions in our experience, *is a real ashtray,* the only one there is, and real only as phenomenal. Both our subjective impression of the ashtray and our conception of "objective" ashtray are abstractions from the experienced ashtray.

Husserl speaks of the subjective and the objective as abstractions from experience in *C* §§ 66–67, but avoids the metaphysical conclusion. For that, see Bowne, *Metaphysics.* Bowne insists on the phenomenality of the sense world but denies the need for a conception of noumenal reality (pp. 137–44) and affirms the sole reality of particulars.

13. See Ian Jarvie, *A Revolution in Anthropology,* as an instance. Jarvie is not a phenomenologist, or at least he does not seem aware of being one.

14. In Husserl's terms, having grasped the experience in terms of its *eidos,* I can proceed to explain its contingent factual form (*I* §§ 2–3). Subsequent examination reveals the *eidos* as a function of the *intentionality* of a subject's being (*I* § 84 and *CM V*).

15. "Edmund Husserl: A Letter to Arnold Metzger."

16. In *I* § 32e Husserl adds what amounts to an important footnote. He speaks of the *epoché* as freeing us of the *Vorurteil* ("prejudgment") about the significance of the existing world for explanation. This confirms our earlier point, that the "natural standpoint" designates not natural necessity but our habitual prejudgment in understanding the world, the *sensus naturalis* or common sense. Unfortunately, the connotations of the word and of its ordinary English equivalent, prejudice, lead to a Baconian misinterpretation. The *epoché* is designed to rid us not of "prejudices" but of the specific pre-judgment that the world explains experience rather than vice versa.

17. The idea of "reducing" constructs to their fundamental experiences leads Husserl to speak of "phenomenological reduction" as an equivalent of the terms "bracketing" or *"epoché,"* from § 56 on. Given the significance that "reductive" has in English, the usage is unfortunate, since in that sense it is the special ("regional") sciences which offer "reductive" explanations

while the purpose of Husserl's *Reduktion* is to present a nonreductive understanding, that is, reality in its experienced fullness, unconstrained by the concepts of special sciences or perspectives.

18. Basically, phenomenological bracketing acknowledges the impossibility of accounting for the order of nature in terms of natural entities. Nature is intelligible only as experience—that is, for a subject. When we go beyond a phenomenological description to metaphysical speculation, we face the choice of either considering the order of the universe as in each case relative to a particular human subject, which is plainly false, or positing an intelligent world-ground as subject. Thus Bowne, *Metaphysics,* pt. 1. Such speculation, however, is in principle illegitimate if it is conceived as providing a transcendent "explanation" which can replace phenomenological understanding of lived experience.

19. Cf. Husserl's analysis of mathematization of nature and secondary mathematization of experience in *C* §§ 8–9c and his subsequent discussion of bracketing of idealizations (analogous to the transcendent structures of *ideas*) and of the life-world in *C* §§ 35–36.

20. This is true unless, without acknowledging it, we posit the scientist as a subject, describe the world as intelligible from his viewpoint, then point out that the scientist as a human being is a part of the world so described, and so present the description of the world as subjectless, "objective." This procedure tends to confuse the subject as pure ego—that is, as the *subject-function* which makes description possible by constituting experience as intelligible system—with the subject as a natural subject, which can indeed be included within the system described. See directly below in the text and also *CM* §§ 41, 45; *C* §§ 54–55.

21. Interpreting Husserl's "transcendental ego" as a substantival entity is the error that leads Sartre to its denial (in *Transcendence of the Ego*) and to the strange ontology of anonymous acts in *Being and Nothingness.* More surprisingly, the same error seems to occur in the work of a highly competent scholar as well—in Aron Gurwitsch's "A Non-Egological Conception of Consciousness" (*Studies in Phenomenology and Psychology*). The puzzlement disappears when we note that Gurwitsch's objection is not to the conception of the ego as transcendental but to that ego as substantival; the substitution he wants to make, speaking of a *transcendental function* of consciousness (p. xxiv), captures, we would submit, Husserl's own intent—hence *I* § 57b.

22. Ricoeur, *Freedom and Nature;* see pp. 186–87, above.

23. This fact provides the solution of the problem raised by idealist philosophers such as T. H. Green or F. H. Bradley, who note that, stripped of all particular, individuating traits, the I as pure I-hood would no longer

be individual, and so they are led to posit a free-floating subjectivity-in-general. The problem makes as little sense as the solution in terms of lived experience. Here I am directly aware of the pure ego as an I, distinctive and individual, since not matter but *act* is the *principium individuationis* in lived experience. Thus, though the idea which just occurred to me might be a cliché, in lived experience I recognize it as individual by virtue of the individual act: *I thought it*. Similarly, the act of adding two and two to get four is individual, not by virtue of its contents but by virtue of my act: *I* am adding. The I, even in its purity as a "pure ego"—sheer I-hood—is individual as act. This is how Husserl in fact resolves the problem in *C* § 54b, though his presentation is not readily intelligible apart from a clear recognition of the act as the principle of individuation.

3   The World As Experience

1. Husserl deals with the first problem in *I* §§ 33–46, and elaborates it at length in *CM*. He deals with the second problem in *I* §§ 47–55, and at length in *C*, whose insight, especially *C* §§ 28–51, Merleau-Ponty in turn elaborated in his *Phenomenology of Perception*.

2. The pivotal points are presented in § 33 (transcendental consciousness as the phenomenological residuum), in § 41 (the way we really experience transcendent objects), and in § 46 (conclusion). Even the reader who so far chose not to follow Husserl's text concurrently with our exposition might do well to read those three sections.

3. Anglican readers will remember the phrase in the Prayer of Consecration—that while doing this "in remembrance" we may be partakers not of symbolic wafers and wine but of the "most blessed Body and Blood." That is not Cranmer's attempt to fuse the Reformed doctrine of remembrance with the Lutheran doctrine of real presence. Rather, it is a recognition that the act-experience (doing in remembrance) constitutes its object-in-experience (again, note, not "in the mind" but *in experience*), the true Body and Blood.

4. Heidegger describes the constitution of objects in experience clearly and accurately in § 15 of *Being and Time*. His presentation, however, ignores the Cartesian *wonder* (which becomes increasingly important in his later work as the "listening to being") as an equally primordial intentional stance. (See Ricoeur, *Freedom and Nature,* pt. 2, chap. 2, sec. 2.1; or Kohák, "I, Thou, and It," § 3.1.)

5. This is easy to overlook in dealing with familiar behavior, some of whose objects—such as snarling dogs—we have come to regard as inherently

threatening. Yet, staying within ordinary experience, there are subjects who manifest no fear of snarling dogs—the Androcles syndrome. To explain this, as we commonly do, by saying that such persons have not "learned to fear dogs" may be an accurate description of the fact, but it is not an explanation that would help us understand such persons' acts. For that, we need to undertake an analysis not of dogs or the subject's feelings about them but of the "dog-*Erlebnis,*" the way snarling dogs function in the context of the person's lived experience. Cf. Bowne's helpful distinction between explanation which describes and understanding which explains (*Metaphysics,* chaps. 2, 4; and *Theory of Thought and Knowledge,* pt. 1, chap. 10, especially pp. 223 f.).

6. The *Husserliana* text incorporates extensive revisions and additions which Husserl prepared for a future edition. Especially in § 33, there are numerous verbal discrepancies between the English translation, made on the basis of an earlier edition, and the German text we are using. (For instance, what we have designated as § 33h and 33i has no counterpart in the English text.) Since Husserl's changes, while introducing the terminology of his later work, do not substantively affect the general meaning of the text, we have not marked them specifically or compared the two versions. A reader wishing to do that will find a comprehensive guide in Biemel's "Textkritischer Anhang" in the *Husserliana* edition, pp. 461 f.

7. Husserl makes this abundantly clear in his insistence that a thing's being-in-experience—and only that—is the "thing in itself," and in explicitly denying any "noumena" (*I* § 43; discussion above, pp. 68–71). This, as Husserl's analysis of the objectivity of the object (what Nicolai Hartmann called *die Härte des Realen* in "Zum Problem der Realitäts-gegebenheit" [*Philosophische Vorträge,* no. 32 (Berlin: Pan-Verlag, 1931), p. 28], and what Husserl describes as the "X" in § 131 and the sections surrounding it), does *not* deny the reality of the transcendent but rather recognizes the *reality* of "the real" is its meaning rather than its thinghood.

8. We are anticipating Husserl's elaboration of the point in §§ 35, 38 (above, pp. 61–65).

9. The philosophical groundwork here was done by Johannes Duns Scotus in a theological context, explicitly in *Quaestiones Miscellaneae de Formalitatibus* (Q.I, V, 338–53b; Q.II, V, 353c–57b), with frequent references to it throughout his work. Dealing primarily with the distinctness of God's attributes and the unity of the divine essence, Scotus points out that to account for both we have to recognize—in addition to the real distinction between *res* and the virtual and logical distinctions in the mind alone—a real distinction not between *res* but between "formalities," that is, modes of being (or our "objects-in-experience"), which he recognizes not merely as *entes rationis* but rather as constituting a *ratio objectiva,*

which is not *res sed rei.* While Scotus never makes such use of his formal distinction, we can utilize it to describe the distinction between objects-in-experience (example in text) as a "formal" distinction, using the term to indicate that the distinction is a *real* one, though not a distinction between *res.* For a clear summary presentation of the Scotist doctrine, see Maurice J. Grajewski, O.F.M., *The Formal Distinction of Duns Scotus,* pp. 67–97; 140–78.

10. In German, this is even a play on words. *Sein* ("being") is an infinitive with the connotations of a verb, the way of being. The word for consciousness, *Bewusstsein,* can be read as *bewusst-sein,* "being-aware," analogously with "being-human." Lest this suggest Berkeley's *esse est percipi,* note that Husserl, in the same sentence, uses *reines Erlebnis,* pure lived experience, as a synonym. The distinctive mode of being of objects-in-experience is being-experienced, and it is as such that they are intelligible. That does not, however, make them "merely subjective." Experience, as we shall see in the next chapter, is still perception, not imagination, and its structure is necessary, not private (thus *I* §§ 47–55; *CM* §§ 45–46; and *C* §§ 54–55).

11. The metaphysical implications of Husserl's observation here, and even more emphatically in *Cartesian Meditations* and *Crisis,* are in fact idealistic. The implications of his arguments or speculations may not be that, but those of the *experience he describes* are. That is something rather different. What Husserl criticizes about idealism—and probably the chief reason for its philosophical disrepute in recent decades—is that it has become speculative, losing its experiential foundations and no longer speaking to experience. But that is not the case with Husserl. His procedure and reference, as he stresses even in *CM* (§§ 4–5), remain rigorously experiential throughout. While rejecting naturalism, Husserl never falls prey to subjectivism (see chap. 4, pp. 94–102, above). His is not an "absolute" idealism, based on the assumption that all *mine* is *me.* Rather, it is a *transcendental experientialism,* recognizing that the (real) object is really an object of consciousness. If that kind of idealism is the product of a rigorous examination of experiential data and deals most adequately with experience, then the objections to it lose all but rhetorical force.

12. Husserl examines this in detail in *CM,* where, in § 33, he even speaks of consciousness as a monad. Consciousness here clearly is not an entity standing over against the world. Rather, it is a way of speaking about the whole experienced world (emphatically including all I experience as *other; CM* §§ 45–53), designed to underline its crucial characteristic: that it is experienced and structured as the unity of my experiencing. That is not a matter of speculation but a straightforword description of my experience and of the experienced world in which I in fact live. Subject acts

are in fact acted *and intelligible* in a world conceived as a subject's experience or, in Husserl's intimidating term, as a monad. To interpret this on the model of a snake swallowing its tail—i.e., claiming that in an objective world there is a special object, consciousness, which in turn subjectively contains the world in itself—is a subjectivistic misreading of idealism (which Husserl rejects explicitly, as in *I* § 55) as well as a subjectivistic misreading of Husserl (which he rejects equally explicitly in *CM* § 41). Husserl's point is experiential, not subjectivistic: the recognition that, in fact as well as necessarily, the actual world of my lived experience, including its otherness, is my experiential world and that I experience even its objectivity as real in the context of my experience. *Lived experience itself, not Husserl's description of it, has idealistic metaphysical implications. Transcendental idealism,* as Husserl notes in *CM* § 41, *is experientially realistic.*

13. Our examples, admittedly, have no analogue in Husserl's writings (unless in the "vocations" passage in *C* § 35). Husserl avoids examples from the social sciences, perhaps because, in spite of all possible caveats, they are always prone to subjectivistic misinterpretation. But he does examine and elaborate the point, in terms of the *Umwelt* (world as subject context), the experiential matrix pre-given by the necessary structure of subjectivity as such (*C* §§ 29–37; it is elaborated in Merleau-Ponty's *Phenomenology of Perception*). The link between Husserl's structural analysis and our *all'zu menschliche* examples is T. G. Masaryk's conception of our shared *humanitas* (*Ideály humanitní;* cf. Kohák, "Tři téze o Masarykovi," and Bowne's conception of Person [in his *Personalism*]).

14. The term *Umwelt,* literally "surroundings" or "environment," is a common term in ordinary German usage. In Husserl, it appears as *terminus technicus* in *Crisis.* The question is not whether "there is" a world, but rather how that world is to be understood. A suicide attempt always has antecedents, but why did these become *reasons for* suicide? Objectively, they are simply facts. How do they become reasons? Or, as Husserl puts it, "the problem is not to secure objectivity but to understand it" (*C* § 55), to render it intuitively available (*C* § 34d).

15. Husserl says a great deal about consciousness in *CM,* though his analysis there needs to be read in light of the caution he gives in *C* § 43.

16. Since Husserl insists that perception is an act, not a passion, the neologism *actum,* favored by Alfred Schutz, might be more accurate than the usual *datum.* However, since neologisms have little immediate intuitive significance, they may sharpen precision at the cost of impairing intuitability. We shall therefore continue using the usual term, *datum,* though in its ordinary rather than its etymological sense.

17. Here note the sentence in § 34a, "jedes individuelle Vorkomnis sein Wesen hat ("every individual *event* has its typical way of being [essence]"). The point is that *events,* not objects, have "essences." The chair-experience, not the transcendent object, is something typical, in itself; the object could be anything. Thus when Husserl speaks of "grasping the typical ways of being" ("intuiting essences" in the usual English translation), he is *not* speaking of some mystical penetration into the inner being of an object but of becoming aware of the structure of our lived experience as subjects in a world. The approach is experiential, not mystical. And, since transcendent objects are what they really are only in subjects' experiences (only in a world of subjects who sit is this object a sit-upon-able, a chair), becoming aware of the necessary structure of our experiences (as chair-experience, situponability) means becoming aware of the world as well.

18. How to associate such acts with a *me* is a separate problem at which Husserl hints when he speaks of things which "because of psychological hindrances I cannot bring to consciousness," an oblique reference to Freud (*I* § 69c). Ricoeur examines it in detail in his *Freud and Philosophy.* Here, however, we are dealing, like Ricoeur in *Freedom and Nature,* with ordinary awareness, within the brackets: the "neutral keyboard" which he describes in brackets which exclude the bondage of passions and the hope of glory (see *Freedom and Nature,* Introduction, secs. 2, 3; also pt. 3, chap. 2, sec. 2).

19. Husserl elaborates on reality and perception later, in *I* §§ 97–101 and again in §§ 128–33, as well as in *Ideen II, Ideen III,* and *FTL* (in the last, note especially §§ 60–61, dealing with objectivity as a correlate of *Evidenz*). The objective reference is also a *consciousness of* something, a noematic nucleus serving as a point of unification. Whether this recognition solves the problem is not clear.

20. Cf. the explication in *FTL* § 86: all predicative primordial grasp (*Evidenz*) must be reducible to nonpredicative givenness. The statement evokes an uncanny echo of A. J. Ayer's criterion of meaningfulness in the Introduction to the second edition of *Language, Truth and Logic.* While Ayer's analysis is wholly uncritical, within a "natural" standpoint, the echo is a reminder that Husserl's phenomenology is genuinely a (transcendental) *experientialism* and, though not a positivism, a *positive* rather than a speculative philosophy.

21. It is worth noting that here Husserl affirms a basic realism. Intentional objects, while objects of consciousness, cannot be reduced to immanent acts of consciousness. It is I who is perceiving, what I am seeing is my intentional object; but for all that, I am seeing, not inventing. Or, as

Husserl explains in *CM V* and in *C* §§ 28–51, reality is given, but it is given in and as experience, in sharp contrast with the Hegelian conception of the *mine* as *me*.

22. Husserl elaborates this in *CM V,* in *C* §§ 54–55, and again in *FTL* §§ 95–96, always insisting both on the genuine otherness of the Other and on the genuine community of subjects as transcendental.

23. *I* § 35e. There is no reason why the same should not be true of plants, and it would not affect Husserl's position if it were true of stones as well. Merleau-Ponty, in *Phenomenology of Perception,* elaborates this in dealing with the body as a subject, noting that being-a-subject, as Husserl notes in *I* § 35, does not require an articulated, reflective consciousness. See also *Ideen II* §§ 19–47.

24. *I* § 43d; also *CM* § 45 or *C* § 54.

25. *Excursus:* Husserl's insistence on the truth as overt, *there* to be grasped and capable of being grasped clearly, in "perfect *Evidenz,*" rather than being hidden, open only to oblique "hermeneutic" uncovering that is also a distortion, is crucial to his phenomenology. (It is, for instance, this insistence on truth as being there for all to see rather than as a privileged realm of the poet, the philosopher, or the ideologue that leads Husserl's followers to a democratic commitment to human rights against the claim of ideology, as with the resistance group Weisse Rose in Nazi Germany or the human rights manifesto, Charta 77, in present-day Czechoslovakia.) Yet there is room for hermeneutics within phenomenology, though in the sense of the *mittelbare Schlüsse* (the mediate conclusions and idealizing procedures of *I* § 75f,g), as a means of reaching an insight, inaccessible in other ways, perhaps *wegen psychologischen Hemmungen* ("due to psy-chological hindrances"; *I* § 69c), which, however, *can be brought* to a clear grasp, once reached (see Ricoeur's conception of self-displacement in the struggle for self-awareness, in *Freud and Philosophy*). Hermeneutics becomes illegitimate, within a Husserlian framework, when it claims that not only the way of reaching insight but the insight itself is esoteric rather than overt.

26. How aware Husserl was of the existential implications of his work is quite unclear. They are there. For instance, the Table of Contents of *Ideen II* reads like a summary of topics in existentialism elaborated by men like Buber, Marcel, Merleau-Ponty, and others. Husserl's presentation, however, retains its measured scholarly tone. His correspondence reveals him as a deeply sensitive man who, for instance, read Kierkegaard with great absorption (Leon Shestov, "Edmund Husserl," in Edie, ed., *Russian Philosophy,* 3:254). In a letter to Lévy-Bruhl, he shows acute awareness of the new barbarism of the Nazis (Spiegelberg, *The Phenomenological*

Movement, 1:84). He saw this as the result of a profound intellectual crisis and set aside the revision of *CM* to write about the crisis of European sciences, traveling, in spite of age and illness, to lecture on the topic in Prague and Vienna, at that time still beyond Hitler's reach (Translator's Introduction, *The Crisis of European Sciences . . . ,* pp. xvi–xviii). It is an intriguing question for a historian, but, because truth is a matter of transcendental rather than natural subjectivity, it does not affect the meaning of Husserl's work.

4   **Experience and Intersubjectivity**

1. Ordinarily, this perspective would be described as "humanistic." Historically, it is a legitimate term; the lofty classical and Renaissance conception of *humanitas,* revived by thinkers like Bolzano, Brentano, and Masaryk, would justify using it. Unfortunately, for too many speakers the term "humanistic" has acquired the connotations of bungling incompetence, the substitution of vague good intentions for rigor and excellence. For that reason, we prefer other terms. When occasionally we do use the term "humanistic," it refers to the ideal of *homo humanus,* not to the *All'zumenschlichkeit* of contemporary usage.

2. Husserl traces the rise of the objectivist bias in detail, seeing it precisely as a quest for intersubjective validity (*C* §§ 8–14).

3. The most familiar example is in Kierkegaard, for whom "subjectivity is the truth" (*Concluding Unscientific Postscript,* trans. D. F. Swanson [Princeton: Princeton University Press, 1941], p. 187) and a moot point is resolved by passionate personal conviction (as immortality, pp. 154–55). It is such subjectivism which leads Feuerbach to write, "It is better to embrace in love the most unworthy, undignified object than to enclose oneself lovelessly in one's own subjectivity" (*Sämtliche Werke,* 2:395; my translation).

4. We use the term "naturalism" because "realism," though sanctioned by usage (including Husserl's own in *I* § 52b), is misleading. As we shall note (above, p. 103), Husserl's transcendental idealism is emphatically "realistic," focusing on experienced *reality* as *really* experienced, but it is not reistic. The point is not whether we deal with "ideas" or "realities," but whether we conceive the reality we deal with as natural, mental, or experiential. Thus while Husserl speaks of "realism," we shall use the term "naturalism" for any philosophy which considers reality as natural.

5. Husserl does not help by adopting, in *CM IV,* the Leibnizian term "monad" to describe the unity of lived experience. The term, strictly speak-

ing, does no more than acknowledge the unity of all experience as mine, an acknowledgment which Husserl repeats in unobjectionably experiential terms in *CM* § 46. But it does carry unfortunate subjectivistic connotations. Husserl's treatment of the constitution of intersubjectivity in *CM* §§ 47–55 (paralleling the common-sense attribution of "objectivity" to objects of analogous experience) and of transcendental subjectivity in *CM* § 56–60 (paralleling the common-sense recognition of the necessary common structure of any subject experience) clearly denies such connotations and leads to his rejection of solipsism except as describing the mineness of experience (*CM* § 62). Still, the fact that the impression has arisen and still lingers suggests that the problem must be dealt with.

6. Csepel is the steel complex in Budapest, Kolben-Daněk the heavy-industry complex in Prague. When the Soviets occupied Hungary (1956) and Czechoslovakia (1968), they encountered the most stubborn resistance to their claim that they were acting in the name of "the working class" among the workers of these two complexes.

7. Metaphysically speaking, the Berkeleyan model, albeit in a rather sophisticated form, might indeed prove more adequate. To say that the world is God's idea may add nothing to its intelligibility, but neither does calling it "matter." The givens are the independent reality and the intelligibility of the world. The first precludes subjectivism; the second precludes materialism: matter as such (as distinct from matter as experience) is not intelligible. The most adequate metaphysical model may well be one which interprets material reality as *created*, that is, as embodying God's idea, and so intelligible. We can use, roughly, an analogy with common sense, which readily understands an artifact, say, a wheelbarrow, that clearly embodies an idea, but which finds a natural object puzzling—or, grimly, understands a pogrom but finds a volcanic explosion or the collapse of the bridge at San Luis Rey incomprehensible, even if it can describe its "causes." Similarly, conceiving reality as ultimately material reduces it to ultimate incomprehensibility; its intelligibility is a strong argument for a creationist metaphysical model (thus Bowne, *Theory of Thought and Knowledge,* pt. 2, especially chap. 2). That, however, takes us far beyond our own concern. Since we are concerned here with reality *as experience,* we can and indeed must bracket out the metaphysical question of its ultimate nature.

8. Lest the assertion seem an isolated slip of the pen, note that, even at his most explicitly idealistic, in *CM,* Husserl insists on the otherness of the world (thus *CM* § 11) and dissociates himself from the Cartesian doubt in that respect (*CM* § 10). His oft-stated aim is not to doubt the reality of the world but to understand it, as he states most clearly in *C* § 55.

9. "Schluss. Alle Realität seiend durch 'Sinngebung.' Kein 'subjektiver

Idealismus.' " As we shall note in detail (p. 103), *Sinn geben*, in ordinary usage, has the force of "making sense," as in the phrase "Das hat keinen Sinn" ("that makes no sense"). Further, Husserl's critique of idealism (above, pp. 161–65 or, for instance, *C* § 57) is throughout aimed at subjectivism and subjective relativism. Thus both language and context justify a rather different English rendering of the title, reading it as asserting that the objects of our experience present themselves to us as real insofar as they *make sense*—constitute a coherent whole—and that no philosophy can be built on private, subjective ideas. A close scrutiny of Husserl's §§ 47–55 will, I believe, bear out this reading.

10. Husserl presents a clear summary of his argument in *CM* §§ 7–8, which is perhaps the best guide for reading the present chapter of *Ideas*. Similarly, the analysis of givenness of object and transcendental intersubjectivity in *FTL* §§ 94–96 is relevant and helpful.

11. We are speaking most imprecisely, for the sake of emphasis. Strictly speaking, we should say that being-real is a characteristic which we attribute to some segments of our experience; that whether such attribution is justified or not is a function of its growing empirical coherence; but that the structure of experience is the same whether or not we make such attribution (thus *CM* §§ 7–8; *Ideen III, Beilage I*, § 6; and *FTL*, e.g., § 99).

12. In his three Introductions (*I, CM*, and *C*), Husserl never satisfactorily distinguishes these two themes, thus giving rise to many unfortunate misunderstandings. But the distinction is clear in principle. When Husserl insists, as he does, for instance, in *CM* §§ 11–12, 34, and 40–41, or again in *C* §§ 48–49 and the entire *C* Part III, on the necessary, universal structure of experience as transcendental, he is speaking to the first theme. When, by contrast, he speaks of the communal constitution of objectivity by a we-subject, as in *CM* §§ 55–56 or in *C* §§ 47 and 66, he is speaking to the second theme. The two themes are not contradictory, nor does one represent "idealism" and the other "realism"; rather, one describes the essential structure of experience, and the other the actual constitution of its contents.

13. Husserl makes an important addition to this point in his analysis of the pregiven world in *C* § 36; this is elaborated by Merleau-Ponty in *Phenomenology of Perception*. Many of the descriptive possibilities of experience, grasped in reflection, articulate prereflective experience. We need not, for instance, try to derive the possibilities of satisfying hunger from the essential structure of the pure ego. But this is not true in all cases. The possibility of normative judgments, ordering rather than describing experience, is contingent on the pure essential possibilities of being-a-subject—Husserl's transcendental subjectivity—as such. The recognition of the Other as Thou and, with it, the possibility of a categorical imperative

and of a normative conception of *Person* embodied by this particular man (*C* § 45; also *CM* § 31) constitute perhaps the most important application of the principle for our purposes.

14. As an instance, see Kautsky's attempt to account for the Reformation in economic terms (Karl Kautsky, "Der Kommunismus im Mittelalter und im Zeitalter der Reformation," in E. Bernstein et al., *Die Geschichte des Sozialismus* [Berlin: Vorwärts, 1902], vol. 1, pt. 1, chap. 3), and Masaryk's critique of it in *Masaryk on Marx* (§ 34); or Freud's attempt to do so in libidinal terms in *The Future of an Illusion* (trans. James Strachey [New York: Norton, 1961] and Ricoeur's critique of it in *Freud and Philosophy*. Karl Jaspers (*Reason and Anti-Reason in our Time,* trans. Stanley Godman [New Haven, Conn.: Yale, 1952]) presents the classic critique of such attempts.

15. See Bowne, *Theory of Thought and Knowledge,* pt. 3, chap. 5, for his argument against skepticism; also in his *Philosophy of Theism,* chap. 6.

16. Ricoeur, *Freud and Philosophy,* p. 28 and passim. Ricoeur's work raises anew the question of the relationship between phenomenology and hermeneutics. The distinction, we would suggest, is misleading. A more adequate distinction may be one between philosophies committed to the conviction that truth can be brought to clear evidence, whether by rigorous phenomenological description or only by the roundabout way of a hermeneutic uncovering (Husserl, Ricoeur), and philosophies which consider all articulated truth as inherently defective and truth itself as something that can be approached only obliquely (Jaspers, Heidegger). Husserl's commitment to bringing truth to full *Evidenz* remains unwavering. Given the dimension of experience which cannot be brought to full awareness because of psychological hindrances (whose reality Husserl recognizes in I § 69c), hermeneutics, as Ricoeur uses it, may be a necessary adjunct to phenomenology. But the goal and normative ideal of clear grasp, as Husserl describes it movingly in the Introduction to *FTL,* still remains.

17. Husserl speaks consistently of *Erlebnisstrom,* the stream of *Erlebnisse,* lived experiences, even though his definition of consciousness would justify his speaking of "stream of consciousness." The reason is implicit in the three works we have been using, *I, CM,* and *C,* and becomes explicit in *Ideen III,* § 8, where Husserl points out that the connotations of "stream of consciousness" are inescapably psychologistic, suggesting something that is "in" consciousness as against what is "out there" in the world. Husserl is calling our attention to reality *as* consciousness—as lived and experienced, not as a stream of subjective images. Hence stream of lived experiences serves better than stream of consciousness.

18. This, again, is implicit in Husserl's insistence on taking lived

experience as our primordial datum. For explicit elaboration of the point, see, for instance, *C* § 66.

19. Husserl notes this explicitly with the conception of passive constitution in *CM* § 38. The term is not a contradiction but rather an acknowledgment of the experience in which the subject constitutes his experience as intelligible but does not determine its order. Thus, in observing objects A and B, the subject constitutes one as to the right of the other, but does not determine whether it is A or B—that is given. See also an analysis of the world as pregiven in *C* §§ 36.

20. In Husserl's view (as Spiegelberg points out in *The Phenomenological Movement*, 1:282), Heidegger's work in *Being and Time* is not so much phenomenology as a "transcendental anthropologism" or "psychologism." Heidegger's work does at times read more like cultural anthropology than phenomenology, but, as Husserl himself recognizes, especially in *C*, we are cultural *anthropoi* as well as transcendental subjects. Thus the distinction is crucial but the opposition unfortunate.

21. This is what Alfred Schutz describes as the "ideal types" of experience, crucial to scientific sociological study (see *The Phenomenology of the Social World*, §§ 38–39).

22. The term "natural subjectivity," referring to a natural subject's set of individual meanings, occurs occasionally both in *I* and in *CM*, but it does not become stabilized as a technical term (at least in the three Introductions we are using) until sec. III.B of *C*. In the passage under discussion here, Husserl still refers to "mere subjectivity." Similarly, the concept of transcendental subjectivity, which emerges as a clearly technical term in *CM*, here still appears under the term "experiential" subjectivity—the subjectivity of experience as such rather than of a particular subject (cf. also the elaboration in *FTL* § 96).

23. § 52e–g was added in a later edition and does not appear in the English text. It can be found in the Biemel edition. The English text resumes with 52h.

24. "Motivation" here functions as a *terminus technicus*. In ordinary English, we would paraphrase it as "good and sufficient reason." A possibility can be said to be 'rigorously motivated' when it is necessary in terms of logical consistence, not of the causality which the term suggests in ordinary usage (see elaboration in *I* §§ 135–39).

25. The term "class" is taken from the writings of Karl Marx, passim, the term "shabby individual" from Friedrich Engels, *Ursprung der Familie,* English translation in Marx and Engels, *Selected Works* (Moscow, 1962), 2:325.

26. Perhaps the most significant development is Husserl's analysis of meaningful constitution of the world and the other in *CM,* of history as

meaningfully constituted in *C,* and of bodily constitution in *Ideen II* (chaps. I.3, II.3) and *Ideen III* ("somatology" § 2). These themes are carried further by Merleau-Ponty, *Phenomenology of Perception;* Ludwig Landgrebe, *Phänomenologie und Geschichte;* Alfred Schutz, *The Phenomenology of the Social World;* and David Carr, *Phenomenology and the Problem of History.* Husserl may be unique, but he is not an isolated phenomenon.

27. *Circumspice!* Note, for instance, Earl Harris, "The Problem of Self-Constitution for Idealism and Phenomenology" (paper presented at the 1975 annual meeting of the American Philosophical Association [East], New York, 28 December); C. A. Campbell, *On Selfhood and Godhood,* pp. 70–83; and P. A. Bertocci, *The Person God Is,* pp. 41–65. Husserl copes with the problem in *CM* §§ 45, 55, and *C* §§ 53–55.

28. Husserl deals with this briefly in the "vocations" passage in *C* § 35.

29. Cf. Gurwitsch, *Studies in Phenomenology and Psychology,* p. xxiv, though he sees the conception of the transcendental function of consciousness as a "non-egological" alternative to, rather than the basic meaning of, Husserl's conception of the I as transcendental.

30. On pairing, see *CM* § 51.

31. Note again the assertion "The point is not to secure objectivity but to understand it" (*C* § 55).

5   Reflection, Intentionality, Constitution

1. "We have learned how to utilize the phenomenological perspective . . . [but] . . . we do not yet know what its *central themes* will be or, more exactly, what the basic areas of inquiry will be once we delineate experience in terms of its modes of being [rather than of its putative object-content]". (My paraphrase of *I* § 76d.)

2. The concept of *Evidenz* ("evident givenness"; sometimes mistranslated as "self-evidence") receives preliminary clarification in *I* §§ 137–40, and further elaboration in *FTL* §§ 58–61.

3. The unavailability of the texts gave rise to the myth that Husserl's work is full of unfulfilled promises. This simply is not true. Like any seminal thinker, Husserl poses a number of open questions, but his work is remarkably consistent and systematic. As for the topics projected in *Ideas I,* Husserl deals with the pure ego in *CM,* with temporality in *The Phenomenology of Internal Time-Consciousness,* with the relation of noema and object in *Ideen II* and *III,* with *Evidenz* and reflection in *FTL,* and with experience and judgment in a volume by that title, *Experience*

and Judgment. Note also the consistency of the three Introductions, *I, CM,* and *C* (below, pp. 229–31.)

4. Heidegger, *Der Satz vom Grund;* Karl Jaspers, *The Perennial Scope of Philosophy,* trans. R. Manheim (New York: Philosophical Library, 1949), pp. 1–23, 156–83; and Jan Patočka, *Úvod do studia Husserlovy fenomenologie.*

5. This *does not* preclude the use of hermeneutics as a "mediate inference" (I § 85), a tool for bringing to clear grasp those aspects of subject being which are not initially present to consciousness. Ricoeur so uses hermeneutics (see *The Conflict of Interpretations,* especially pp. 260–66). The goal, however, as his conclusion on p. 266 indicates, remains explicit grasp. Contrast this with Heidegger's treatment in, for instance, "Das Ding," in *Vorträge und Aufsätze,* pp. 163–85. Ricoeur's "long road" (*Conflict . . . ,* p. 6)—his criticism of a premature shift from epistemology to ontology, and the proposal to proceed through a hermeneutic analysis of psychology and language—seems more reminiscent of Husserl's criticism of the "Cartesian way" (*C* § 43) and the cure he proposes in *C* pt. III than of Heidegger's "Dasein analysis," in spite of his generous interpretation of Heidegger (*Conflict . . . ,* pp. 223–35).

6. Jean-Paul Sartre captures this feeling in numerous passages (see *Being and Nothingness,* pp. 55–56, 59) dealing with what he calls false consciousness (*mauvais foi,* usually translated verbatim as "bad faith").

7. As *locus classicus,* see Bowne, *Theory of Thought and Knowledge,* pt. 2, chap. 5; also his *Philosophy of Theism,* chap. 5; for a contemporary statement, Bertocci, *Introduction to the Philosophy of Religion,* chap. 3, §§ 3–5; for critical elaboration in a phenomenological context, Ricoeur's distinction between trust and suspicion in *Freud and Philosophy,* pp. 463–64, and in *The Conflict of Interpretations* (noted by Don Ihde in Editor's Introduction, p. xvii).

8. Ricoeur, *Freedom and Nature: The Voluntary and the Involuntary,* pp. 444–56. Since evil is an existential rather than an essential aspect of being-human, a fact rather than an essence, the consideration of it requires a methodological variation which Ricoeur describes as "grafting a hermeneutics" onto phenomenology (*The Conflict . . . ,* pp. 6–10), but the raising of the question clearly presupposes a prior rigorously eidetic description (*The Voluntary . . . ,* pp. 4–16), the descriptive phenomenology which Husserl proposes in *I.*

9. See the concept of *Leibesauffassung* (roughly, "bodily awareness") in *Ideen III,* § 5, and Merleau-Ponty's equivalent, *practognosie,* in *Phénoménologie de la perception,* p. 164 (p. 140 in the English translation).

10. In this sense, as Husserl explains in § 78, reflection is a *modification* of consciousness, not affecting its content but changing the *mode* of

presentation. Reality, however, is essentially *presented reality* (chaps. 3, 4 above), so that the presentation itself is not inherently a distortion but its intrinsic way of being. See also the elaboration of the concept of *Evidenz* in *FTL* §§ 58–61.

11. *I* §§ 81–82; for an elaboration, see *The Phenomenology of Internal Time-Consciousness,* especially §§ 11, 12. This is why Husserl does not consider the traditional problem of the experience of succession particularly difficult. The experience of succession is already there in the present, as retention and protention, prior to reflective recollection and anticipation.

12. To the extent that we can speak of a phenomenological "method" in a narrow sense, clear grasping of the evidently given—in our metaphor, seeing—is that method (as *C* § 7), and seeing again is the only elaboration of seeing (*FTL* § 59).

13. In *C;* note especially §§ 1–7 and the appended Vienna Lecture.

14. It is crucial to remind ourselves constantly that phenomenology yields no factual knowledge whatsoever. It brings to light essential structures of being-human which make it possible for us to understand rather than simply record facts, but it gives no information as to what those facts are in any particular case. On rigorously phenomenological grounds we can show, for instance, that any social order which denies the subject the opportunity for meaningful self-determination is intrinsically dehumanizing, no matter what other benefits it may offer. We cannot, however, on phenomenological or intuitive grounds, claim that this is what a particular regime does. Thus *I* § 4, but also § 79.

15. Since we are concerned with Husserl's basic insight and project of phenomenology, we are passing over (as Husserl does in *I*) the problem of grasping the full, lived density of being-human in a world. This shortcut is justified in a basic presentation, but the problem remains. Husserl points it out in *C* § 43 and seeks to remedy it in that work and in *FTL.* See also Ricoeur's "Existence and Hermeneutics," in *The Conflict of Interpretations,* pp. 3–24.

16. For intentionality as act-character of perception, see *Logical Investigations;* also note in *I* § 84e,f.

17. Cf. Heidegger's elaboration of the concept of *being-in,* in *Being and Time,* §§ 29–31. In this specific aspect, Husserl's perception is strictly analogous to Heidegger's being-in, *not* to our uncritically empiricist conception of perception as passive recording.

18. In this sense, consciousness can be described as self-enclosed and monadic, as Husserl does in *CM* § 33—not that the world is excluded from it, but rather that it includes all the world within itself.

19. We are treating the concept of hyletic data as nonproblematic, as Husserl does in *I,* since, as he tells us in *FTL* § 107, on a naive first level it is unproblematic: as a matter of ordinary experience, in perceiving an

object we are also tangentially aware of brown, hard, square, *into which* we can analyze the content of the perception. The conception would become highly problematic if we were to treat hyletic data as "sensations" in the technical British sense, as Harmon M. Chapman does in *Sensations and Phenomenology,* considering them as bits of reality *out of which* we construct a perception and which guarantee its transcendent status. That they cannot do, as Chapman points out (pp. 109–13), since they are themselves immanent. Chapman sees this as the fatal flaw of Husserl's phenomenology, and even as faithful a disciple of Husserl as Aron Gurwitsch concludes that the distinction between *morphē* and *hylē* is untenable (*Studies in Phenomenology and Psychology,* pp. 253–58). While writing *I,* Husserl may not have been aware of the ambiguity (though *I* §§ 97 ff. suggest otherwise). However (in light of *Ideen II,* pt. I and *FTL* § 107 and App. I), he clearly conceived of hyletic data as something *into* which we analyze a perception rather than something *out of* which we build it up. As for the transcendent status of the percept, that is not derived from the hyletic data but confronts us directly (as the "X" of *I* § 131 or the other of *CM* V). Chapman admits as much in his own chap. 6. However, it remained for Ludwig Landgrebe (*Phänomenologie und Geschichte,* chap. 6) to resolve the issue definitively.

20. Husserl presents a detailed analysis in the remaining chapters of *I.* To keep our presentation within reasonable limits, we shall not follow him there but finish our analysis with his conclusion of the general presentation of the project of phenomenology in § 96d. The reader, however, might find it useful to refer to subsequent texts (here, for instance, §§ 98–100, 129–33).

21. The use of the term "works" is startling, if at all, only in English. The German term *fungieren* ("to function" or "to work") is used in most mundane contexts, as of a public phone which *fungiert nicht* ("does not work," or "is not functioning"). Husserl stresses this, in § 86b, in emphasizing that he does not intend the term in the passive mathematical or logical sense of a function but in the active sense of functioning. See also concept of act, § 115.

22. For "success" of modern science, note *C* §§ 1–4.

23. Husserl cites the experimental phenomenology of Karl Stumpf (*I* § 86g) as a study of appearances—ways of appearing—rather than of constitutions, ways of bestowing meaning. In a perhaps unconscious bow to Stumpf, the publishers adorned the jacket of *Phenomenology in America* (James Edie, ed.) with a picture of an American flag printed in black, green, and orange. If a subject stares at it intently, then closes his eyes, he will see an image of the flag in its usual colors.

24. Heidegger's lapse into anthropologism is brief and specific. In the description of average everydayness (as in *Being and Time,* pp. H. 346–47)

he at times identifies the superficial mediocrity of the Weimar Republic's bourgeoisie, as caricatured by the national socialist critics, with the ordinary human condition, and mistakes the posturing radicalism of the revolutionaries for authentic existence. Unlike lesser thinkers, Heidegger quickly saw his error; in his later works, "dwelling poetically in the earth" replaces the *Entschlossenheit* ("anticipatory resoluteness" in the Richardson and Macquarrie translation) as the basic metaphor of authentic existence.

25. As with substituting the neologism *actum* for the conventional *datum,* we could, given the emphasis on subject as actor, substitute the neologism "pragma" for Husserl's "noema." For reasons already given (p. 206, n. 16), we shall use Husserl's term, but compare Ricoeur's examination in *Freedom and Nature: The Voluntary and the Involuntary,* pt. I, chap. 1, sec. 2.

26. This is not a repetition of the distinction between *noēsis* (*morphē*) and its "primary contents," *hylē.* Husserl considered hyletic data—like the noetic act—primordial givens of direct awareness. The noema designates not a given but the product of the intentional act (see *I* § 90). However, as we noted in note 19 above, the distinction is subject to misinterpretation and so to doubt.

27. Transcendental phenomenology can be considered "idealistic" in this sense—not as holding that "reality is mental" but as holding that the reality of the actual is its meaning rather than its brute existence (see Bowne's definition of idealism, in *Philosophy of Theism,* chap. 5). The usual objections aimed against Berkeleyan or Hegelian idealism (reality as mind dependent, mine as me) do not hold against Husserl's transcendental experientialistic "idealism."

28. In a more detailed analysis in *I* § 131, Husserl will point out that, strictly speaking, the nucleus is simply the thereness, the presence to which we attribute more or less closely related characteristics. It is this sense of the thereness of the object which naturalistic philosophy sought to capture with terms like "substance" or "matter," said to be itself devoid of any qualities but to "underlie" all attributes.

29. This is also the point of Husserl's much misinterpreted assertion that the "noema does not burn" (§ 89a). The noema is not a fireproof double of the tree; it is, as Husserl notes in § 99c, the way the tree is present in our experience. When the tree changes—say, burns—so can the noema: we now experience the noema "burning tree." But it is not the noema that is burning—or fireproof. The noema *isn't;* objects are, present as noemata.

30. The passage cited (§ 97) is, strictly, beyond the scope of our examination, since it comes after Husserl concludes his presentation of the project of phenomenology with § 96d. We cite it in the text rather than in a

footnote because it is thematically continuous with the passage under discussion.

31. For a detailed treatment, see *Experience and Judgment,* §§ 58–65.

32. Husserl never examined this in detail, but Max Scheler did, in *Formalism in Ethics and Non-Formal Ethics of Values,* and Husserl operates with a distinction closely analogous to Scheler's *Ziele* and *Werte.* Whatever Husserl's misgivings about Scheler's phenomenology (see Spiegelberg, *The Phenomenological Movement,* 1:230), the latter's analyses of the constitution of value, together with his phenomenology of emotion in *Nature of Sympathy,* make a valuable contribution. Along similar lines, though in a rather different area, see also Adolf Reinach, *Zur Phänomenologie des Rechts.*

6	**Method in Phenomenology**

1. Richard Zaner, for instance, presents the project of phenomenology as an essay on method in *The Way of Phenomenology* (New York: Pegasus, 1970), especially pp. 125–74.

2. *Gebende Anschauung.* Cairns (*Guide for Translating Husserl,* p. 56) suggests "giving" or "presentive" as a translation for *gebend;* Boyce Gibson had coined the latinate neologism "dator." Either way, the point is that in such apprehension something is presented, given; it is, adapting a term from Kant, a *synthetic* apprehension. In "seeing" the necessary relation of the opposite angles of the parallelogram or the goodness of love and the badness of hate, the subject is neither inventing nor judging; he is genuinely *seeing.* Thus *I* § 3 and pp. 15–19, above.

3. Cf. the elaboration in *FTL* § 59.

4. While Husserl normally draws his examples from the formal rather than the moral sciences, he clearly means to apply the principle to both. See Alois Roth's useful compilation of texts, *Edmund Husserls ethische Untersuchungen.*

5. On apodicticity of eidetic perception, see *CM* § 6, the entire *CM III,* but also *I* § 44, the elaboration in *FTL* §§ 58–61 (note the possibility of error, *FTL* § 58), and throughout Husserl's work. The whole project of *Fundierung* ("the grounding of science") partakes of this spirit. On the specific topic, Hans Ulrich Hoche, *Nichtempirische Erkenntnis* (Meisenheim: Hain, 1964), is helpful.

6. While we cannot hope to give a list, we can give an example. Max Weber's *verstehende Soziologie* falls into this category, enabling Alfred Schutz to use it as a springboard for a self-conscious phenomenological sociology in *The Phenomenology of the Social World.*

7. For the distinction between cause and motive, see Bernard Hang, *Kausalität und Motivation;* Paul Ricoeur, *Freedom and Nature,* pt. I, chap. 2, and chap. 3, sec. 4; cf. also Bowne's somewhat idiosyncratic conception of "volitional causality" (*Metaphysics,* chap. 4).

8. Here Alfred Schutz in sociology and Aron Gurwitsch in psychology provide clear examples; see also Bernhard Waldenfels, *Das Zwischenreich des Dialogs.*

9. I am borrowing the phrase from Bowne (*Principles of Ethics,* p. 39). Husserl, in *C* (especially § 6 and the Vienna Lecture), speaks of the "European" ideal; earlier thinkers (Masaryk, Brentano, Bolzano) spoke of the "ideal of humanity," reviving the Renaissance and Roman ideal of the *homo humanus.*

10. Ricoeur (*The Conflict of Interpretations,* pp. 17–19) sees an analogy between this centrality of the subject and Freud's conception of narcissism. The point, however, would seem more persuasive if applied to Sartre's "non-ego" (*The Transcendence of the Ego*) rather than to Husserl's "sheer I-ness," the *reines Ich,* who is always intrinsically *with an Other* (*CM V; C* § 55) and so is a *moral* subject rather than a solipsistic one. Husserl's subject would seem to be displaced from moral solipsism by his own transcendental dimension; his apparent solipsism is methodological only, not moral (*CM* § 62; *FTL* § 95).

11. There are more modest, positive examples as well; see Gerhard Husserl, "Die Frage nach dem Geltungsgrund des Rechts," pp. 153 ff., and Vladimír Kubeš, *Grundfragen der Philosophie des Rechts,* especially pp. 25–54.

12. In § 63 Husserl speaks of "observing the norms," which, he clearly assumes, have already been presented adequately and now need only be applied; § 63a, the opening of a chapter on method, is actually a summary of a method already presented.

13. In *Ideas I,* Husserl stresses the novelty of phenomenology (as in § 33), both because, in an experiential perspective, it is always novel and because of the need for a methodological vacuum (*I* § 18). He is, however, aware of the continuity of phenomenology with the history of Western thought and traces it out in *C* §§ 28–34.

14. The reader will recognize Husserl's "golden rule" from *I* § 24 or *CM* § 5 and repeated in all his works. For a succinct presentation of Husserl's experientialism, see Dorion Cairns, "An Approach to Phenomenology," pp. 3–18; on experience as *Evidenz,* see Husserl's *Experience and Judgment* § 6.

15. *I* § 83, especially pars. e, f; also "vocations" passage in *C* §§ 40 f.

16. Husserl presents a helpful summary in *FTL* § 95.

17. Husserl's § 65 served as the methodological model for this study.

Following his strictures, we have sought throughout not to argue or speculate but to *see* and point out, step by step, grasping and articulating clearly even at the cost of belaboring and resorting to un-Husserlian examples. For detailed guidance, we relied on *CM* §§ 24–26 and on Husserl's credo in *C* § 7.

18. In Husserl, elaborations of the concept of *Evidenz* ("evident givenness," *not* "evidence" in the English sense, *not* "self-evidence") are in *CM III, CM* § 41; *FTL* §§ 58–61; and *E&J* §§ 3–6. Also relevant are David M. Levin, *Reason and Evidence in Husserl's Phenomenology,* and Emmanuel Levinas, *The Theory of Intuition in Husserl's Phenomenology.*

19. In his later work, Husserl increasingly came to regard this method of *freie Phantasie*—a free variation of hypothetical examples—as crucial to phenomenology (see *CM* §§ 19, 27, 36; *FTL* §§ 87–88; and *E&J* §§ 39–42). The principle, however, is already fully contained in the passage under examination, *I* § 70.

20. *Deskriptive Wesenslehre der reinen Erlebnisse,* rendered by Boyce Gibson as "descriptive theory of the Essence of pure experience." Following Cairns's *Guide to Translating Husserl,* it would be "descriptive eidetic doctrine of pure mental processes." Instead of attempting a translation, we shall speak of a descriptive study of the necessary structures of lived experience (see a consideration of the terms *Wesen* [above, p. 197, n. 12] and *Erlebnis* [above, pp. 157–59]).

21. This, at least in Ricoeur's generous interpretation of Heidegger in *The Conflict of Interpretations* (pp. 230–33), is the conclusion at which Heidegger hints when he interprets the task of humans as one of fusing together the four dimensions of Being—the sky, the earth, the gods and the mortals ("Das Ding," in *Vorträge und Aufsätze,* pp. 163–81) or as the articulating of Being in language (*Introduction to Metaphysics*). Ricoeur himself reaches that conclusion explicitly (pp. 234–36). In that sense, the subject (and so phenomenology) remains central. Hermeneutics does not replace it; rather, in Ricoeur's phrase, it is "grafted onto" it (pp. 6–11).

7   Phenomenology and Philosophy

1. The claim that language carries a cultural bias is distinct from the claim that linguistic expression distorts (certain aspects of) reality simply by articulation (Jaspers, Heidegger). The latter claim, to the extent to which it is legitimate (Husserl's "twilight zone," *I* § 69c; Ricoeur, *Freud and Philosophy*), calls for a hermeneutic extension of phenomenology.

The former claim, by contrast, does no more than acknowledge a generic characteristic of *all* experience, in no way peculiar to its linguistic articulation—the "parochialism of the particular" which Husserl calls "natural" subjectivity. Here the transcendental bracketing applies to language as well as to experience, leading Husserl to the conclusion that language can, but need not, distort: univocity is possible as transcendental (Lothar Eley, "Afterword" to Husserl's *E&J;* and Husserl on language as clear articulation, *I* § 66; *FTL* § 3 and passim).

2. While the text must speak for itself, clarified only by the experience it articulates, the reader might, subsequently, consult Dorion Cairns's classic summary of Husserl's critique of empiricism and idealism in "An Approach to Phenomenology," pp. 3–18. Here (p. 3) Cairns also makes the point that a study of phenomenology must itself be phenomenological, letting the text speak rather than speculating about it.

3. Husserl explicitly authorized Eugen Fink's characterization of phenomenology as a "radical empiricism" (Fink, "Die phänomenologische Philosophie Edmund Husserls in der gegenwärtigen Kritik," pp. 319 ff; cited in H. Spiegelberg, *The Phenomenological Movement,* 1:136; see also *I* § 20b).

4. Please note: We are offering a paraphrase designed to bring out the point of the passage rather than a translation designed to re-present it. For a translation, consult the Boyce Gibson edition or the new translation by Fred Kersten, as of this writing in preparation by Martinus Nijhoff of The Hague.

5. This sentence sums up most succinctly Husserl's conception of language. It assumes that experience is already articulate: language brings its structure to expression rather than imposes one on an experience inchoate without it (see n. 1 above and chap. 8, pp. 180–81).

6. Translating *Sache* as "thing" would be inaccurate in this context. *Die Sache* is a "thing" in the sense of "the thing of it is that . . ." It is "the matter" in the phrase "getting to the heart of the matter," or, as Dorion Cairns suggests (*Guide for Translating Husserl,* p. 96), the "affair." Husserl certainly is not suggesting a turn to some "thing-itself," in the sense of *Ding an sich,* but rather a return to experience. The colloquialism "getting down to cases" may be the most faithful rendition.

7. It is this stabilized technical usage which Dorion Cairns treats as definitive (*Guide for Translating Husserl,* p. 46) as "mental process (*or* occurrence) . . . ," though he notes the second, nontechnical, sense as well —"loose sense, rarely: 'experience.' "

8. There is a reason for this. In the first part of *I,* Husserl is concerned with stressing, against naive objectivism, that experience is *a subject's experience* (*not* "subjective" experience!). Not until §§ 85 ff. does he get

around to distinguishing, within a subject's experience, the noetic (the experiencing) and the noematic (the experienced) aspect, thus creating a need for a technical terminology.

9. That is why Husserl can say, in *E&J*, that evident givenness (*Evidenz*) is *Erfahrung* (§ 6), even though, in terms of the usage of *Ideas I*, the entire section simply cries out for *Erlebnis* as the term for experience.

10. The term *Anschauung* again translates with ease into Czech (*nazírání*) but with difficulty into English. Cairns (*Guide to Translating Husserl*, p. 8) suggests "intuition," which we find utterly unacceptable for reasons given in the text. The etymological equivalent would be "onlooking" (Cairns: "(loose sense:) view"). We have wavered among the loose metaphor "seeing" (suggested by *I* § 19c), "grasping," and, perhaps least problematically, "awareness."

11. That is also why Husserl insists that philosophy cannot generalize the results of the special sciences (that is, build on experience as interpreted by the sciences) but must have independent access to experience (see Husserl's essay, "Philosophy as a Rigorous Science").

12. Husserl's critique of idealism in *Ideas I* may appear superseded by his later treatments of the topic (see the critique of "logicism" in *FTL* §§ 73–80 and his elaboration of transcendental philosophy in *CM*). The *Ideas* treatment is indeed cursory and superficial, but perhaps for that very reason it clearly exhibits Husserl's basic insight: the givenness of eidetic structures which leads him to a transcendental experientialism equally critical of any denial of the reality of "ideas" *and* of any denial of the primacy of experiential *Evidenz*.

13. Husserl's text here is complicated by the fact that he has not yet presented the distinction between "natural" and transcendental subjectivity. That is why we have inverted his order of presentation, examining his second chapter, which is still introductory, only after presenting the project of phenomenology itself.

14. It is precisely Husserl's experientialist insistence that immanent *eidē* are objects of awareness, analogous to sense awareness, that enables him to speak of both certainty and error. Thus the entire elaboration of awareness as *Evidenz* in *FTL* §§ 58–61; *E&J* §§ 70–79; and throughout Husserl's work.

15. The incorporation of the objective, capable of presentation only as the "twilight zone" of *I* § 69, does, as we have been noting, require the incorporation of a hermeneutic dimension (see Ricoeur on linguistics and psychology, "Existence and Hermeneutics," *The Conflict of Interpretations*, pp. 3–26 and passim).

16. Comparison of Kosík's work with classical Marxist works graphically illustrates the impact of phenomenology on Marxism.

17. Bowne, *Philosophy of Theism;* note especially his assertion that "mechanism is simply teleology read backwards" (p. 94).

18. "Dogmatic" here has no pejorative connotations. It is a *terminus technicus* which Husserl uses to describe any science that works uncritically within a particular regional perspective, in contrast with sciences of the "philosophic" standpoint that question their own assumptions. In practice, any science has its "dogmatic" and its "philosophic" aspect. (See the discussion of theory and metatheory, above, pp. 169–70.)

19. Merleau-Ponty, Preface to *Phenomenology of Perception,* pp. vii–xxi.

20. Here we are not gainsaying Dorion Cairns's presentation of phenomenology as a method (see "An Approach to Phenomenology"). Rather, we would hold that claim to be valid precisely because Cairns extends the meaning of "method" to the extent of what we prefer to describe as *metatheory*.

21. See Kohák, "Physics, Meta-Physics and Metaphysics."

22. An analysis of the success and the crisis of Western science can be found in *C* §§ 1–3. Note also the contrast between "indirect quantification" (*C* § 9b) and the world of lived experience (*Lebenswelt*) (*C* § 9h).

23. The opposite of "real" is not "unreal"; the unreal, strictly speaking, would not be at all. Kant's real 30.00 thalers are given in primary original experience; the imaginary 30.00 thalers are not originally given but are, in Husserl's term, *fundiert,* based upon or derivative from lived experience or imagination.

24. Husserl in fact explicitly labels both metaphysical conceptions, the "subjective" and the "objective," as abstractions from the unity of primordial awareness, as in *C* § 10 and elsewhere.

25. Husserl expanded his Paris lectures into the *Cartesian Meditations.* His lecture notes have also been published as *The Paris Lectures.* See the Bibliography at the end of this volume.

8   **The Horizon of Phenomenology**

1. Here the *locus classicus* is Sartre's *Transcendence of the Ego,* with its interpretation of the sheer subject dimension of experience as a homunculus called "the transcendental Ego" (which Sartre then rightly rejects). Gurwitsch (*Studies in Phenomenology and Psychology*) offers a far more perceptive reading when he speaks of the "transcendental function" of consciousness (p. xxiv), though he then misleadingly labels his conception of the self "non-egological" (pp. 287–300).

2. Following the American Personalist usage, we shall use *Person* as a

terminus technicus, in the sense of an "existential" (in Heidegger's sense) designating the transcendental dimension of subjectivity in its fullness as a presence rather than as an epistemological vanishing point. Person thus designates a way of being rather than a type of entity. See also Husserl, *Ideen II,* pt. III and app. XII.

3. The process, as we shall note (pp. 184–85), was initiated by Husserl himself, who notes the problem in *C* § 43c and sets out to explore the personal (*Ideen II*), physical (*Ideen III*), and historical (*C*) density of subject presence.

4. Though we shall not elaborate it here, that is also the answer to the criticism of Husserl implicit in Heidegger's claim (as in *Introduction to Metaphysics* or in *Unterwegs zur Sprache*) that speech conceals as it reveals. Were experience in its immediacy in-articulate, receiving articulation only in speech, that would be so. Husserl's point, however, is precisely that experience is already articulate as lived so that speech can be its faithful expression, the *getreuer Ausdruck* we noted above. See also *FTL* §§ 1–3 and elsewhere throughout Husserl's work, as in *CM* § 62b where he stresses that phenomenology "tut . . . nichts anderes . . . als den *Sinne auslegen, den diese Welt für uns alle vor jedem Philosophieren hat* ("does nothing except articulate the prephilosophical intelligibility of the world of our lived experience").

5. "Das *'Ich denke' muss alle meine Vorstellungen begleiten können"* ("The 'I Think' must be capable of accompanying all my appresentations"; *I* § 57c). This is why the phenomenological ego can, as Husserl points out in *CM* § 15, establish himself as a "disinterested onlooker" above the naively interested ego.

6. This is why we have preferred the term transcendental "experientialism" rather than transcendental "idealism" as a description of Husserl's philosophical stance. It is also why we see a closer kinship between Husserl's work and the European "humanism" of, say, Masaryk or the American "personalism" of Bowne (in spite of the anthropologism which, as Husserl warns it would [*I* § 51], affects their work) than between Husserl and traditional idealists like Green or Bradley.

7. Note that Husserl consistently spells "ego" with a lowercase "e." Since a native German speaker will quite automatically capitalize any noun, this supports our contention (see pp. 44–45, above) that Husserl thinks of "ego" as a personal pronoun, "I," what I am, rather than as the psychologistic homunculus, "the Ego," which I could be said to "have." Note also that Ricoeur's later criticism of Heidegger's "short route" to ontology (*The Conflict of Interpretations,* p. 6) strictly parallels Husserl's criticism here of his own Cartesian shortcut.

8. Landgrebe, *Phänomenologie und Geschichte,* p. 142.

9. The phenomenological significance of James's work has, however, been recognized, for instance by James Edie in his "Notes on the Philosophical Anthropology of William James," pp. 110–32.

10. "Ein Brief über den Humanismus," *Platons Lehre von der Wahrheit,* pp. 53–119.

11. For a recent summary of a Personalist analysis, see P. A. Bertocci, "The Essence of Person."

12. Note especially the *Beilagen*—appendixes which make up almost a third of the volume and which Husserl never worked into the text. In this context, see especially app. 12.ii.

13. Husserl's personalism is also immune to Ricoeur's gentle critique (*History and Truth,* pp. 133–61). Ricoeur deals with a psychological presentation of personalism (Emanuel Mounier's) rather than an explicitly philosophical one, writing in appreciation rather than in criticism.

14. As evidence that not all are misled by the metaphor of power, see Landgrebe, *Phänomenologie und Geschichte,* pp. 145–47.

15. "The self is a relation which relates itself to its own self, or it is that in the relation [which accounts for it] that the relation relates itself to its own self; the self is not the relation but [consists in the fact] that the relation relates itself to its own self" (Kierkegaard, *The Sickness unto Death,* p. 17).

16. For "retention" and "protention" see *I* §§ 81–82; an elaboration is in *The Phenomenology of Internal Time-Consciousness,* §§ 10–16.

17. On self-contradiction, see E. S. Brightman, *Moral Laws,* chap. 6, secs. v–viii.

18. That is why, in constituting temporality, the subject inevitably constitutes a historicity as well (see David Carr, *Phenomenology and the Problem of History*).

19. Husserl's analysis, *Ideen II* §§ 1–18; see also Jan Patočka, *Přirozený svět jako filosofický problém.*

20. Even in *Ideas I,* Husserl acknowledges the recalcitrance of reality implicitly in recognizing the privileged status of our "natural" as contrasted with "ideal" world. (§ 3), in introducing the notion of *hylē* (§ 85), and explicitly in speaking of the "X" in § 131. For, as we noted above, "the noema does not burn" (see p. 218, n. 29).

21. Ricoeur, *The Conflict of Interpretations,* pp. 6–11.

Bibliography

Husserl subtitled three of his works "introductions" to phenomenology: the first volume of *Ideen, Cartesian Meditations,* and *Crisis.* In our text, we have followed Husserl's presentation of the project of phenomenology in the first two-thirds of *Ideen zu einer reinen Phänomenologie und phänomenologischen Philosophie; Erstes Buch, Allgemeine Einführung in die reine Phänomenologie (Ideas Towards a Pure Phenomenology and Phenomenological Philosophy; Book One, General Introduction to Pure Phenomenology*—hence *Ideas I).* The reader can gain a sufficient working grasp of phenomenology—though by no means of the full scope and richness of Husserl's thought—from that presentation.

The German text of *Ideas I* we have used is the most readily available one, prepared by Walter Biemel, which appeared as volume III of the *Husserliana* series in 1950. It is not simply a reprint of the three earlier editions but incorporates Husserl's proposed revisions and additions as well. Since Husserl's marginal notes and "improvements" frequently seem out of context and use the terminology of later works, which is often misleading when inserted in *Ideas I,* the reader might want to check the text against the textual notes appended to the volume.

An English translation, prepared by W. R. Boyce Gibson in 1931, is readily available in a Collier paperback edition, reprinted several times since 1962. Since that translation is not without some problems, we have refrained from citing it, instead citing the German of the Biemel edition, along with our own translations or paraphrases, as most convenient. A reader bewildered by the English translation but not at home in German might find it worthwhile to consult Paul Ricoeur's French translation, *Idées directrices pour une phénoménologie* (Paris, 1950), which adds a helpful commentary to a beautifully lucid text. A new English translation by Fred Kersten is in preparation by Martinus Nijhoff and should be available shortly.

The text of *Cartesian Meditations* is also available both in the original and in an English translation. During Husserl's lifetime, however, only a French translation appeared in print, as *Méditations carté-* **227** *siennes* (Paris, 1931); the lectures were delivered at the Sorbonne on 23 and 25 February, 1929. Husserl held back the German text and continued to revise it until, sometime in 1935, he set it aside in order to concentrate on his last work, *Crisis*.

The German text available today was edited by Stephan Strasser on the basis of the original German typescript, the French translation, and Husserl's subsequent revisions. It appeared as the first volume of the *Husserliana* series, *Cartesianische Meditationen und Pariser Vorträge,* in 1950. *Pariser Vorträge* presents the text of the lectures, expanded later as *Cartesian Meditations*. Both works are available in English, *CM* in a translation prepared by Dorion Cairns (*Cartesian Meditations*) and published by Martinus Nijhoff in 1960, and *Pariser Vorträge* in a translation by Peter Koestenbaum (*The Paris Lectures*) also published by Nijhoff, in 1967, with a rather handy translator's introduction.

Crisis, or, to give its full title, *Die Krisis der europäischen Wissenschaften und die transzendentale Phänomenologie,* is Husserl's last work. Husserl presented its major theme in lectures in Vienna and Prague in 1935 and published what are Parts I and II of the present text in the Yugoslav journal *Philosophia* in 1937. In August of that year, Husserl's terminal illness set in and the work remained unfinished.

The text presently available is Walter Biemel's reconstruction based on Husserl's manuscript. It appeared as the sixth volume of the *Husserliana* series in 1962, together with the text of related lectures and papers.

The text is available in English in David Carr's translation (*The Crisis of European Sciences and Transcendental Phenomenology*) published by Northwestern University Press in 1970. Carr's translation has come in for some criticism, for instance for the rather misleading rendering of Husserl's *Evidenz* ("evident givenness") by the English "self-evidence." Still, it has the virtue of a fresh, readily comprehensible English which makes up for whatever it may lack in technical precision by conveying the spirit of the work to an average reader more faithfully than many technical translations. To be sure, for specific points of the text, it is crucial to consult the original, but that is true even of the work of the grand old man of Husserlian translation, Dorion Cairns, whose rendering of *Anschauung* as "intuition" can also lead to misunderstanding. Ultimately, though for precision there is no substitute for the original, Carr's work has the great virtue that even the uninitiated can read it with comprehension. That, rather than the possibility of flawless retranslation into the original, is the mark of a great translation.

The three volumes—*Ideas I, Cartesian Meditations,* and *Crisis*— do, in broad outline, present the same insight and follow the same pattern of presentation. In all three cases, Husserl sets out by noting the intrinsic structure of lived experience and the quasi-theoretical bias of common-sense interpretation which obscures it, then proposes to bracket that bias and shows how this is done, explains the structure of consciousness and its correlates in brackets, and presents his conclusion as the propaedeutic for philosophy and science in a radically experiential perspective.

The emphasis, however, varies markedly from volume to volume. In *Ideas,* Husserl is writing under the full impact of his discovery of the possibility of a fundamental shift of viewpoint from the conventional reism of common sense and science alike to a radically experiential perspective. Much of the work is devoted to an analysis of ordinary experience, of its bias, of the possibility of bracketing it, and of describing self and world as experience. Husserl seems unconcerned about the special problems posed by the conception of the pure ego or by the relation of such a radically experiential view of the world to the public world. Even the crucial topic of intentionality comes up only halfway through the work, almost as an afterthought. Husserl is not speculating or analyzing here. His overriding concern is to present phenomenology as tool and perspective to the reader.

As Dorion Cairns points out in his *Conversations with Husserl and Fink* (and as is suggested, for instance, in *FTL* § 107c), Husserl came to regard all three volumes of his *Ideen* as an early and naive attempt which needs to be brought to the level of sophistication that marks *CM* or *FTL,* and not without reason. Yet precisely the naiveté and freshness of *Ideas I* makes them far less obscure and more readily intelligible than Husserl's later works. While the full depth of Husserl's work can by no means be found here alone, we would still— Husserl to the contrary—consider this the key, presenting the basic insight which unlocks the later works, including *CM.*

In *Cartesian Meditations,* the pattern remains constant but the emphasis changes radically. The presentation of natural standpoint and its basic bracketing, which occupied Husserl throughout the first half of *Ideas I,* is mentioned only as a preface and dispensed with in barely seven sections. Husserl's preoccupation here is with the pure subject which, in *Ideas I,* warranted only the short § 57. It would not be altogether inaccurate to say that Husserl is here concerned with the metaphysical foundations of the project of phenomenology, though he would surely reject that adjective. In *CM II,* he distinguishes the natural subject from the transcendental subject-function and analyzes intentionality as the basic structure of the latter. *CM III* presents an intentional analysis of the world, *CM IV* that of the transcendental ego. Finally, in *CM V,* Husserl tackles the crucial problem of inter-subjectivity.

Altogether, *Cartesian Meditations,* perhaps Husserl's most polished, tightly argued work, may also be the best introduction to phenomenology for philosophers whose concern is not experience and the basic assumptions of social and human science but rather the possibility of a philosophy which is neither materialistic nor subjectivistic. For that is what Husserl presents here. For all the familiar landmarks, Husserl's conclusion in *I* § 56, "no subjective idealism!" holds unchanged. What Husserl is presenting is a transcendentalist alternative to naturalism and subjectivism.

Yet, as Husserl noted in *Crisis* (§ 43), the abrupt transcendental turn of *Ideas I* and *Cartesian Meditations* can be misleading. If the transcendental turn is not preceded by the thorough phenomenology of *Ideas I,* which fixates experience in its lived unity within phenomenological brackets, it can easily appear as the kind of subjectivism Husserl is vehement in rejecting throughout his work. The point is not to substitute "mental objects" for the putative transcendent objects of the natural standpoint, but to substitute a radically experiential, transcendental perspective for the naive realism, whether physicalistic or psychologistic, of common sense. The *Cartesian Meditations,* finally, are a fine introduction to phenomenology for readers who have already grasped the point of *Ideas I.*

Husserl's third Introduction, *The Crisis of European Sciences,* returns to some of the themes of *Ideas I,* though in a broader context. While in *Ideas I* the initial context was ordinary experience, in *Crisis* it is the whole history of Western thought, tracing the physicalist and transcendental alternatives since the Renaissance. Only in part III does Husserl return to familiar ground, dealing with the bias of common-sense interpretation and proposing a bracketing.

The problems are now familiar, but the presentation is far broader, dealing with the question of the *Umwelt* rather than of particular object. Thus when the problem of the pure ego arises, as in due course it must, Husserl is able to resolve it by recognizing the pure ego as *Ich als Ur-Ich,* in the context of a "we."

Husserl did not live long enough to edit, much less to criticize, his *Crisis.* When the manuscript was finally published, after the war, numerous scholars took on the criticism, with reason. *Crisis* is a rushed, unfinished work. But it is also a work of grand vision. Since we find Husserl's true greatness not in his undeniable competence as a philosophical technician but in the significance of his work as a reaffirmation of the European ideal of *humanitas,* of the veridicity, value, and intelligibility of subject experience, against both epistemological and moral skepsis, we consider *Crisis,* together with the Vienna Lecture, a uniquely valuable work, a testimony to the greatness of his spirit.

To be sure, that greatness is not to be found in *Crisis* alone, or even in the three Introductions taken together. Much of the significance of Husserl's work lies in the fact that he gave the humanistic vision rigorous philosophical substance—and that is to be found in the investigations of *Ideen II* and *III,* in the detailed analyses of *FTL, E&J, LU,* as well as in the special focus of works like *The Phenomenology of Internal Time-Consciousness.* The reader who has followed us in our analysis of Husserl's first presentation of the project of phenomenology in *Ideas I* cannot yet claim to "know Husserl." We do believe, however, that he has gained the key, the basic insight, which makes Husserl's other works accessible.

For a full bibliography of Husserl's writings, consult the following:

Eley Lothar. "Husserl-Bibliographie (1945–59)." *Zeitschrift für philosophische Forschung* 13 (1959): 357–67.

Jan Patočka. "Husserl-Bibliographie." *Revue internationale de philosophie* 1 (1939): 374–97.

Jean Raes. "Supplément à la bibliographie de Husserl." *Revue internationale de philosophie* 4 (1950): 469–75.

Husserl's Works Used in
This Study

Cartesianische Meditationen und Pariser Vorträge. The Hague: Martinus Nijhoff, 1950; reprinted 1973. *Cartesian Meditations.* Translated by Dorion Cairns. The Hague: Martinus Nijhoff, 1960. *The Paris Lectures.* Translated by Peter Koestenbaum. The Hague: Martinus Nijhoff, 1967.

Erfahrung und Urteil. Edited by Ludwig Landgrebe. Prague: Academia, 1939; Hamburg: Meiner, 1974. *Experience and Judgment.* Translated by James S. Churchill and Karl Ameriks. Evanston, Ill.: Northwestern University Press, 1973.

Formale und transzendentale Logik. Halle: Niemeyer, 1929; The Hague: Martinus Nijhoff, 1974. *Formal and Transcendental Logic.* Translated by Dorion Cairns. The Hague: Martinus Nijhoff, 1969.

"Edmund Husserl: A Letter to Arnold Metzger" (opposed German and English text). Translated by Erazim Kohák. *Philosophical Forum* 21 (1964): 48–68.

Die Idee der Phänomenologie. Edited by Walter Biemel. The Hague: Martinus Nijhoff, 1950. *The Idea of Phenomenology.* Translated by W. Alston and G. Nakhnikian. The Hague: Martinus Nijhoff, 1968.

Ideen zu einer reinen Phänomenologie und phänomenologischen Philosophie
  Vol. I: *Allgemeine Einführung in die reine Phänomenologie.* Halle: Niemeyer, 1913; The Hague: Martinus Nijhoff, 1950. *Ideas towards a Pure Phenomenology and Phenomenological Philosophy.* Translated by W. R. Boyce Gibson. New York: Macmillan, 1931; Collier, 1962, and reprints.
  Vol. II: *Phänomenologische Untersuchungen zur Konstitution.* Edited by Marly Biemel. The Hague: Martinus Nijhoff, 1952.
  Vol. III: *Die Phänomenologie und die Fundamente der Wissenschaften.* Edited by Marly Biemel. The Hague: Martinus Nijhoff, 1971.

Die Krisis der europäischen Wissenschaften und die transzendentale Phänomenologie. Edited by Walter Biemel. The Hague: Martinus Nijhoff, 1962; reprinted 1969. *The Crisis of European Sciences and Transcendental Phenomenology.* Translated by David Carr. Evanston, Ill.: Northwestern University Press, 1970.

Logische Untersuchungen. Tübingen: M. Niemeyer [1913], 1968. *Logical Investigations.* Translated by J. N. Findlay. New York Humanities Press, 1970.

Phänomenologische Psychologie (1925). Edited by Walter Biemel. The Hague: Martinus Nijhoff, 1962.

Philosophie als strenge Wissenschaft [*Logos* I (1910)]. Frankfurt: Klostermann, 1965. "Philosophy as a Rigorous Science." Translated by Quentin Lauer. In *Phenomenology and the Crisis of Philosophy,* edited by Lauer. New York: Harper, 1965.

Die Vorlesungen zur Phänomenologie des inneren Zeitbewusstseins. Edited by R. Boehm. Halle: Niemeyer, 1929. *The Phenomenology of Internal Time-Consciousness.* Translated by James Spencer Churchill. Bloomington, Ind.: Indiana University Press, 1964.

Zur Phänomenologie der Intersubjektivität. Edited by Iso Kern. The Hague: Martinus Nijhoff, 1973.

Secondary Sources

Given the methodological strictures within which we have conducted our inquiry, the use of secondary sources requires justification. We had, after all, set out to *see,* to grasp in evident givenness what there is to be seen in the text itself, not to reconstruct the project of phenomenology from a jigsaw puzzle of secondary sources. The sole legitimate reference beyond the text, we had said, is to lived experience itself; the sole legitimate question is, "What *in experience* is Husserl pointing out?" Accordingly, in the initial presentation of the project of phenomenology (chapters 1–5 above), we have relied solely on Husserl's text and our experience, restricting other references strictly to the notes and even there only to Husserl's other two "introductions" and to his elaboration of *I* in *FTL.*

Phenomenology, however, works in a context of philosophy and has philosophical significance as well. For that reason, having completed the initial presentation, we gradually broadened our range of references, first in the notes and then the text of the last chapter, where we referred to Husserl's other writings, to the works of his successors and commentators, and to authors whose thought is relevant to Husserl's project without being neccessarily continuous with it. The purpose of the bibliography of secondary sources is to acknowledge our indebtedness and to offer some guidance to those works.

Works which are directly relevant to Husserl's project of phenomenology have been marked with an asterisk (*). Those without an
asterisk include works continuous with Husserl's project as its horizon
but not necessarily relevant specifically to it. Finally, we have included
(in parentheses) all authors mentioned in the text, indicating which of
their works occasioned the mention. In no sense do we wish to make
the least pretense to completeness. That was not the purpose of our
study, which was *seeing,* a confrontation of the *Evidenz* rather than a
gathering of evidence. We offer our bibliography solely as we have
used it—as an incomplete and unsystematic glance over the horizon of
the project of phenomenology.

*Adorno, Theodor, *Zur Metakritik der Erkenntnistheorie.* Frankfurt:
Suhrkamp, 1970.
(Ayer, Alfred J.) *Language, Truth and Logic.* London: Gollancz,
1946 (note especially the description of experiential grounding in
the introduction to the second edition).
*Berger, Gaston. *The* Cogito *in Husserl's Philosophy.* Translated by
K. McLaughlin. Evanston, Ill.: Northwestern University Press,
1972.
Bertocci, Peter. "The Essence of Person," *Monist,* in press.
———. *Introduction to the Philosophy of Religion.* New York:
Prentice-Hall, 1951.
———. *The Person God Is.* New York: Humanities Press, 1970.
(Bolzano, Bernard). *Ueber die Wohltätigkeit. O pokroku a dobročin-
nosti.* Translated into Czech by Vladimír Hořejší. Prague: Vyšeh-
rad, 1951.
Bowne, Borden P. *Metaphysics.* 2d ed. New York: American Book,
1910.
———. *Personalism.* Boston: Houghton Mifflin, 1908.
———. *Philosophy of Theism.* New York: Harper, 1887.
———. *Principles of Ethics.* New York: Harper, 1892.
———. *Theory of Thought and Knowledge.* New York: American
Book, 1897.
(Bradley, F. H.) *Appearance and Reality.* London: Sonnenschein,
1893.
Brentano, Franz. *Grundlegung und Aufbau der Ethik. The Founda-
tion and Construction of Ethics.* Translated by L. Schneewind. New
York: Humanities Press, 1973.

————. *The Origin of the Knowledge of Right and Wrong.* Translated by C. Hague. Westminster: Constable, 1902.

————. *Wahrheit und Evidenz.* Leipzig: Meiner, 1930. *The True and the Evident.* Translated by R. Chisholm et al. London: Routledge, 1966.

(Brightman, Edgar S.) *Moral Laws.* New York: Abingdon, 1933.

————. *Nature and Values.* New York: Abingdon, 1945.

————. *Person and Reality.* Edited by P. Bertocci. New York: Humanities Press, 1957.

*Cairns, Dorion. "An Approach to Phenomenology." In *Philosophical Essays in Memory of Edmund Husserl,* edited by M. Farber, pp. 3–18.

*————. *Conversations with Husserl and Fink.* The Hague: Martinus Nijhoff, 1976.

***————. *Guide for Translating Husserl.* The Hague: Martinus Nijhoff, 1973.

(Campbell, C. A.) *On Selfhood and Godhood.* New York: Humanities Press, 1957.

(Carnap, Rudolf.) *Der Logische Aufbau der Welt.* Berlin: Weltkreis, 1928. *The Logical Structure of the World.* Translated by F. George. Berkeley, Calif.: University of California Press, 1967.

Carr, David. *Phenomenology and the Problem of History.* Evanston, Ill.: Northwestern University Press, 1974.

*Chapman, Harmon M. *Sensations and Phenomenology.* Bloomington, Ind.: Indiana University Press, 1966.

————. "The Transcendental Standpoint and Method." Ph.D. dissertation, Harvard University, 1933.

(Chomsky, Noam.) *Language and Mind.* New York: Harcourt, Brace, 1972.

*Christoff, Daniel, ed. *Edmund Husserl ou le retour aux choses.* Paris: Seghers, 1966.

*Claesges, Ulrich, ed. *Perspektiven transcendental-phänomenologisher Forschung.* Festschrift for Ludwig Landgrebe. The Hague: Martinus Nijhoff, 1972.

*Diemer, Alwin. *Edmund Husserl: Versuch einer systematischen Darstellung seiner Phänomenologie.* Meisenheim: Haim, 1956.

Edie, James. "Notes on the Philosophical Anthropology of William James." In *An Invitation to Phenomenology,* edited by J. Edie, pp. 110–32.

Edie, James, ed. *An Invitation to Phenomenology.* Chicago: Quadrangle, 1965.

————. *Phenomenology in America.* Chicago: Quadrangle, 1967.

*Eigler, Gunther. *Metaphysische Voraussetzungen in Husserl's Zeitanalysen.* Meisenheim: Haim, 1961.

*Eley, Lothar. "Nachwort" to *Erfahrung und Urteil.* Re-edition. Hamburg: Meiner, 1974. "Afterword" to *Experience and Judgment.* Translated by Karl Ameriks. Evanston, Ill.: Northwestern University Press, 1973.

(Ellenberger, Henri.) *The Discovery of the Unconscious.* New York: Basic Books, 1970.

*Embree, Lester E., ed. *Life-World and Consciousness: Essays for Aron Gurwitsch.* Evanston, Ill.: Northwestern University Press, 1972.

*Farber, Marvin, ed. *Philosophical Essays in Memory of Edmund Husserl.* Cambridge: Harvard University Press, 1940.

(Feuerbach, Ludwig.) *Sämtliche Werke.* Edited by W. Bolin and F. Jodl. 13 vols. Stuttgart: Frommann, 1903–11.

*Fink, Eugen. "Die phänomenologische Philosophie Edmund Husserls in der gegenwärtigen Kritik." *Kantstudien* 38: 319 ff.

*————. *Phänomenologie—lebendig oder tod?* Karlsruhe: Badenia, 1969.

*————. *Sein, Wahrheit, Welt.* The Hague: Martinus Nijhoff, 1958.

*————. *Studien zur Phänomenologie, 1930–39.* The Hague: Martinus Nijhoff, 1966.

(Gadamer, Hans-Georg.) *Kleine Schriften.* Tübingen: Mohr, 1967.

(————.) *Wahrheit und Methode.* Tübingen: Mohr, 1965. *Truth and Method.* Translated by G. Baden and J. Cumming. New York: Seabury, 1975.

(Grajewski, Maurice J.) *The Formal Distinction of Duns Scotus.* Washington, D.C.: Catholic University of America, 1944.

(Green, T. H.) *Prolegomena to Ethics.* Edited by A. C. Bradley. Oxford: Clarendon Press, 1883.

(————.) *Works of T. H. Green.* Vols. 1–2. London: Longmans, Green, 1894.

*Gurwitsch, Aron. *Phenomenology and the Theory of Science.* Edited by Lester Embree. Evanston, Ill.: Northwestern University Press, 1974.

*————. *Studies in Phenomenology and Psychology.* Evanston, Ill.: Northwestern University Press, 1966.

*Hang, Bernhard. *Kausalität und Motivation.* The Hague: Martinus Nijhoff, 1973.

Heidegger, Martin. *Basic Works.* Edited by D. F. Krell. New York: Harper & Row, 1977.

————. *Die Einführung in die Metaphysik.* Tübingen: Niemeyer, 1953. *Introduction to Metaphysics.* Translated by Ralph Manheim. New Haven, Conn.: Yale University Press, 1959.

*————. *Die Grundprobleme der Phänomenologie* [1927]. Frankfurt: Klostermann, 1975.

————. *Kant und das Problem der Metaphysik.* Bonn: Cohen, 1929. *Kant and the Problem of Metaphysics.* Translated by James Spencer Churchill. Bloomington, Ind.: Indiana University Press, 1962.

————. *Platons Lehre von der Wahrheit. Mit einem Brief über den "Humanismus."* Bern: Francke, 1947.

————. *Poetry, Language, Thought.* Translated by A. Hoffstadter. New York: Harper & Row, 1977.

(————.) *Der Satz vom Grund.* Pfullingen: Noeske, 1957.

*————. *Sein und Zeit.* Halle: Niemeyer, 1927. *Being and Time.* Translated by John Macquarrie and Edward Robinson. New York: Harper, 1962.

(————.) *Unterwegs zur Sprache.* Pfullingen: Neske, 1959 (especially pp. 157–268).

(————.) *Vom Wesen des Grundes.* Frankfurt: Klostermann, 1955. *The Essence of Reasons.* Translated by Terrence Malick. Evanston, Ill.: Northwestern University Press, 1969.

————. *Vorträge und Aufsätze.* Pfullingen: Neske, 1954 (especially phenomenology of object presence in "Das Ding," pp. 163–85; cf. *I* § 131).

(————.) *Zur Seinsfrage.* Frankfurt: Klostermann, 1958.

*Hoche, Hans Ulrich. *Nichtempirische Erkenntnis: analytische und synthetische Urteile* a priori *bei Kant und bei Husserl.* Meisenheim: Haim, 1964.

*Holenstein, Elmar. *Phänomenologie der Assoziation.* The Hague: Martinus Nijhoff, 1972 (especially on the concept of passive genesis).

Husserl, Gerhard. "Die Frage nach dem Geltungsgrund des Rechts." *Zeitschrift für Rechtsphilosophie in Lehre und Praxis* (erroneously cited in most sources as *"Zentralblatt für Rechtsphilosophie"*) 5, no. 3 (July 1931): 151–84.

————. *Recht und Welt.* Leipzig: Meiner, 1929.

Ihde, Don. *Sense and Significance.* New York: Humanities Press (for Duquesne University Press), 1973.

*Ingarden, Roman. *On the Motives which Led Husserl to Transcendental Idealism.* Translated by A. Hannibalson. The Hague: Martinus Nijhoff, 1975.

(James, William.) *Essays in Radical Empiricism.* New York: Longmans, Green, 1912.

(————.) "The Essence of Humanism." *The Journal of Philosophy, Psychology and the Scientific Method* 2, no. 12 (8 June 1905).

(————.) *The Principles of Psychology.* New York: Holt, 1890.

(Jarvie, Ian.) *A Revolution in Anthropology.* London: Routledge, 1964.

Jaspers, Karl. *The European Spirit.* Translated by R. G. Smith. London: SCM, 1948.

————. *Existenzphilosophie.* Berlin: deGruyter, 1938. *Existentialism and Humanism.* Translated by E. B. Ashton. New York: Moore, 1952.

————. *Philosophie.* Berlin: Springer, 1932. *Philosophy.* Translated by E. B. Ashton. Chicago: University of Chicago Press, 1969–71.

Kierkegaard, Søren. *The Sickness unto Death.* Translated by W. Lowrie. Princeton, N.J.: Princeton University Press, 1951.

*Kohák, Erazim. "I, Thou, and It." *Philosophical Forum,* n.s. 1, no. 1 (Fall 1968): 36–72.

————. "Physics, Meta-Physics and Metaphysics." *Metaphilosophy* 5, no. 1 (January 1974): 18–35.

(————.) "Tři téze o Masarykovi" [Three Theses on Masaryk]. *Svědectví* (Paris) 13, no. 50 (Fall 1975): 225–41.

*Kołakowski, Leszek. *Husserl and the Search for Certitude.* New Haven, Conn.: Yale University Press, 1975.

(Kosík, Karel.) *Dialektika konkrétního.* Prague: ČSAV, 1964. *Dialectics of the Concrete.* Translated by K. Kovanda. Doortrecht: Reidel, 1977.

Kubeš, Vladimír. *Grundfragen der Philosophie des Rechts.* Vienna: Springer, 1977.

*Landgrebe, Ludwig. *Phänomenologie und Geschichte.* Gütersloh: Gerd Mohn, 1968.

*————. *Phänomenologie und Metaphysik.* Hamburg: Schroeder, 1949.

*————. *Philosophie der Gegenwart,* Bonn: Athenaeum, 1952.

Major Problems in Contemporary European Philosophy. Translated by K. Reinhardt. New York: Ungar, 1966.

*————. "The World as a Phenomenological Problem." Translated by Dorion Cairns. *Philosophy and Phenomenological Research* 1, no. 1 (September 1940): 38–58.

*Levin, David. *Reason and Evidence in Husserl's Phenomenology.* Evanston, Ill.: Northwestern University Press, 1970.

*Levinas, Emmanuel. *La Théorie de l'intuition dans la phénoménologie de Husserl.* Paris: Alcan, 1930. *The Theory of Intuition in Husserl's Phenomenology.* Translated by André Orianne. Evanston, Ill.: Northwestern University Press, 1973.

*Lowenstein, Alfred. *Das Erlebnis.* Stuttgart: Kohlhammer, 1966.

(McCall, Dorothy.) *The Theatre of Jean-Paul Sartre.* New York: Columbia University Press, 1969.

*Mall, Ram Adhar. *Experience and Reason: The Phenomenology of Edmund Husserl and Its Relation to Hume's Philosophy.* The Hague: Martins Mijhoff, 1973.

*Marbach, Edward. *Das Problem des Ich in der Phänomenologie Husserls.* The Hague: Martinus Nijhoff, 1974.

Masaryk, Tomáš G. *Ideály humanitní.* Prague: Čas, 1901. *Ideals of Humanity.* Translated by P. Warren. New York: Arno, 1971.

(————.) *Otázka sociální.* Prague: Čin, 1936. *Masaryk on Marx.* Translated by E. Kohák. Lewisburg, Pa.: Bucknell University Press, 1972.

(————.) *Rusko a Evropa.* Prague: Laichter, 1911. *The Spirit of Russia.* Translated by E. and C. Paul. London: Allen & Unwin, 1918.

Merleau-Ponty, Maurice. *Phénoménologie de la perception.* Paris: Gallimard, 1945. *Phenomenology of Perception.* Translated by Colin Smith. New York: Humanities Press, 1962.

————. *Les Sciences de l'homme et la phénoménologie.* Paris: Centre de documentation universitaire, 1965.

————. *Le Visible et l'invisible.* Edited by Claude Lefort. Paris: Gallimard, 1964. *The Visible and the Invisible.* Translated by A. Lingis. Evanston, Ill.: Northwestern University Press, 1969.

(Mounier, Emmanuel.) *Traité du caractère.* Paris: Soleil, 1946. *The Character of Man.* Translated by C. Rowland. London: Rockliff, 1956.

(————.) *Le Personalisme.* Paris: Presses Universitaires de France,

1950. *Personalism*. Translated by P. Mairet. London: Routledge, 1952.

*Natanson, Maurice. *Edmund Husserl: Philosopher of Infinite Tasks*. Evanston, Ill.: Northwestern University Press, 1973.

*————, ed. *Essays in Phenomenology*. The Hague: Martinus Nijhoff, 1966.

————, ed. *Philosophy of the Social Sciences*. New York: Random House, 1963.

*Patočka, Jan. *Edmund Husserl zum Gedächtnis* (with Ludwig Landgrebe). Prague: Academia, 1938.

*————. *Existencializmus a fenomenologia* [Existentialism and Phenomenology]. Bratislava: Obzor, 1967.

*————. "Pojem evidence." *Česká Mysl*. 1934.

*————. *Přirozený svět jako filosofický problém*. Prague: Laichter, 1939. *Le Monde naturel comme un problème philosophique*. Translated by Jaromír Daněk. The Hague: Martinus Nijhoff, 1976.

*————. *Úvod do studia Husserlovy fenomenologie* [Introduction to the Study of Husserl's Phenomenology]. Prague: Státní Pedagogické Nakladatelství, 1966.

*Pivčević, Edo. *Husserl and Phenomenology*. London: Hutchinson, 1970.

Reinach, Adolf. *Was ist Phänomenologie?* Munich: Kösel, 1951 (reprint). "What Is Phenomenology?" Translated by Derek Kelly. *Philosophical Forum*, n.s. 1, no. 2 (Winter 1968): 231–56.

————. *Zur Phänomenologie des Rechts*. Munich: Kösel, 1953 (reprint).

Ricoeur, Paul. *Le Conflit des interprétations*. Paris: Seuil, 1969. *The Conflict of Interpretations*. Translated by Don Ihde, et al. Evanston, Ill.: Northwestern University Press, 1974.

————. *De l'interprétation*. Paris: Seuil, 1965. *Freud and Philosophy*. Translated by D. Savage. New Haven, Conn.: Yale University Press, 1970.

————. *Histoire et vérité*. Paris: Seuil, 1955. *History and Truth*. Translated by Charles Kelbley. Evanston, Ill.: Northwestern University Press, 1965.

*————. *Husserl: An Analysis of His Phenomenology*. Translated by Edward G. Ballard and Lester Embree. Evanston, Ill.: Northwestern University Press, 1967.

————. *La Métaphore vivre*. Paris: Seuil, 1975.

————. *La Philosophie de la volonté (The Philosophy of of the Will)*.
Vol. 1: *Le Volontaire et l'involontaire*. Paris: Aubier, 1950. *Free-dom and Nature: The Voluntary and the Involuntary*. Translated by E. Kohák. Evanston, Ill.: Northwestern University Press, 1966.
Vol. 2: *Finitude et culpabilité (Finitude and Guilt)*.
Part I: *L'Homme faillible*. Paris: Aubier, 1960. *Fallible Man*. Translated by Charles Kelbley. Chicago: Regnery, 1965.
Part II: *La Symbolique du mal*. Paris: Aubier, 1960. *Symbolism of Evil*. Translated by E. Buchanan. New York: Harper, 1967.
*Robberechts, Ludovic. *Husserl*. Paris: Editions universitaires, 1964.
(Rosensohn, William.) *The Phenomenology of Charles Peirce*. Amsterdam: Grüner, 1974.
(Ross, W. D.) *Foundations of Ethics*. Oxford: Clarendon Press, 1939.
*Roth, Alois, ed. *Edmund Husserls ethische Untersuchungen*. The Hague: Martinus Niffhoff, 1960.
*Röttges, Heinz. *Evidenz und Solipsismus in Husserls CM*. Frankfurt: Heiderhoff, 1971.
*Saraiwa, Maria Manuella. *L'Imagination selon Husserl*. The Hague: Martinus Nijhoff, 1970.
(Sartre, Jean-Paul.) *Critique de la raison dialectique*. Paris: Gallimard, 1960. Translation of first part only: *Search for a Method*. Translated by Hazel Barnes. New York: Knopf, 1963.
————. *L'Etre et le néant*. Paris: Gallimard, 1943. *Being and Nothingness*. Translated by Hazel Barnes. New York: Philosophical Library, 1956.
*————. *La Transcendence de l'ego*. Paris: Vrin, 1965. *The Transcendence of the Ego*. Translated by Forrest Williams and Robert Kirkpatrick. New York: Farrar, Straus, Noonday Press, 1957.
(Scheler, Max.) *Der Formalismus in der Ethik und die materiale Wertethik*. 2d ed. Halle: Niemeyer, 1921. *Formalism in Ethics and Non-Formal Ethics of Values*. Translated by Manfred Frings and Roger Funk. Evanston, Ill.: Northwestern University Press, 1973.
————. "Das Ressentiment im Aufbau der Moralen." in *Gesammelte Werke,* vol. 3. Bern: Francke, 1954. *Ressentiment*. Translated by Wm. Holdheim. New York: Free Press, 1961.
————. *Wesen und Formen der Sympathie*. Bonn: Cohen, 1923. *The Nature of Sympathy*. Translated by Peter Heath. Hamden, Conn.: Archon, 1970.

Schutz, Alfred. *Der sinnhafte Aufbau der sozialen Welt*. Vienna:
Springer [1932] 1970. *The Phenomenology of the Social World*.
Translated by George Walsh and Frederick Lehnert. Evanston,
Ill.: Northwestern University Press, 1967.

*Shestov, Leon. "Edmund Husserl." In James Edie, ed., *Russian
Philosophy*, vol. 3, pp. 254–67. Chicago: Quadrangle, 1965.

*Sokolowski, Robert. *The Formation of Husserl's Concept of Con-
stitution*. The Hague: Martinus Nijhoff, 1970.

*————. *Husserlian Meditations*. The Hague: Martinus Nijhoff,
1974.

*Son, B. H. *Science and Person: A Study in the Idea of "Philosophy as
a Rigorous Science" in Kant and Husserl*. Assen: van Gorcum,
1972.

*Souche-Dagues, Denise. *Le Développement de l'intentionalité dans
la phénoménologie husserlienne*. The Hague: Martinus Nijhoff,
1960.

*Spiegelberg, Herbert. *The Phenomenological Movement*. 2 vols.
The Hague: Martinus Nijhoff, 1960.

*Szilasi, Wilhelm. *Einführung in die Phänomenologie Edmund Hus-
serls*. Tübingen: Niemeyer, 1959.

Waldenfels, Bernhard. *Das Zwischenreich des Dialogs: Sozialphiloso-
phische Untersuchungen im Anschluss an Edmund Husserl*. The
Hague: Martinus Nijhoff, 1971.

(Weber, Max.) *Die protestantische Ethik und der "Geist" des Kapi-
talismus*. Tübingen: Mohr, 1904. *The Protestant Ethic and the
Spirit of Capitalism*. Translated by T. Parsons. New York: Scrib-
ner's 1958.

(Wittgenstein, Ludwig.) *Philosophische Untersuchungen*. In *Schriften*,
vol. 1. Frankfurt: Suhrkamp, 1960. *Philosophical Investigations*.
Translated by G. E. M. Anscombe. New York: Macmillan, 1958.

(————.) *Tractatus Logico-Philosophicus*. Edited by B. Russel. London: Routledge, 1960.

*Zaner, Richard. *The Way of Phenomenology*. New York: Pegasus,
1970.

*————, and Kersten, Fred, eds. *Phenomenology: Continuation and
Criticism, Essays in Memory of Dorion Cairns*. The Hague: Martinus Nijhoff, 1973.

Index

243